LOVE LIKE LIGHT

plays & performance texts
by Daniel Alexander Jones

53 SP 35

August 2021
Brooklyn, NY

Love Like Light
© Daniel Alexander Jones 2021
53rdstatepress.org

ISBN Number: 978-1732545243
Library of Congress Number: 2021938971

Book design: Kate Kremer
Cover design: vind datter

Printed on recycled paper in the United States of America.

The text of *Duat* was first published in a performance edition by Soho Rep.

Love Like Light is made possible by the New York State Council on the Arts with the support of Governor Andrew M. Cuomo and the New York State Legislature.

LOVE LIKE LIGHT

plays & performance texts by Daniel Alexander Jones
with an introduction by Omi Osun Joni L. Jones
53rd State Press | Brooklyn, NY | August 2021

I dedicate this book to these 5 lightbearers:

Zehline A. Davis
who expected excellence

Patricia A. Keenan
who dared me to leap

Karen "Poochie" Madison
for my first quiet lessons in craft

Bernice "Bunny" Leslie
for circles and fires and portals

&

Jeannie Jones
for unerring angelic heart

"Here is ecstasy in death and certainty in life.
We are gods in the body of god, truth and love our destinies.
Go then and make of the world something beautiful,
set up a light in the darkness."

– Normandi Ellis, *Awakening Osiris*

CONTENTS

BLACK
JOY: :LOVE
LIGHT

an introduction
by Omi Osun Joni L. Jones

JOY:

"I like this dream, it speaks to me.
It tells me I will always be.
Have always been and am right now."

> "Regenerating"
> Lyrics by Jomama Jones, *Flowering*

At this distinctive time in which I pen these ideas—as Black people around the diaspora are once again directing the moral compass of humanity—Daniel calls us, with *Love Like Light,* to follow his persistent dance to Joy. Joy as Divine pulse. Joy, not as the absence of pain, but as a declaration of aliveness. Joy as an irrepressible always. Daniel is forging paths to Freedom, and Joy is the train that will take us there—but as Jomama reminds us, not everyone will make it. Not everyone is ready for the work that Freedom requires. Even in the midst of a pandemic that tantalizes us with the possibility of relinquishing the arrogance of our misguided independence, even as the Earth's steadily rising temperature implores us to see the absolute interconnectedness of all things, even as the real matter of Black lives once again rallies us to claim Love and the Joy it can bring, some will resist this Joy as naïve or apolitical. While in fact, it is the heart of political truth. These truths are so profound, so necessary, that Daniel can gracefully navigate a willingness to be not understood.

When *Black Light*—"a musical revival for turbulent times"—was produced in 2018, the times were not nearly as turbulent as they have become, which gives us some sense of the prescience of Daniel's vision. Jomama opens with "What if I told you it's going to be alright?" and the cynics will run away from Freedom and Joy because being cramped and outraged has become so habitual that the very thought of melting the cynicism seems like a fantasy. "Who should listen to Jomama?" some might ask—but she is precisely who we should heed in this time. She of indeterminacy of identity and promulgator of Joy. As we live more deeply in "the break" of possibility we are currently facing, the wisdom from someone who transgresses all identity markers and knows the Joys and perils of doing so is precisely the guide for the Next Now. Toni Morrison tells us, "writers who construct meaning in the face of chaos must be nurtured, protected,"[1] and the publication of *Love Like Light* provides the protection of legacy that the material fact of a book can bestow.

This volume is our opportunity to do our own dance through Daniel's inspiration, and in so doing, we not only imagine the physical productions of his work as described in the "altar notes" that accompany these texts, but we also have the opportunity to experience the literariness of his work. In Daniel's writing there is a compelling precision that looks like nonchalance—each word and image sharp, crisp, no excess or dross—what Sharon Bridgforth calls, "A beauty that looks soft but really cuts."[2] His deftness with language demonstrates a command of sound that is understood as music when Jomama sings—but is also vibrating in every spoken exchange. The people in his worlds are always singing even as they chat. So, this volume allows us to savor language, to underline passages that make us gasp, to map the structural landscape, to read and re-read and re-read into the pleasure of text—thereby giving us the saturation reading affords.

Love Like Light is our sacred grove where Daniel has gathered several of his longtime interlocutors, from vital 1990s formulations in Austin with Vicky Boone to even earlier university explorations with Shay Youngblood and to more recent collaborations with Eisa

---

1   Morrison, Toni. *The Source of Self-Regard*, New York: New York, Alfred A. Knopf, 2019, p. viii.

2   Bridgforth, Sharon. Personal Communication.

Davis, Jacques Colimon, and Deborah Paredez. These long-standing companions are rounded out by newer acquaintances *cum* kin, korde arrington tuttle and Aaron Landsman—a good party always has a few new guests to ensure some heat. This gathering is a potent Black Feminist move, creating a collective, bringing people together for a convening, a ceremony of celebration, an enactment of Joy through honoring each contributing voice.

BLACK:

"Sink into the darkness.
Make stardust of your bones.
Dissolve into potential.
Release all that you hold."

"Dark Matter"
Lyrics by Jomama Jones, *Radiate*

"What if Joy *is* Black?" It's as if Daniel's work is directly responding to this question that I posed in my book, *Theatrical Jazz*.[3] Black has occupied such a narrow space in the collective imagination—and Daniel insists on Black that is deeply inclusive and resistant to the rigidity of singular definitions. He asks us to live inside unfixedness. The song "Black Light" rings with "veils all lifting showing us the darkest night"—for Black is the space of the unknown yet to be known, rather than an empty cavernous void. Black is the fertile soil of invention. In considering *Black Light*, Deborah Paredez tells us

---

3   Jones, Omi Osun Joni L. *Theatrical Jazz: Performance, Àse, and the Power of the Present Moment*, Columbus, OH: The Ohio State University Press, 2015. p. 222.

that the work "calls us to meditate in the darkness." Here, we can see more, not less—as somatic scholar Amber McZeal reminds us, our pupils *expand* so we can see in the dark.[4]

Like the doorway in *clayangels*—a passage to an Egyptian-laden underground where the entire experience takes place; or the portals that Eisa Davis notes as Spiritually significant in *Phoenix Fabrik*—megaphones of communication between then and now; or the alcove in *The Book of Daniel*—a birth canal from which Daniel emerged in a 2005 production at allgo; or the netherworld interlude in *Duat*—an icy Black world where Osiris must make choices—Black offers infinite possibilities, and Daniel revels in presenting them.

LIGHT:

> *"I'm here to remind you: look within for your melody;*
> *shine your light no matter what the cost;*
> *burn brighter; brighter still"*
> > "Lone Star"
> > Lyrics by Jomama Jones, *Lone Star*

Black and Light are aspects of the same experience. Both illuminate in their own way. Black is "what if," while Light is "is." Black is where Light is born. And, a blacklight as a tool causes a glow that can authenticate currency and art, and identify medical disorders. A blacklight, then, detects that which is not visible to the naked eye. In this way, Daniel's work is a BlackLight, pushing us past the world as we know it into what the world could so beautifully be.

---

4   McZeal, Amber. *Revival: Millennial reMembering in the Afro NOW*, written and directed by Amara Tabor-Smith, 2019.

The very simile that grounds the title of the work bends toward physics—where the curvilinear nature of spacetime that abounds in Daniel's work has been well known for at least a century. Physicist Carlo Rovelli tells us, "All things are continually interacting with one another, and in doing so each bears the traces of that with which it has interacted: and in this sense all things continuously exchange information about one another."[5] Energy moves as heat. Molecules energize each other. Rovelli's discussion of the relationship between humans and the principles of physics describes the very embodiment of theatre and how we are made anew through it.

Light, and its many refractions, is a central force and theme in Daniel's productions. The sparkling cabaret and disco ball of *Black Light*, the moody crumbling spaces where light lands just right on the faces and keeps so much else in intriguing shadows in *Phoenix Fabrik*, the chilly mustiness (here, light evoking scent) in *clayangels*, and the individual intimate spatially dispersed locations of *Book of Daniel Chapter 10: Wonder Us*—all reveal the importance of illumination in his work. Daniel acknowledges the gifted lighting designer Mike Wangen—a frequent Theatrical Jazz collaborator—with bringing forth "the soul of the piece." Mike lent his skills to productions of Laurie Carlos, Sharon Bridgforth, Robbie McCauley, and so many others.

And then, there are the character names (Luna and Light of *Blood:Shock:Boogie*), performance titles (*Black Light*; *Bright Now Beyond*; *Hera Bright*), CD and New Music Theatre titles (*Radiate*, *Qualities of Light*), Song titles ("Future Light," "Sunbeam," "Daybreak," "Brightly Shining")—Daniel is as enthralled with Light as he is with sound.

Light moves us into the stratosphere from whence we all came as particles of stardust. There's *Lone Star*, "Dark Matter," "Rings of

5   Rovelli, Carlo. *Seven Brief Lessons on Physics*, New York: New York, Riverhead Books, p. 70.

Saturn," "Sister Moon," "Sirius"— all celestially encapsulated by the chorus to "Stardust,"

We are Stardust full of light

We are Stardust resonating

That glow is irreplaceable

Now begin

LOVE:

> *"Don't you know you're free, when you live in love, my dear"*
> "Sunbeam"
> Lyric by Sharon Bridgforth, *Radiate*

We can't get to Freedom with the strategies that have maimed us. To imagine and *be* beyond what we know, Daniel tells us in an interview with music journalist Christian John Wikane, "We often look to external systems to be agents of our collective transformation and it really must begin within. There's something that happens when you let go of the old and you allow yourself to be undone, completely."[6] *Love Like Light* invites this undoing with the sonic inventions throughout that often defy genre classifications, and with the insistence to courageously re-birth ourselves, or as Daniel states in his altar notes for *Phoenix Fabrik*, "we rebuild the dead into the flying free." Borrowing Barbara Ann Teer's coinage in her Black actor training

---

6   Wikane, Christian John. Liner Notes, *Flowering*. Jomama Jones and Bobby Halvorson, 2017.

program, there is a "decrudding" that must take place.[7] Hearts are righteously suspicious, are rusted with rage and grimey with fear, and still, Daniel beckons us to reveal the heart as the sturdy life-generating force that it is. He encourages a bone-deep transformation through what korde arrington tuttle calls Daniel's "gift for alchemy." In true Theatrical Jazz fashion, Daniel's virtuosity is in his courage to map a decidedly singular path. And that singularity can have a price. In considering *The Book of Daniel Chapter 10: Wonder Us*, Aaron Landsman notes the "practiced courage" that fuels Daniel's work, in which "liberation remains central." Daniel cares enough about Humanity that he challenges us to do the hardest thing—to re-invent ourselves through Love.

Black cultural theorist Richard Iton asks, "How do the excluded engage the apparently dominant order?"[8] I think *Love Like Light* offers up some possibilities. In keeping with performance artist Gabrielle Civil's mandate to "let joy shift from a feeling to a practice,"[9] Daniel's work gives us multiple "hows"—from Benjamin's wrenching commitment to being his full self in *Bel Canto,* to the cosmic lessons of Mother Dixon in *Phoenix Fabrik,* to the necessary family confrontations and even tentative resolutions in *The Book of Daniel* and *clayangels,* to Jomama's sage counsel in *Blood:Shock:Boogie, Duat,* and *Black Light*—each work in this volume is a primer for those students willing to open, willing to yield to what Shay Youngblood calls his "superpowers as a creative visionary." Daniel presents possibilities—pledges of reciprocating Love between humans and nature and all that might be.

7   Teer, Barbara Ann. "The Great White Way Is Not Our Way—Not Yet," *Negro Digest*, April, 1968.

8   Iton, Richard. *In Search of the Black Fantastic*. New York: Oxford University Press, 2008, p. 3.

9   Civil, Gabrielle. *Experiments in Joy: A Workbook*. Los Angeles, CA: Co-Conspirator Press, 2019, p. 6.

By the time you read this we will know if humans were brave enough to follow the call to Joy proffered throughout this volume. As Vicky Boone so aptly suggests, Daniel's work is "an event. A revolution." Can we join this particular brand of a life-affirming Love-commanding insurgency? Will Love be the Light?

Or, as summoned into Daniel's work by Jacques Colimon, "Welcome to the crossroads."

The choice is in our hands.

– Omi Osun Joni L. Jones, 2020

tell

a

free

story

field notes from an altar-building practice
by Daniel Alexander Jones

This morning I put sunflowers on my altar. I still tend to use old glass juice bottles or mason jars to hold flowers. After balancing the wide, heavy blooms with their electric gold penumbras and deepdark centers, I add them to the mantle in this bright and beautiful room where I've worked nearly every day this past year. Los Angeles's distinctive sunshine blesses their faces with a streak. Some objects on this altar have been with me for decades and are often the first things carefully packed when I'm going to travel. Others are collected just for a period of time; some of those, like these flowers, are intentionally ephemeral. Each object has an apparent purpose, as well as uses and meanings yet to be revealed. Each object contains stories. There are other stories welling up from the spaces between and among them. Each of the pieces in this book is an altar. May they evoke free stories.

I was born into a lineage of lightbearers who were wholly devoted to freedom. They had already been done cleared space. I took their utterances as givens—sure and pulsing stars in my firmament. See, I began my career after Ntozake Shange and the women who created *for colored girls who have considered suicide/when the rainbow is enuf* had irrefutably reminded us of the truths of multivalent voice (individual, collective, and ever-changing). Shange and my own mentors—Laurie Carlos, Rebecca Rice, Aishah Rahman, Jessica Hagedorn, and Robbie McCauley among them—repeatedly demonstrated to me the imperative of creating sacred ceremonies to offer lucent, medicinal maps. These awakened senses and suggested pathways for movement while also confronting the work of healing across time, within the loftiest macrocosmic realms and inside the most granular microcosmic materialities. I'd already been baptized by Betty Carter's distinctive vocal expressions that bent, stretched, snapped, and spun temporality, cautioning us—always—not to mistake content for form, nor to be seduced away from sui generis expressions by the familiarity of recordings of any sort, even the ones that brought her voice to my speakers!

Indeed, Dr. Constance E. Berkley, another of my great mentors, taught me that the nature of freedom is elusive. It must be cultivated and remembered through consistent, devotional practice. She imagined freedom as a living dynamic unfolding within a moving and shifting field of consciousness. Freedom consistently adapts to embrace an unpredictable series of utterances within an expansive whole. She, like Carter, drew my attention to the fact that forms can be liberatory in one configuration and caging in another. Abbey Lincoln had written "Throw it Away" to remind us that breathing is not just about air and lungs, but is a lifelong attentive activity, releasing what you hold, giving your love liberally, to make space for what your open hands will receive. And as my ears had become attuned to the range of sound I could hear, and my eyes had become accustomed to the spectrum of visible light, my mind's eye had embraced the fact that I saw and heard but a fraction of what is or what was, let alone what was becoming.

I had other glorious examples in literature and theatre (Toni Morrison, Alice Walker, Audre Lorde, Lucille Clifton, Robert Hayden, Essex Hemphill, Adrienne Kennedy, Amiri Baraka, Virginia Hamilton, et. al.) music (Carter and Lincoln, Josephine Baker, Lena Horne, Sarah Vaughan, Sun Ra, Prince, Stevie Wonder, Patrice Rushen, Teena Marie, Angela Bofill, Sade, Sylvester, Labelle, Billie Holiday, Diana Ross, Bob Marley, Aretha Franklin, Joni Mitchell, Joan Armatrading, Sweet Honey in the Rock, Laura Nyro, to name but a tiny handful) visual and conceptual art and film (Betye Saar, Yoko Ono, Charles White, Adrian Piper, Marlon Riggs, Julie Dash, Charles Burnett, et. al.) as well as from family and community. Each in their own ways cleaved to freedom and by doing so were often experienced by the society as iconoclastic. Each, also in their own ways, demonstrated that the pursuit of freedom will inevitably lead to innovations in form because one must dance with both the known and the unknown. The light of consciousness, directed at the seemingly known, can reveal new details, make more space, and suggest shadow. Nothing alive is static. No thing remains the same. And, as noted in the song "The Man Who Talks to Flowers," which I wrote with Samora Pinderhughes for *Duat*, "if you love a thing enough, it will reveal its secrets to you. Open up its codes and keys and send its message through you." That love. That intentional love. That love as attention. That love as the light of consciousness. They all had that love. And they all, in their own ways, beamed it toward possibilities heretofore unimagined collectively. By doing so in public performance, in community, they made maps for others, to guide folks consciously into the flow of lifeforce, and, as a natural consequence, away from predetermined, limited, and limiting realities. When I name my work as belonging to traditions of Blackness and Queerness, I do so because both these dynamic domains have held evidence of flow beyond imposed boundaries and singular narratives. I make this distinction during a historical moment in which we seem to be slipping away from the kind of freedom espoused by my forebears and toward dangerous rigidities and neo-essentialist reductions. I remind myself daily that I come from traditions of transgression, improvisation, and marronage and if you don't keep it porous to the flow of life, the thing that freed you can ensnare you.

Energy is my true medium. Whether I am putting words on a page or moving bodies on a stage, it's all about energy. All these pieces-as-altars are temporary houses for the conjuring, transmission, and release of energy. These altars are intended to reorient us toward the multiverse, perhaps by affirming capacities of perception and communication that have been belittled or besieged, perhaps by disorienting us or confronting us with ways of seeing and being that invite us to think or feel outside our habits. If energy is my medium, making altars is my consistent practice.

If there was a time before I made altars, I cannot remember it. My earliest memories are altars built in my mind's eye from gathered bits of light, sound, and touch: the precise frequency of a pale blue wall in the nursery, a trace of my grandmother's vocal cadence, the toasty smell of afternoon sunlight heating the dust in the air, the weight of parents' arms enfolding, the press and pulse of our hearts and lungs, our smooth skin humming under worn bleached cotton. I became an archivist collecting signs and signifiers, then arranging the structures to invite an intimate encounter later on; I became an arkivist transporting feelings across time. And when I say feelings, I mean the multivalent experiences of embodied presence in context. Tucked into real time, in plain sight, altars invite a world within a world to reveal itself, and by so doing, draw our attention to a dynamic field of interdependent worlds, multiple undulating dimensions, and multivalent connections made of countless covalent bonds.

Fragments evoke wholes—multiplicities, potentials, and concurrencies. Fragments signify absences, even as they remind us of the presence of the unseen-yet-felt. Among my greatest teachers of this way of seeing and being was the late Alice Coltrane. While I never had the honor of meeting her in life, her recorded music (Carter's caution about records, noted) had long-ago taken up residence in my bone marrow. I attended Coltrane's memorial service at Saint John the Divine in Manhattan and was bathed in the sound of her former bandmates, devotees, and other loved ones filling that space with her words of wisdom and her compositions. In her elegant consideration of Coltrane's life, *Monument Eternal*[10], the late musicologist Franya J. Berkman noted, "Her boundary-crossing aesthetics and her inspiring spiritual autobiography—documented in sound, text, and ritual—tells a free story, testifying to her faith and extraordinary personal history. Perhaps most of all, it reveals an understanding of herself that transcends earthly constructions." In their "astral expansion," John and Alice Coltrane modeled an exploration in time through sound of realities that lie within and outside time. I

---

10   Berkman, Franya J. *Monument Eternal: The Music of Alice Coltrane*. Wesleyan University Press, 2010.

absolutely consider their work to have been altar-building, placing fragments within a field of presence, mapping pathways to awaken, invite, remind, and conjure. They left the comfort of the known in service to freedom. They remembered. We remember.

AFROMYSTICISM

This is the opening of my play *Earthbirths, Jazz & Raven's Wings* (1994):

> (*Darkness. Sound of distant footsteps. In the recess of the space the movement of a lantern. Softly, light focuses on* HARPER, *who appears to be floating in space.*)

HARPER. Only time I know my father?
I'm sitting at the bottom of the stairs.
Don't know even if he know I'm there.
Twilight.
Outside sounds
hum low.
Nicky, Ako,
jump rope.
Keiyan shouts from five houses down about somebody's mama.
Wind turns the leaves—shows the silver—tells of coming rain.
Sitting on the bottom stair.
Don't know even if he know I'm there.
Twilight.
Mom upstairs
feeding my brother,
washing my brother
getting my brother ready for bed.

Warm water,
talcum powder,
hang in the hallway.
Not dark, just deep.
Curtains are ghosts.
Twilight.
My father in the black chair.
Feet, hand, chin, eyes almost closed.
I'm a shadow on the stairs behind
Don't know even if he know I'm there.
Just know him cause
she's
here.
Her voice lifts out the record player
in the corner,
with the scratch and pop of needle in groove.

Them that's got shall get,
them that's not shall lose ...

Only time I know my father ...
she
haunts the room,
makes the breathing easy,
makes the softness on his face,
slow and steady.
Eyes closed almost ...

And it still is news ...
Then blue
and almost not at all,
the sound
comes
from him.

Bass notes catch in the wood. *Mama may have...*
Notes set in my eyes. *Papa may have...*
Sound of my father and her together.
Flood the room full night comes on
First drops
of rain
fall.
I am safe.
Something about my father and Billie
makes sense.
Something holy
for which there are no words,
only sound.

I first uttered the term Afromysticism when I was looking for a way to describe and evoke (not limit) the connective tissue among works of art I loved for their ability to open inter-dimensional portals and create experiences of the numinous in the everyday. Because many of these works (others' and my own) straddled aesthetics that might easily and correctly be identified as Afrofuturist, the question was posed to me, "why don't you just say Afrofuturism?" I loved the question.

Certainly, Afrofuturism is multivalent and pliable. Yes, it fabulously includes the delight of the Mothership and all manner of metallic lamé. As it pertains to the Settler Colonial project, Afrofuturism has deployed powerful imaginative therapy, asserting the continued presence of the African diaspora on the planet and in any collectively envisioned universal future. I recall the legendary story of Nichelle Nichols being told by Dr. Martin Luther King, Jr. that she must stay on *Star Trek*, despite her dissatisfaction with the amount and quality of work she was able to do on the show, because her presence on the weekly series about future space exploration enshrined Black folk in the speculative imaginations of a rising generation and had redemptive impact for prior generations who'd been excluded from such representation. The Settler Colonial project is future-oriented. It erases or distorts evidence of complex pasts, overlays narratives affirming colonial authority over a singular, aggregate present truth rooted in materialism. It views the past solely as prologue. It emphasizes the pursuit of the yet-to-be as having greater value than the pursuit of accord with current circumstances. Yet Afrofuturism has posited the multifold emancipation and liberated expression of historically oppressed and marginalized groups. One need only consider the silver-suited nightbirds themselves, Labelle, to witness the embodiment of an Afrofuturist sovereignty nimbly envisioned beyond conformist tendencies and limited habits of sight. And of course, the watershed work of science fiction writers like Samuel R. Delaney and Octavia E. Butler squared off with dystopia through courageous and unsentimental world-building and clarion-calling. While not always, there are often elements of technology employed within Afrofuturism (note that technology includes cultural and spiritual technology, not just machines); and a sense of struggle that continues to engage the colonial hydra in its imagined future iterations.

There are traces of Afrofuturism in my work. Still, my heart's roots sprawl beyond the boundaries of the term. The codes of my conjure are transtemporal and translinear. They are sourced before, through, and beyond the Settler Colonial project, even as I have only known a material world defined by its centuries-long fever. I remember otherwise. I always say: *every act of imagination is simultaneously an act of remembrance.* My work roots in the freedom dreams and deeds of generations of beings from a range of cultural and historical lines. My own mystical journeys and my evolving spiritual acumen have since early childhood led me toward an ontology of immanence. My embodied understanding of time was born of oft-revisited experiences beyond "the veil." I was not second-sighted from birth as were some folks I knew and many of the forebears I'd read about; rather, I grew into it through unintentional rites of passage encoded in a series of life events that had the commensurate impact of initiations, trainings, and transmutations. Consequently, I see multiply—the many in the one, the concomitant truths, all in motion. My inquiries and imaginings are what I term *ancientfuture*. My longings are unabashedly mystical.

Afromysticism is an experiential, embodied aesthetic. It is born from and produces practices containing African diasporic philosophies. I apply the term Afromystical, broadly, to work I have encountered in the Black American cultural continuum that activates interdimensional portals, evokes the numinous, communicates on multiple levels of perception simultaneously, and continuously reorients perceptions of time and space. Afromysticism emphasizes the centrality of those reorienting perceptions to the lived experience of freedom and further-more posits freedom as an ever-unfolding process of being indivisible from universal expansion. Afromysticism's felt states of becoming contain discernible forms that occur both inside and outside the present moment and inside and outside of the self and community. Afromysticism reveals concurrency. Afromysticism recognizes states of play as sites for co-creative consciousness. Afromysticism is indivisible from the ancestors.

ANCESTORS

I maintain active relationships with my ancestors. I state unambiguously that I experience direct collaboration with them. This is neither an abstraction nor a colorful story. It is a commonplace truth, true at root for the vast majority of humans on the planet throughout history. This truth has consistently been deemed superstitious or primitive by a Settler Colonial project, which—in service of future-focused consumption—benefits from the severing of relationship between the living and dead. In the continuum I am a part of, ancestral legacy is an active, responsive field and "the work" extends beyond any individual lifetime. I belong to a constellation of people who continue to recollect our wholeness even during the most fractious, divisive, and dispiriting juncture I've yet experienced culturally, socially, and politically. I have within me a vigilant hawk, eyes out for extractive behaviors or reductive approaches; yet I am witness to the fact that despite my own best intentions I am ineluctably acculturated toward both. This is why the work *of* the work is holy, the ceremonies that *beget* the ceremonies are holy. By holy I mean a state of interdimensional encounter that is entered intentionally and with humility. In this work, what is holy contains the sacred and the profane.

An interesting observation occurred when I was compiling the list of gratitudes for this book. I filled the pages of a notebook, somewhat anxious about the likelihood I'd neglect to include folks, but determined to call as many names as I could. With each name listed, a glistening web was revealed, replete with nodes of memory, and pulsing with vital connection, even with and to those who were no longer embodied. In many cases I could perceive a weave among many of the names akin to a living tissue, which upon closer examination contained countless clusters of other names and places and stories. What struck me particularly was that I could hold the vast expanse of this field and simultaneously perceive it in minute detail. By diving into one spot I could activate a fractal expansion that allowed me to perceive and distinguish innumerable specificities in the story while always maintaining a sense of the larger, moving whole. In short, there was no limit on my capacity to feel love. I could imagine love at a galactic scale just as I savored the remembered nuances of conjunctions past.

The texts contained in this volume represent a selection of works from my career thus far. Each is true to its time and place of genesis and contains evidence of a community that brought it into being. Each continues to speak in its own way. This is what we made when we made it, how we made it, and why. Much of the work in this collection has happened in performance spaces or on stages. But it's like folk who congregate in a public park—some are there to play, some to pray. Sometimes a bit of both. You know why only through doing. When I have been disciplined in my attentions to grounding all aspects of the process in love, the results have been palpable. When I have not, dry rot has destabilized the foundations of a project and sometimes led to catastrophic failure. I have screwed up royally several times in my career by mistaking interest in my work on the part of others (collaborators or producers) for fluency with my ways of making it. As my grandmother used to say, when you assume you make an *ass* out of *u* and *me*. Your attention and your care must extend to every person and every aspect of the process of creation, or the conjure won't come correct.

There are instances where a story shows up or a symbol appears in multiple pieces. That's not for lack of imagination. It is congruent with my roots in theatrical jazz, wherein multiple meanings are evoked through retelling—repetition with variation, amplified by the particularities of context. Sarah Vaughan singing "Misty" with the sniffles in Sweden in the early 1960s is deliciously different from Sarah Vaughan singing "Misty" in Tokyo in the mid-1980s; Joni Mitchell singing "Both Sides Now" on *Clouds* in 1969 played in sequence with her exquisite inhabitation of it on the album that shares its name from 2000. Each is replete with the heart wisdom abiding in them in those particular times and places. The familiar chords and words of the songs become points of communal contact, vantages from which to experience the differences in the singers' utterances and invitations. A taxonomical approach to life impedes our capacity for love, and the relentless pursuit of the singular exemplar occludes the healing power of unguarded presence (i.e. free of expectation and assumption). What is evoked from you will of necessity be distinct from what is evoked from me. And rather than seek the dissolution of those distinctions in pursuit of a false narrative of uniformity and conformity, can we see multiply? An ecosystem, like a web, depends on points of contact, divergence, and space among and between. A taxonomical approach mistakes material specificity in time for the full scope of being and suggests an erroneous and ultimately toxic essentialism (i.e. form dictating content). It avoids what it deems contradictory and often employs some form of violence to eliminate contradictions in service to a singular truth.

"Always seek to house contradictions, not to resolve them."

   – Robbie McCauley

Among the contradictions I happily house? I am at once a hermit and a social animal. My work contains cross-currents moving toward deep and precise interiority as well as generative external engagement. It has always been my intention to welcome the seen and the unseen, to create portals for others to experience multiplicity and multivalence and, in my typically Uranian way, to invite a collective recollection. It is a given that that recollection will include the specific and often contradictory consciousnesses of all the individuals who participate; it is also a given that the power of congregational perception and utterance is inimitable and formidable. There is, by default, a recuperative and reparative aspect to my practice which involves a conjure of multiplicities within a moving whole. That includes multiple meanings.

Normandi Ellis notes in her book *Hieroglyphic Words of Power*[11], "Symbols accrue meaning, expanding with endless, interrelated diversity and aspect. A symbol swims in the waters of endless possibility, and those who understand the power of symbol use it as a raft to float from meaning to meaning in a vast ocean of consciousness." The political and social implications of "moving from meaning to

---

11   Ellis, Normandi. *Hieroglyphic Words of Power: Symbols for Magic, Divination, and Dreamwork.* Bear & Company, 2020.

meaning" can be life and death in the United States, particularly for the crossroad communities to which I belong. From the earliest, I have wondered and explored whether the artwork I created could be in service to this movement and its emancipatory potential. I recognized the destructive force of the ontological occupation which we all have to navigate even as I celebrated those lightbearers who charted courses through and beyond it. I sought those who understand the relationship between aesthetics and the practices of freedom. I was blessed by those who boldly articulated the imperative of moving beyond the material with integrity, openness, and care.

RECORDS & ALTARED STATES

I'll be delighted if you consider this volume the book version of a record collection. In honor of Betty Carter's warning, don't take these recordings as gospel. Play with these plays. Please dip and dive among the pieces and the pieces of the pieces as you might move among songs and sides of vinyl albums splayed around you like planetary rings. Make a mixtape. Know that these are records that are symbols containing symbols, all of which, as Ellis reminds us, intentionally evoke multiple meanings. Your attention makes these works anew, your presence animates them and engenders new associations alongside any I intended. May they conjure something in you of the intersecting, lived worlds that bore them; may they help you remember what you might not have experienced firsthand.

Go with me here. The legendary actress Beah Richards once said she believed identity had something to do with love—with the degree of love that can be absorbed. Some questions for you: What do you look like when you are loved? How do you move? How do you breathe? What can you see that you might not otherwise? If I extend "you" from one to many (y'all) I might ask: What do we look like when we love ourselves? What can we move together when we are loved and when we love? Can we alter/altar our states of being to welcome it?

I was loved. That may be the defining aspect of my being. I was loved by a family and a community fractured by the seismic wake of the serial assassinations of the Civil Rights Era and the subsequent rightward political landslide; a family and a community whose commitment to love was greater, for a time in time, than the impediments they faced. I was forged in a multivalent environment that held a distinctive Blackness borne of the meeting of Great Migrants and their children and their children's children with New England Blacks and Caribbean folks; that also, however improbable this may seem to readers today, held a range of white folks including immigrant and first-generation workers, and, as in the case of my own mother and grandmother, folks who transgressed their whiteness in intimate and transformative ways through radical acts of love and surrender. The dignity of work was centered and the currency of local connection and community responsibility were upheld. I have said a million times this love didn't have anything to do with people necessarily liking one another. It was not a shallow, sugary love. It was the love that asked us to face blind spots and willful ignorance, and to dare to name the unspeakable horrors in our histories. The sound of that love echoed through the air even as the occluding and corrupting force of Reaganomics strangled the vitality of the Northeast corridor and forced people into dire choices born from cruel material circumstances. It was the love worth dying for because it was the love worth living for. It was the love spun between upheaving Uranian sparks and limiting Saturnine rings.

I was loved. And I loved. That love was an extension of will. A clear-eyed intention. That love was a choice—a series of choices, in fact. That love was a bedrock bond of community that depended on each individual's contribution to the jam. That love was a force—a revelatory, binding and animating force. If identity has something to do with the degree of love that can be absorbed, as Richards pronounced, I say remembering and rememory (Morrison's concept) has something to do with the force of love's light. The clarifying fire that allows us to see trans-temporally, to crack open the silences, and to, as the *Egyptian Book of the Dead* says, "give a mouth to Osiris." The myriad violences of the United States's meta-narrative deform not only our capacity to prefigure but also the health of our memories. May light shine for all we who communicate across the ragged edges of our corrupt inheritance, who know that scrapes and deep cuts await, but who trust the scars as warrior marks, the near misses as echolocation, the continued practice as prophecy.

The newest permanent object on the altar is a photograph of my Mom, Jeannie Jones, who died in November of 2020. In the photo, taken in the mid-1970s, she smiles with wide open eyes. She's wearing the fancy dress she'd use on the rare occasion when she'd go out to an event with my Dad. She's framed against vibrant red wallpaper with a floral pattern. As we've finished this volume, grief has loosened many of my temporal mooring posts and long-recessed memories have popped up like little riffs. Today I recollect a late-summer afternoon from around the same time as the photograph, standing outside with Jeannie Jones, looking up at what seemed an impossibly tall sunflower. She places her forearm across my chest from behind and nudges my face with her finger. She teaches me how the sunflower turns to follow the sun. Standing with her, watching the flower's fiery eye, I imagine the lifeforce flowing.

Today I place sunflowers on my altar. I remember love like light.

> – Daniel Alexander Jones
> Los Angeles, July 2021

Blood:Shock:Boogie

FOREWORD | holy nourishment

in preparation for penning my response to *Blood:Shock:Boogie*, a kaleidoscopic, cosmic offering + assemblage by Daniel Alexander Jones, eye drew a couple of tarot cards for meditation. the first card eye pulled was THE ALCHEMIST (14), from the major arcana. it speaks to seeking balance. it asks where stagnation might be lurking. "what," the alchemist asks, "is in need of purification by fire?" it challenges us to identify what needs grounding. what might benefit from exposure to what is soft + cool? the alchemist calls us to the deep, internal work of transformation by reminding us that magic exists in the most basic elements: air, water, fire + earth. to begin—or further progress upon—the journey of metamorphosis, we need look no further than where we stand. as the ancient axiom intimates, as above, so below. as within, so without. as we seek balance, we recognize that we come equipped with all the tools we need to blend, conjure, transmute + dance our way into being.

the digital copy of Daniel's performance text eye was fortunate enough to spend time with utilizes a black background. the white letters, symbols + images appear suspended on the screen. each gesture, every syllable speaking to me as if from the depths of the cosmos. in a multitude of ways, they are. LUNA + LIGHT serve as our guides through this multi-dimensional collage of the mind + soul. in the tradition of black, black-feminist + queer avant-garde + experimental performance, *Blood:Shock:Boogie* is lovingly confrontational. that is not to suggest cuteness. rather, because the artist loves you, they tell you the truth. coursing through the text, eye feel a kinship with the work of luminaries such as Ntozake Shange, Robbie McCauley, Rhodessa Jones + Anna Deavere Smith. one of many realities that Daniel shares with these incredible women is the structurally dynamic, virtuosic ability to shape-shift. a perfected, embodied practice of alchemy.

LUNA is described as, "The boy," and LIGHT, "Two embodied aspects of electromagnetic radiation." together, they comprise the trilogy that metamorphose into fourteen (14) different characters throughout the course of *Blood:Shock:Boogie*'s prismatic journey. the play's grounding in a trinity is fitting for many reasons; some readings of which may sit comfortably near the surface of understanding + and others that make themselves known only in retrospect.

in the context of christian doctrine, its situation in relation to god as holy trinity (father/son/holy spirit) is striking. like the holy trinity, simultaneously unseen + omnipresent, the life force of LUNA + LIGHT inhabit characters spanning a panoply of racial, ethnic, gender, age + anachronistic identities, to name only a handful. the utilization of minimalist design elements + the actors' bodies as primary materials evokes immortality. like the cosmos, mirroring my experience of the pale letters set in relief against the text's background, everything emerges from a backdrop of blackness. all life onstage is birthed through a 'holy trinity' of black queerness. this rearticulation of mythology + radical articulation of spirit, through movement, music, text, breath—even on the page—eye experienced as a powerful conjuring. the ancestors are called into the space. laughter is called into the space. liberation is called into the space.

within the framework of christian mythology, jesus makes the choice to come to earth + lead a human life. through his suffering, death + resurrection, the teachings he leaves behind make way for the redemption of all people. in the architecture of *Blood:Shock:Boogie*, although we encounter LUNA's earthly parents, like jesus, his origins are not of this world. unlike jesus, LUNA did not consent to the journey. nonetheless, through enacting the ritual of his creation story, we are presented with the keys to salvation. embracing his humanity, LUNA loves, breaks, heals + bleeds. out loud. in public. and survives.

"I KEPT ON," JOMAMA JONES avows, on an episode of *Soul Train*, in all her soulful splendor.

> "knowing my success would be a beacon,
> and someday, somewhere, some little red-headed stepchild
> would reach out, reach up from the mud to me,
> here,
> glowing among the stars on high, like a Afro-American
> astronaut perched on top of the Empire State Building;
> and it's my duty—no, my pleasure,
> to shine my light on y'all."

prior to making this declaration, JOMAMA's physical embodiment exits the playing space as LUNA. at the end of the scene, through alchemy, JOMAMA's physical embodiment is replaced by LUNA. their characters are distinct, however, LUNA's survival is no less a beacon of light.

in a different tarot deck than the one from which eye pulled THE ALCHEMIST (14), that same card is dominated by a gorgeous broad-winged angel. they are depicted as possessing both masculine + feminine characteristics. balance. drawn onto their flowing light blue robe is a triangle framed by a square. the square represents earth. the triangle is symbolic of humanity. the angel places one foot in the water + the other firmly planted on the rocks. from a chalice they are holding, living water tumbles to the ground, splashing between the two elements. in the background, behind the angel, a majestic mountain range rises in the distance. between the mountains + the angel winds a golden path. if the card were big enough, eye am positive that above the mountains, sliced high in the purple sky, we would find the moon.

                    – korde arrington tuttle

ALTAR NOTES | self-portrait as us in motion

The cold penetrates. Yet, we radiate nervous anticipation this dark February night in Austin. Jason Phelps, Daniel Dodd Ellis, and I huddle in the tiny sliver of space behind the masking, a whisper of space between our bodies. I am nursing a cold, and we just snuck down the road to Hyde Park Bakery to get Lemon Zinger tea. Dellis (as we call Daniel) got a banana muffin. I always trip out watching him eat food; he tastes things with his whole being, short circuiting whatever he had been about to say. And Jason, so tall and limber and graceful, laughs his inimitable laugh, as clear as spring water. I love them both so much. I'm grateful that they opened themselves to this exploration. They have taken the postures, rhythms, melodies, and fragments of my language into their cores. Together we have played in a rehearsal space warmed by a hissing open flame gas heater, figuring out the signals and gestures, sharing the secrets and spelling the spell. I love Austin, this low-slung southern city full of contradictions that welcomed me unexpectedly two years earlier, and to which I've found myself returning again and again.

We had limited rehearsal time. (We always have limited rehearsal time!) So it was all about how we inhabited the time we did have. We had to dilate the hours, and access immediacy and potency. I am grateful I have that old-school thing in me: get in there, drop in, get it done. It helps me, always, to know that I can be responsive to circumstances with great or limited resources, and keep the integrity of the work. I laid out the pieces, provided visual and sonic references as needed, but did not run my mouth about it. I trusted that the elements would transmit their particular energies to Jason and Dellis. We played from the heart with short-burst phrases full of saturated color, spontaneous shared movements, and deeply felt renderings of the people in the piece. When something clicked, we all memorized its contours on the spot, then moved on. Happily, they were seeing the emergent system, and we found a synchronous flow that I can still feel all these years distant.

I assembled the elements of *Blood:Shock:Boogie* with zeal, beginning in the fall of 1995. I closed my eyes and saw the whole in my mind's eye. It looked like a moving model of a solar system, with the spinning "planets," "moons," and "comets" being the people, stories, and songs that would orbit through view as we swept through the moving whole. Some elements were quick-spinning and simple—for example, a single line or phrase of sound and movement that I could imagine repeating infinitely like a musical loop as it traversed space. Characters in this assemblage would need to transmit their essence instantaneously, so the performers had to render a complicated being without flattening them, and figure their way to signify the whole through spare language and gestures. Other elements were more complex, and spun slowly with a heavier gravity about them. I knew it was crucial to bring each part into razor sharp focus, whatever its relative size, and to listen for the trajectory that we all would take through the material (which meant considering sequence, duration, and proximity).

As the house lights begin to dim, Dellis, Jason, and I embrace one another and begin the low hum that will start the whole thing off in the dark. I am excited to see how this "music of the spheres" dramaturgy works in performance.

○

Kimberlee Koym-Murteira (Kimberlee Koym at the time of our first acquaintance) has been a vital collaborator across my career. A visual artist whose work bridges scenic design and installation, she and I first met in Austin when Vicky Boone suggested her as the designer for a double-bill I was to direct of Shay Youngblood's play *Black Power Barbie* and my own *Earthbirths, Jazz and Raven's Wings* at

Frontera. I was nervous about our meeting, as I didn't know how I was going to describe the aesthetic approach I wanted to take; I was so used to folks "not getting it" on the page, I was unsure how she would respond to the scripts Vicky had shared with her. Earlier that day I'd identified an indigo-saturated collage by Romare Bearden in the library that I thought had the feeling of the work, and had written down the name of the piece along with a couple other pieces of his and some work by Betye Saar. When Kym arrived at Mojo's cafe, my nerves instantaneously evaporated; the glint in her eye and her distinctive laughter accurately signaled her capacious brilliance. She had read both pieces and she said, "let me show you something!" She reached into her huge canvas bag and pulled out a big book of artwork by Romare Bearden, and opened to a page she'd marked with a small slip of yellow paper. She turned it toward me, and there was the precise collage I was going to tell her about. She started talking about identity and fragmentation and about her belief in the use of collage and assemblage as dramaturgical structures. The environment she created for those two plays haunts me to this day, it was so beautiful. Of course I asked her to design *Blood:Shock:Boogie* (she designed five other productions for me over the years and has remained a vital creative interlocutor). I didn't need to see sketches; just bring it! I knew her offering would bring us many invitations and challenge us to respond and incorporate her statements as part of our common text.

Sure enough, Kym walked into the space the first day with a sculpture she'd made of a crescent moon inside a bicycle wheel! The moon was made of materials similar to the rectangular reflectors that are usually attached to the spokes. In performance the moon could glow with just a whisper of light, or it could bounce light like a beacon across the space. It was rugged, everyday, and absolutely mystical. Kym hung it just above our heads. Then she pulled out white chalk and as we showed her the places where each element happened, she began to draw the anchor visual elements on the walls and on the floor: the window panes, the streetlamp, the hopscotch grid, etc. Her drawings had the feel of a show that was on Saturday mornings when we were kids, *Simon and the Land of Chalk Drawings*, about a boy who draws things in chalk that become real in an alternate dimension he can access. They also suggested vévés and other such ceremonial markings made on the ground, animated through practice, then swept away upon conclusion of a ritual. The light sat on a spectrum from incandescent electric to the cool soul blue of moonlight. As our bodies moved among Kym's elements, I was elated to see that the whole thing was a constantly unfolding multidimensional collage. Kym was, and remains, no joke.

– DAJ

Blood:Shock:Boogie
Premiered at Frontera@Hyde Park Theatre
Austin, Texas
February 1996

Directed by Daniel Alexander Jones
Installation by Kimberlee Koym
Lighting Design by Scott Segar
Sound Design by Kevin Freedman

FEATURING:
Daniel Alexander Jones as LUNA
Jason Phelps & Daniel Dodd Ellis as LIGHT

These three:

>LUNA. The boy.
>LIGHT. Two embodied aspects of electromagnetic radiation.

become the others:

>JOSEPHINE BAKER. Flamboyant, expatriate artist and activist.
>BROTHER:SAGE. Young Black man under a streetlight.
>DAD. New England Black man.
>GENIE. New England white woman.
>NICKY. Intrepid nine-year-old Black girl.
>JULIA CHILD. Popular American cooking show host.
>EUGENE. Teenaged gay Black boy.
>TRAGIC MULATTO. Á la Lena Horne from the cutting room floor.
>DON CORNELIUS. Silky smooth host of television's *Soul Train*.
>JOMAMA JONES. Soulsonic super star.
>THE VIGNETTES. Jomama's relentless background singers.
>YANKEE GRANDMOTHER. 84-year-old New England white woman.

Note:

>Scene titles may be projected or chalked into the space.
>/ indicates the point at which a speaker is interrupted.
>Italics indicate a line is sung.

BLOOD

(*Darkness.* LUNA *sings.*)

LUNA.
Sister moon
you are so quiet
hanging back
in your infinite sky.
Your soul
spins in silence,
you turn your face
to the darkside to cry.

(LUNA's *notes catch the slowly-revealed edge*
of a looming crescent moon.)

LUNA.
The part of you we see
hides all that you be.
In the shadow
do you feel at home?

Let the angels touch your hair,
wipe the silver from your eyes,
bring comfort to you by and by.

(*Footlights snap on along the edge of the*
moon, illuminating JOSEPHINE BAKER, *who*
looks down from the crescent and smiles.
She is naked, save for a cut of fine silver
cloth spilling like moonlight through her
hands. She dances wildly along the cres-
cent's edge, to tease the sad faces into smil-
ing. She plucks a nearby star and blows it

*like a kiss. The star floats gingerly down
through a waiting window frame. The star
bursts and becomes* LIGHT. *Pleased,* JOSE-
PHINE BAKER *winks at them. They wink
back. Lights out on the moon. Swelling
organ tones from an old-fashioned radio
serial.* LIGHT *speaks as* LUNA *intones from
the shadows.* LIGHT *each speaks with their
own timing and phrasing, listening to one
another, but not deliberately seeking unison
or uniformity.)*

LIGHT. This is the story of a boy.

LUNA.
  Blood sound, pressing.
  Rush of visions.
  Premonitions.

LIGHT. The creation story of a boy.

(*Lights rise on* LUNA, *staring up at the window frame.* LUNA *turns to the two figures
of* LIGHT *and gestures. They gesture back
in kind. As they do so, the light in the space
blooms, incandescent. Two more gestures
establish playful physical communication
among the three players. The three huddle
together, vaudeville style.* LIGHT *speaks,*
LUNA *sings.)*

LUNA.
  I become at once old:new.

LIGHT. Made for a world which never came.

LUNA.
Looking in the mirror...

LIGHT. Mind:body:spirit.
Made for the darkness, under the light.

LUNA.
I become you for me.

> *(Silver flash.* LUNA *demonstrates how to "become you for me," gesturing to each aspect of* LIGHT *as the telling unfolds, calling forth the characters each is to portray. They must "vibrate" the essence of each, even though they might say very little.)*

LUNA. (*Gesture*) Mother. Genie.

> *(One aspect of* LIGHT *becomes* GENIE, *a New England white woman, middle-aged, with big eyes.)*

GENIE. I wondered what you looked like when you were inside of me.

STREET

LUNA. Jazz. Brother:Sage.

> *(One aspect of* LIGHT *becomes* BROTHER:SAGE, *a young man standing under a streetlight, on the sidewalk below the window frame, and gestures with his hands. The streetlight flickers.)*

BROTHER:SAGE. Jazz? I guess syncopations, music …real music, heartfelt music …music that's alive, you know, live not dead, you know? Jazz is not about saxophone, string bass, a piano and some drums …it should be about constantly new instruments—using today's instruments …Jazz begins of …like …voice, you know, utterance …Jazz is that John Henry man-can-stand-on-his-own-two-feet-and-be-what-it-is-and-still-be-Jazz. You know? That's Jazz …*Jazz.*

LUNA. Strong.

> (BROTHER:SAGE *snaps his fingers and the streetlight snaps off. Warm morning light fills the space.* LUNA *is a five-year-old boy. Shy, yet confident, he sits on the floor of his room, as* LUNA *tells this part of the story over the melody to "Lift Ev'ry Voice and Sing," which is hummed earnestly by* LIGHT. *Slowly over the course of the story,* LUNA's *window frame rises into the air, and the street is revealed.*)

LUNA. A long long time ago there was a planet called
Krypton.
And on Krypton were people.
And the people were not strong, or …anything else.
And they were very very unpowerful.
So, one day there started to be earthquakes all around
and all the earthquakes were getting harder and harder
and everytime they went
it was getting harder and harder.
And so,
this…
Superman's mother?

was helping Superman's father do all these kinds of things
and one day
Superman's father...
—well first Superman was a little boy—
well
Superman's father
was looking in the microscope
and
he saw that the sun was getting closer to Krypton
so he thought the best thing to do was to send the
little boy
off to space.
So, he built this rocketship and he sent him off
and the minute he landed at Earth
the planet exploded
and all the people were died
because of the explosion.

(*In the distance behind* LUNA, *the shape of a
yellow school bus is articulated. Its engine
revs hungrily.* LUNA *stands, bravely, and
gestures to* LIGHT.)

LUNA. Parent testimony. Yellow bus. Dad.

(*One aspect of* LIGHT *becomes* DAD, *a New
England Black man in his thirties.* DAD
*holds his face in his hand, thoughtfully,
standing on the sidewalk, on the morning
of the first day of school.*)

DAD. So, Tapley was a perfectly good school.
Perfectly good. Three blocks away.
So, you went to kindergarten there.
So, I knew most of the teachers.

So, now, with the bussing, you're going to Pottenger.

So, Labor Day comes and goes...
So, they send out the assignments for the bus stop
and, HEY, it's right down at the corner.
So, I can see you get on the bus. See you get off.

> (*Not convinced,* LUNA *gestures to* LIGHT's
> *other aspect.*)

LUNA. Yellow bus. Genie.

> (LIGHT's *other aspect again becomes* GENIE,
> *the young mother in her thirties, who stares
> down the revving engine.*)

GENIE. Boston was just last year. I put you on the bus at the corner. I have decided that you are going to be just fine. And you will be.

> (*The yellow school bus is washed away
> into a rush of street sounds. Jelly shoes on
> pavement, double-dutch ropes smacking the
> sidewalk, handclaps and muted songs from
> distant radios. Edges of buildings and city
> houses sketch themselves in the air, from a
> child's twilight perspective.*)

BRICK

LUNA. Alright. (*Gestures*) Nicky.

> (LIGHT *becomes* LUNA. LUNA *portrays*
> NICKY. NICKY *is a nine-year-old Black girl.
> She is the girl who used to beat you up.*

During the following text, she demon-
strates her skill at hopscotch. She speaks
to LIGHT *and* LUNA *while keeping an eye*
on her street.)

NICKY. Alright.
    If you gonna fight,
    you got to tell the difference between real and fake.
    Cuz if you can't tell the difference,
    you ain't gonna know who to bother fighting.
    Most people are fake.
    All the way through.
    Most people that's fake try to act like they real.
    Perpetrate.
    If you real, you could see right through them.
    And they could tell.
    If you fake, or a sucka, they can tell
    and they gonna try and play you.
    Huh?
    No, you ain't fake. You just shy.
    But you gotta bust out of that.
    And you can't be being nice to everybody up front like
    you do.
    Everybody say, "you so nice."
    Well, you so nice you will keep getting played,
    'til you played out.
    Hold on!

              (NICKY *executes a masterful hop-through.*)

NICKY. Now, real and fake.
    You need a example.

              (*She quickly surveys the street. Her eyes*

burn toward a particular stoop at the end
of the block. Her shoulders set back a bit.)

NICKY. You could look right here on this block.
Look at Tasha ...
She fake for real.
Umm-hmm.
First, cuz she think she better than everybody.
She think she cute.
Plus, cuz Tasha always bitin'.
Like, look-look at see-see-see
how she always be sayin', "fresh?"
Like, "that's a fresh jacket, Sylvia ..." or
"oh, girl I like the way you wear that dress, that's fresh ...
oooh, Tanita, girl, you could sing, you fresh!"
And you KNOW I was sayin' it first!
Now she say it so much I can't hardly use it.
I should slap her upside her head ...
but I feel sorry for her
cuz she can't think up nothin' herself.
Ooooh, and you remember when she got extensions?
BITE.
Cuz Jameica had had them two weeks before—
in that same exact style, too.

(LIGHT/LUNA *gestures.*)

Please!
Tasha ain't my friend.
She hang around, but it ain't deep.
I will give her the papers at any time.
That's another part of fighting.
You got to remember
you could always send anybody walking.

Real or fake.
Whenever you want.
Just give them papers and move right on.
I don't know, though.
You too nice.
You act like a girl.

(Sound of a television being switched on. The buildings vanish; the window frame of LUNA's *room is articulated. The static snap of a television knob being turned. The theme from* The French Chef *plays.* LUNA *resumes his role, and sends one aspect of* LIGHT *into a waiting television screen to become* JULIA CHILD, *the popular host of the American television cooking show. She is tall and bony with an extremely expressive voice and speaks with a gently instructive tone.* LUNA *huddles in front of the television screen with the other aspect of* LIGHT. *As* JULIA CHILD *speaks, they mimic some of her gestures and practice some of her postures.)*

JULIA CHILD. Cakes! These marvelous confections are found throughout culinary history in most every culture. With a bit of flourish and imagination this staple confection undergoes a metamorphosis, becoming a universal symbol of ceremony and celebration. Once you know the basics of cake-making, you may tailor them to your specific needs. Today we will get to baking and make sure that our cakes rise to their fullest potential. Let's begin...

BOY

LUNA. Boy. Eugene.

(*A cord drops from the sky.* LIGHT *pulls the cord and a distant moon is switched on. It waxes.* LIGHT *becomes* EUGENE, *a teenaged gay Black boy. He is refined and strikingly beautiful; his speech and movement are precise. His presence is informed by an awareness of being observed at all times.* EUGENE *prepares for his house party by rifling through* LUNA's *record collection. They sit under the window frame. He periodically scrutinizes* LUNA, *who blushes when he does.*)

EUGENE. This isn't all of your records. You still listen to her? I test people about music, you know. If somebody doesn't like Stevie, they got a bad heart. If somebody doesn't like Patti—you know something is wrong with them. And you know they are frigid. I mean she is so passionate. And you know she is too much for that tired husband of hers. She's got to get off—that's why she does like she does. Now, what you gonna wear to my party? You can't be serious. If you gonna call yourself my friend, I got standards to uphold. You can't come in there dressed like that, Ms. Sugar. If you gonna come to my party, you gonna have to lose the white shoes, comprende? You got to have your drag correct. And rainbows would be cute if this was 1981 and your name was Stacy Lattisaw, but neither of those things is true. Now let me in this closet. Hmmm. You could wear these black pants and this shirt and these suspenders. You need to be classy, like Sade. You need to throw this out. Now, try it on. What you mean you can't take your clothes off? Boy, take off your clothes! We ain't got time for all of this drama. And the tee-shirt, cuz it's gonna bunch under the white one.

> (LUNA, *facing* EUGENE, *lifts up his shirt.* EUGENE *circles closer, cat-like. He smells* LUNA's *embarrassment like fresh blood. The waxing moon tears slightly at the seams, scoring its surface.*)

What's that? How did you get them? Do they hurt? I ain't never seen stretch marks like that. Mmmm—I ain't giving it back. Stand up.

> (*Stopping the moment with a finger in* EUGENE's *face,* LUNA *pulls the cord and turns out the moon. He counters.*)

LUNA. Birthday cake! Nicky.

> (*With a flurry,* LUNA *and* LIGHT *all become* NICKY. LUNA *speaks her words and both aspects of* LIGHT *refract and echo her movement.* NICKY's *tale is a record-breaking 200-meter race.*)

NICKY. No-no-no let me tell it, let me tell it! Your cake was chocolate and your mother had that little shiny boat on top with all them little shiny Japanese people cuz...who? Yeah, cuz her friend had brought them from Japan—your brother look like he Japanese. Don't neither of y'all look Black—you look like your mama—but anyway she put them on the cake and then put all these candles on there and anyway we had had some cold pizza cuz your father had to walk and get it in the snow and we had ate that when they go in there to get the cake and we all start singing Happy Birthday and then they walking in with the cake and your father went like this and one of the candles knocked into that boat and that boat blew up and caught all them little Japanese people on fire and they started melting and the fire was all high and your father was like "Dammit, Dammit!" and I was like you betta put that down and finally your mother grabbed it and threw it in the sink and put it out. I didn't eat none of that cake!

PUBLIC

> (*One aspect of* LIGHT *fills a television screen, becoming* JULIA CHILD, *who details a recipe. As she speaks, textbook images of bones connecting to bones, muscular patterns, venous systems, nerve networks, etcetera, flash behind her.*)

JULIA CHILD. Dry Ingredients:
   one cup cocksucker, sifted
   2/3 cup candied hands, held so
   one box powdered, cocoa-flavored, mama's boy milk
   pinch of salt
   grated rind of one mulatto
   zest of hand-on-hip

   Liquids:
   3 tablespoons boy spit
   8 "faggot"s up against the locker, juiced
   2 tsp. extract of "faggot" w/knife-in-face

1/2 tenderized queer
2 tsp. semen (best frustrated and fresh)

Mix dry ingredients. Add liquids. Stir. Pour into pans lined with fresh morning sheets, dream-stained. Note: you can test them for freshness by smelling; if you sense confidence, discard. Bake in a slow oven until it bounces back when you touch it, or until a stick inserted into its center comes out clean. Bon Appétit.

> (*Television light falls into static, which falls onto* LUNA *who is a ten-year-old boy lying on his bedroom floor. The window frame under which he sleeps rises into the air. As he speaks, pale blue-green light seeps up from the floor and fills the space.*)

LUNA. I lie in pain. Sleepless, as my bones grow. My father enters silently in the darkness. With cool alcohol, he anoints my legs. He anoints my ankles. He anoints the soles of my feet.

> (LUNA, *bathed in static television light, stretches and bends as though swimming underwater. Tiny moons, like fish, school through the space around him. He reaches for them in his sleep. They slip through his fingers. In the foreground, a street light flickers on. An aspect of* LIGHT *stands as* BROTHER:SAGE *beneath it.*)

BROTHER:SAGE. I used to love the wolfman. Serious. When I heard that there was a man that could turn into a wolf? Yo. There was nobody who could tell me that couldn't happen. Yeah, I saw the movie, but ...the story was older than the movie.

> (*Howl of a wolfman, and the space is plunged into momentary darkness. Sound*

NICKY, *who practices the steps to a homemade dance routine, which* LIGHT *tries
vainly to learn.*)

NICKY. Tomboy?
Psssh!
Eric call me a tomboy cuz I ain't no pussy.
And Eric know all about being a pussy.
You crazy—I don't like old monkey-face Eric!
That's nasty.
I'ma marry me a Puerto Rican.
Not no Dominican, not no Jamaican and not no
chump nigga.
My mama said, "I can't stand me no whining niggas."
Like Eric.
He always whining.
And then he try to act mean like he somebody.
Psssh.
Please.
He know-he know better than to try that mess with me.
Cuz I got no problem with kicking his behind.
And you know he'll come crying,
snot dripping out his nose,
talking 'bout "Stop, sto-o-op!"
Punk. Me liking Eric. Shoot.

(*Bored with her dance,* NICKY *squats on
the sidewalk and stares down the street.*)

I'll kiss Michael Jackson but I ain't gonna marry him.
Jameica say he a faggot, but I don't care
cuz I ain't gonna marry him.

And, plus, my mama said, "I don't trust no man lay up in no
beauty shop longer than I do."

Like Ray?
No, that don't count cuz Ray *work* there.
Plus, he my cousin.
He a faggot *for real*, though.
His boyfriend is cute, too! André.
He look like Leroy off of "Fame."
He could dance good.
Faggots could dance good.
André could dance the best, though.
He taught me how to kiss.

> (LIGHT *gestures a request.* NICKY *is dumb-founded.*)

I ain't showing you!
You too young, and plus, you can't even fight
and you talking 'bout *kissing*?!

JAM

> (*One aspect of* LIGHT *becomes* EUGENE.
> LUNA *resumes his role, and stands uncom-
> fortably in his "new clothes."*)

EUGENE. It looks good. This party is going to be the jam. What's
wrong?

> (LUNA *hangs his head.*)

EUGENE. I know. I like you, too. What? I don't like to say that, it's
cliché. What? "Nothing." You're lying to me; I don't like it
when you lie to me. How do I "hurt you?" You "don't know?"
What do you want?

(EUGENE *moves closer and closer still to* LUNA. *His breath a whisper on* LUNA's *neck.*)

EUGENE. Do you want to hold me? Do you want to kiss me? Do you want to touch me? Where? My chest? My back? Down here? Do you want to kiss me all over my body? That must be hard.

(EUGENE *walks away.*)

EUGENE. These are the records I want to borrow.

MESS

(LUNA *snaps into* NICKY. *A red moon waxes further, overhead. Nighttime on the street.* LIGHT *curls into shadow.*)

NICKY. Now, who's messing with you? Jeremy?
Figures. Jeremy know better than to mess with me
cuz I'll make him bleed.
Like one time, he called my mama a ho?
I was like, you better take that back you Jamaican boo-ty-scratcher!
And he didn't and I was on him like BAM! UHH! DOOZSH!
I beat him so bad, his mama, his daddy, his whole generation felt it.

Psssh.

Everybody think he all tough. He ain't nothing.
Jeremy just know how to perpetrate.

You know, basically, there ain't a whole lot of people it's worth for you fight.
But, when it comes time? You got to go—you can't back down.
You can't just sit by. Cuz if you don't fight, you ain't worth nothing,
cuz you don't think you worth fighting for.
If you let people put you down, you gonna be down.
And people always gonna be trying to put you down.
Especially you, because you too nice.
And that ain't gonna work.

(NICKY *moves toward* LIGHT, *turns her face to the reddening moon. She grows more scrappy with each word.*)

NICKY. Boy, I'm telling you. You got to do whatever you got to do. You could scratch at they eyes, hit at they privates and bite down hard on whatever you could get. But, my thing is, just kick they butt!
My mama said, "I don't ever want to hear about how you lost a fight. If you ever come in here having lost a fight, I will tear you up myself."
So I don't lose.
Ever.

SHOUT-OUT

(*An old-school shout-out.* EUGENE *rides the mic, tearing up and down the street, reverberating. The moon is supplanted by a giant blue lightbulb. Muted waves of slow-*

jams collapse into one another percussively under EUGENE's *words.*)

EUGENE. My house-house. My party-party. All that, and more.
Speakers in every corner; you can feel the music all around you.
Barbecue kickin' all out back and potato salad and kool-aid
and whatever else you like to drink. Blue Nile incense. Boys
with curls who tie their shirts up at the bottom. Girls who go
to barber shops and wear their father's shirts, buttoned down.
My house-house. My party-party. Randy has his hands in Tony's
back pockets—again. Jody is crying cuz Tanya and Deniece was
kissing. Lights dim and dancing slows. *If only you knew.* Air
thick with coconut oil, sweat, and dreaming. My house-house.
My party-party. All that, and more.

MARKINGS

(EUGENE's *voice has the texture of smooth
warm skin, molasses sweet. The lightbulb
dims and the red moon spills out from
behind it, revealing* LUNA, *next to* EUGENE.
*The edges of their bodies seem to fit like
pieces of a puzzle.*)

EUGENE. I let him hug me before he leaves.
I let him hold me and move us
slowly transforming into trees.
Entwined, rippling
the inside of our moment.
He drinks from me thirstily.
Sweet leaf drops.
Willing infinity

through
caresses
indulged,
unspoken.

TRUTH

> *(The hiss of a record ending, and the sound of a record arm lifting.* EUGENE *is gone and* LUNA *is left, contorted. He looks like a cross between a mermaid and a figure from Picasso's "Guernica." He confesses.)*

LUNA. I am a liar. I have been taught well. I don't like to lie, so I forget sometimes. I forget myself, and dance in the world for which I was made; the world which does not exist. The world which I remember. I forget myself and tell about the light I see surrounding some people, about the spirits who tell me things, about the sound of trees singing. For telling such things, I am chastised in one way or another. Therefore, most times, I lie. Well. Though my blood blisters beneath my skin, my words are chosen. My silences, thick. I am a liar. I tell stories that are dances with ill-rehearsed steps. With practice they will be smooth.

SHOCK

> *(*LIGHT *becomes* GENIE *and* DAD. LUNA *crawls back into the periphery to observe.* GENIE *and* DAD *wind through one another's*

words, like two instruments playing the same melody, differently.)

GENIE. You were bigger...

you couldn't...

you were still...

you were always beautiful.

I couldn't see what they...

you were changing, growing, everybody does at that age...

your face changed...you were changing...

you were not a...

you were...

DAD. I heard the bike skid and fall on the sidewalk and I knew it was your bike because...I just knew. You fall off the bike...I'm saying that's a good thing...not hurt or anything...a couple scrapes...and you get up not crying and I know... I know that that is how you're gonna deal with it...your mother brings all that talk about..."are you okay?"...I'm saying, big, "Genie, he's okay, just some scrapes," but you start going inside... and Band-aids...and iodine...all that...all it really needed was some air...you know, I tell her, I was a medic in the army in Texas, and I seen how you deal with that kind of thing...I'm saying...I'm saying he needs to get-back on that bike...then I see the wheel got bent,

you looked like your
brother more so than...

sometimes I couldn't
see either your father or
myself...sometimes both
of us...sometimes more...

you...what was I sup-
posed to do...

I couldn't hurt you more.

so I'm all about let's fix
the bike, fix the bike so
he gets on and rides.
I was downplaying the
whole thing, and I said...
"are you alright," and he
started to cry and I could
tell...he was really hurt
and of course you're not
gonna cry right off cuz
you're in shock.

(*From the back of the space,* NICKY *tells
it straight.*)

NICKY. Shoulda seen it. Bloody knees. Blood mark on the sidewalk.
Knees all messed up from falling. Blood mark on the sidewalk.
There was blood everywhere. Red sticky juice pouring out his
knee holes, it was damn nasty. All over everything, running
down all in his socks, soaked up all thick red, dripping leaving
a trail. It was so. Damn. Nasty. That's all I got to say.

(NICKY *rushes forward to make plans.*
LIGHT *resists.*)

NICKY. When they get back from the store, you know I need to be
Wonder Woman. First of all, cuz y'all boys, and Jameica, she
can't hardly run and, second, cuz I'm badder than all y'all and
y'all know it's true! Don't even, don't even, please, don't EVEN,
okay? Like, remember the time when you said you could skate
faster than me, right, and we was racing, and then Eric tried
to cut me off, and I took him out and still kept skating and
then I came up from behind, and right when we got past the

pole I beat you so don't E-VEN!? ...? ...? ...Yeah, you fell. But that ain't my fault that's your fault cuz you was bragging and it still count. Yeah, that was nasty cuz your knees got messed up. I know you didn't cry. But that don't mean you could be Wonder Woman. You could be the Hulk, though.

THIS FUTURE NIGHT BOY

> (LUNA *resumes his role.* LIGHT *brings a step-ladder for* LUNA *to climb. He does so and sits atop the ladder. Night falls. This is a picture of his grown self.*)

LUNA. I felt his plane land and I hadn't even met him, officially. I was sitting in this meeting for the project and all the hair stood up on my body and I suddenly couldn't hear anything anyone was saying. I walked out into the room where he was standing and I saw his aura. I had always wanted to see someone's aura and yet, I felt somehow embarrassed, as though people could see me seeing it. I introduced myself and he touched my hand and there was this chill over my whole body but not cold exactly, more like a charge, and I was embarrassed again and all that I could say was, "Oh, God, you're beautiful look at you you're family ..." but, I didn't mean like a cousin or even in the queer sense but the word just felt right and we stumbled through the work and in the blink of an eye we were at dinner. Talking like water spilling on the table between us about art, and focus, and "wow, what is this thing," and about the moon, which oh, look, is so full, and he's talking about boyfriends and New York and I'm saying things about being a vegetarian, too, and not being able to look at him too long, but he's touching my hands and my arms and it's feeling so good, and we both say, let's go for a walk, at the exact same time, and then laugh, because we said it at the exact same time, and we're walking, and I don't know what time it is, but just that the sky is ...I can see him against the moon while we walk through this park and it feels like we are both floating and the next thing I know, we are standing with our backs to this beautiful tree, enveloped by her branches, and he tells me how he used to climb trees when he was a kid, to get away from the places of pain, and I understand and tell him about the energy relationship between us and trees and he takes my hand again and curls into me and we are holding one another and I start to cry ...I think ...but ...all pulling silver ... skin ...bleeding ...light and I'm shaking ...his tears on my cheek and there is only color and the breeze and I hear a melody that I realize we are both humming which is the song that I hear the tree humming to us and softly ...softly ...he kisses my mouth ... and I wonder, in that moment ...am I home?

> (LUNA *climbs down the ladder, shakes it all off, and leaves the space. His voice, in voice-over, is left behind.* LIGHT *begins to dance together. The dance is angular, vulnerable, sensual and improvisatory.* LUNA's *childhood story is the dance's contrapuntal score.*)

LUNA. One day a science teacher was in Egypt and she
dug up a treasure.
And ...well
one day
when she opened the treasure
and she found out
that she had the powers of Isis.
And then
she put her amulet on.

And there was a little piece of paper in the box
that said
hide your amulet under your shirt
or your dress cover
or it shall be seen
and the secret shall be tooken—
taken—
away.
So she hid it.
And one day
there was some trouble around the world
and she didn't know about anything—
so she didn't—
and she read the paper again
and it said whenever trouble, say
"O, Mighty Isis"—
that's all it said.
And all of a sudden
something repeated her
"Isis, Isis, Isis…"
all again.
And she was took up into the sky
by an amazing powerful blast-of-something—
I don't know what.
And there was fog all around and smoke
and everything.
At first her face was showing
and the smoke and fog covered her right up
and she turned from a regular person into a
immortal.
And her name was Isis the Immortal.
She will never die like the Egyptians.
Well,

one day
she met a friend, Billy Batson.
Well...
he...
she didn't tell him anything about the amulet.
Well
he knew that she was Isis
because
he was really a superhero, too—Captain Marvel.
And
so by mistake she um
she was um
shaking his hand and the amulet just fell out.
And so he saw the amulet.
And she said "Uhh..."
And...but Billy said, "don't worry because I'm a superhero, too."

SHOWS

> (*With* LUNA *absent,* LIGHT *becomes* NICKY,
> *each aspect jockeying for center stage.*)

NICKY. My friends and me, we play Star Wars and Superfriends.
Sometimes, we fight over who could be Spiderman, the Hulk,
or over who will get to be Wonder Woman. We like the way
she turns into herself. We watch *The Bionic Woman.* And *Soul
Train.* That ain't how you do that. This is how you do.

LIGHT. It's the Soooooul Train!

SOULSONIC SUPERSTAR

(LIGHT *expertly dances a few challenging steps. Sound of a television being turned on. An episode of* Soul Train, *the 1970s American musical variety show, spills from the television. The space gets candy-colored and lights flash. One aspect of* LIGHT *becomes the inimitable host,* DON CORNELIUS, *and speaks with a silky bass voice.*)

DON CORNELIUS. Hey, hey, hey! How y'all doing this evening? That's right. Uh-huh. Dig it? Dig it? DUG. Tonight it gives me the greatest pleasure to announce the presentation of the Soul Train Lifetime Achievement Award for Outstanding Contribution to the Entertainment Industry by an Afro-American Black Performer. Let me say, simply, that our honoree has created some of our favorite tunes here on the *Soul Train*. Let me run some titles down on ya: Tonight, Tonight (I know that's right), Afromatic, and Too Fierce For You (Oooh-Oooh)—to name a few. Yes, I imagine you've guessed by now, so without further adieu, I present to you the incomparable, the amazing, the downright baaaaad...JOMAMA JONES AND THE VIGNETTES!

(LUNA *enters as* JOMAMA JONES, *a relentless soul diva with a massive afro and sequins for days.* LIGHT *snaps to attention, becoming* THE VIGNETTES, JOMAMA's *background singers, who rival the Ikettes for attitude.*)

JOMAMA. Thank you. Before I accept this fabulous award, I'd like to do what comes most naturally to me. Vignettes?

(*A stupefyingly funky bass line fills the*

air. THE VIGNETTES *strike a variety of dra-*
matic, impoverished poses. JOMAMA *takes*
the stage like a tigress, singing with all her
heart and soul.)

JOMAMA.

> *I was born a love child*
> *didn't have no daddy to pave my way*
> *I had to stand on my own two feet*
> *ain't gonna back-track, sugar, not today*
>
> *So I, sho' nuff, sho' nuff*
>
> *Got to keep on rising up*
> *Got to keep on moving up*
> *Got to keep on climbing up*
> *From that...ghetto in my mind*
>
> *Was concrete ever your playground?*
> *Was roaches ever your toy?*
> *Did you ever fall down to your knees and pray*
> *every day*
> *for a teeny tiny little taste of joy*
>
> *Oh I, sho' nuff, sho'nuff*
>
> *Had to keep on rising up*
> *Had to keep on moving up*
> *Had to keep on climbing up*
> *From that...ghetto in mind*
>
> *So, baby I can't love you*
> *cuz you surely ain't worth my time*
> *I am on a mission sugar*
> *I'm truly gonna get what's mine*
>
> *Oh, I, sho'nuff, sho'nuff*

Gonna keep on rising up
Gonna keep on moving up
Gonna keep on climbing up
Just a little bit higher

Keep on
rising
moving
climbing
fro-o-om that
ghetto-o-o
in your mind...

(JOMAMA *basks in the light of applause,*
then speaks with as much sincerity as she
can muster.)

JOMAMA. Thank you.
I'd like to share something with you tonight.
Even as a scorned love child
in Hardtimes, Miss'sippi City USA
I prayed
reached out, with hope
to the heavens above.
A little ebony daisy
in her tiny garden patch
always strivin', always reachin' for that freedom time...
help me now!
I came up talking

Umgawa, Black Power
Umgawa, Black Power
Umgawa ...well
Black Power got turned off,
somebody didn't pay the bill.

Left us all sitting in blackness with no lights on.
But, did I let that stop me?
I said…did I let that stop me?
Jomama's here to tell the story, now isn't she?

It was a long haul up this hill.
I had to fight at an early age.
A little Vaseline kept my nails clean
when I'd pluck me a patch of naps on the playground.
I'm still fierce. Don't doubt it.
Why, I had to snatch some weave backstage tonight
with the folks they got around here.
I kept on!
Brothers tried to pimp me…or wear my clothes.
Sisters dissed my drag, my yellow, my nose.
Had the white men running like a leaky hose.
And the white girls? I was on they ass.
I went to diction class.
I KEPT ON,
knowing my success would be a beacon,
and someday, somewhere, some little red-headed stepchild
would reach out, reach up from the mud to me,
here,
glowing among the stars on high, like a Afro-American
astronaut perched on top of the Empire State Building;
and it's my duty—no, my pleasure,
to shine my light on y'all.

So, I accept this award. But I've got news for you, Mr. Don
Cornelius.
If you think for one moment that by giving me this Lifetime
Achievement Award you gonna knock me off my building and
into an early-career casket
like you tried with Diana Ross last year, you got another thing

coming. The Millennium approaches, and Jomama's got a brand-new drag!

> (JOMAMA *rips off her sequined gown to reveal a skin-tight, space-age micro mini-dress. Things get dangerous as the* Soul Train *derails.*)

JOMAMA. I ain't gonna let nobody turn me around!

You won't catch me eating turkey and mashed potatoes at the Kmart cafeteria—my name is not Aretha Franklin!

You won't catch me making the *Jet* magazine weekly almanac for shooting little twelve-year-old white boys in France—my name is not Nina Simone.

You won't catch me defending my use of AIDS research money on limousines and moving to Brazil to start me a psychic network—my name is not Dionne Warwick.

You won't catch me pulling a rake through my Jheri curl, greasin' up the back of a yellow cab on my way to sing at the Essence awards, talkin' to the cabbie about, "man, you single?"—my name is not Gladys Knight.

Tell me I'm lying!

And you won't catch me marrying no thuggish-ruggish-bone, birthing me no little hoodlum baby in a misguided attempt to cover up my lesbian identity—my name is not Susan, so watch what you say!

I ain't gonna let nobody turn me around
I ain't gonna let nobody turn me around
I ain't gonna let nobody turn me around
Cuz

Ain't no bitches bold enough
Ain't no niggas cold enough
Can't nobody hold enough
To take me away from you!

> (THE VIGNETTES *fall to their knees at* JOMA-
> MA's *sides as she hurls her arms, victori-*
> *ously, into the air.*)

JOMAMA. Who's got your love?!

THE VIGNETTES. Jomama!

> (*Television snaps off.* LUNA *pulls off his afro*
> *wig and speaks in a covert tone. Behind*
> *him,* LIGHT *enacts various web-spinning*
> *poses, as a massive silvery spider web is*
> *sketched behind them in the space.*)

LUNA. One day
    a long time ago...
    a few days...
    I mean a long time ago
    there was a scientist named
    Peter Parker.
    And they...
    And he was this...
    studying
    about spider...
    spiders and how they make their webs.

> (LUNA *rushes from the space. Both aspects*
> *of* LIGHT *finish the story.*)

LIGHT. And
    well

one day
he got bitten by ...
no that ...
he um got bitten by a spider.
And
he he he
he was he was
got all these amazing
he was he felt
very strange.
Then he found ...he looked in the dictionary
it said "spider ... "
he looked up on
"bad spider bite"
it said "you will get amazing strength
and strong
you will have a amazing color
of spider
and you will—if you are a man
you shall be Spider Man."
And then
he heard the
a long
a few
a few days later
he heard a voice.
He heard a scream from a little girl.
And
he he he thought he thoughted thought that the
he had to had to get the girl.
So he and he went like he put all his hands his
fingers up
and webs shooted up from his hands.

And he thought
that was one way he might as well get the girl.

> *(One aspect of* LIGHT *becomes* JULIA CHILD,
> *who stares up, gamely, at the massive web
> unfolding in the space. As she speaks,* LUNA
> *pulls the stepladder out, and quietly, almost
> furtively, climbs to once again look toward
> the future.)*

JULIA CHILD. The problem of timing enters in for any chef worth
their salt. Of course, there are cooking and cooling times listed
for each recipe, there are timers to keep you apprised of these
chronological roadmaps. There are detailed charts to adjust
these times; there are even times estimated. But, it all boils
down to timing, if you ask me. You've got to have a sense of
when a thing is coming along right in time and when it is not.
You may be folding a soufflé, sautéing a pan of mushrooms or
boiling eggs and all the while you must remain keenly aware
of its progress every step of the way. A minute, a second lost,
can mean the difference between a towering triumph and a
floundering flop. In my experience, I have found that relying
exactly on times listed is about as rewarding as taking the
weatherman's word as gospel: everything works out fine—just
as long as it stays sunny. But the minute that custard starts to
curdle, or that butter starts to burn, you'll wish you'd brought
your yellow slicker. Every good cook must rely on an innate
sense of timing. They must hone their powers of observation.
They must develop a keen understanding of the phrase...cook
it 'til it's done.

> *(A tight spot falls on* LUNA, *who sits high
> in the air atop the stepladder amidst the*

chalked web. JULIA CHILD *has left the building.*)

LUNA. Standing in your room, faces pressing.
I've been carrying this glow for you—heavy—in my stomach,
since that night by the tree.
Night after night,
when you hold my hand and pull me to you, rocking.
When you kiss me soft like in movies.
Standing here, I imagine the taste of your open mouth,
through this humid ascension.
Flash away from your nipples, taut stomach,
your obscene neck, light burgeoning sweet gold under your skin.
Feel myself pouring through my vessels. You say, "we have to
deal with this."
Yeah, we…stand here and hold one another and wait.
Faces pressing.
You say you've got to brush your teeth and I am shaking.
My rawness stains me like peeing emotion on myself.
I cannot leave, I stand, hear water running. And wait.
You return, twenty minutes later.
Towel wrapped, and sit at the edge of your bed.
You say, "I don't want to fuck you.
I don't want your tongue in my mouth."
I am wet and cold.
I am aware of my penis.
I don't know where to put my hands.
Emptied of words. I lie down.
You curl into me. Secure in my stillness.

(*Both aspects of* LIGHT *crawl down the web to either side of* LUNA. *They place flowers in his hair. Black-and-white music swells and* LUNA *is the* TRAGIC MULATTO, *caught*

in a web on the seafloor, staring up at the
rippling moon. The three players begin sing-
ing in the style of a Hollywood musical
spiritual, but truth ruptures the form.)

TRAGIC MULATTO.
    I've been touched
    I've been touched
    I've been touched
    by your spirit.

    When I'm falling down
    into the water,
    when I'm bleeding
    from my hands and knees

    I've been changed
    I've been changed
    I've been changed
    by your spirit.

    When I'm cutting my hair,
    when I take your photographs
    when I take my bedsheets
    and I burn them all up

    I will recall
    I will recall
    I will recall
    your spirit.

(The streetlight flickers on. Time to pack
up and go home soon. One aspect of LIGHT
falls under the light and becomes BROTH-
ER:SAGE *who watches* LUNA *and the other*

aspect of LIGHT *begin to brush away some of the chalk drawings.*)

BROTHER:SAGE. I wonder…if this music was really played, then people would see that like yo…you could be a hundred different ways and still be and it still be music, you know, you could be a hundred different ways and still be human, you know that's what all those things are talking about to me, you know? And there was a hip-hop song I remember. It was by Gang Starr, he…it says "I'm the ma'fuckin' man," and it's not so much that the lyrics are like-a-like, uh, yeah, I'm the man, but it's three guys…it…with…in the song it's three different rappers and they get on and say, "I'm the ma'fuckin' man," the next one gets on after him, he says, "I'm the ma'fuckin' man." So, it would seem that like, well, if he's the man, the other one can't be the man, but, Naaaaah. It's not about that. We all ma'fuckin' men and we…they all flow differently. They all had different things to say about why they were the man, or why they could be a man. And that to me was like, yo…tha's, tha's, tha's beautiful.

(*The other aspect of* LIGHT *has become the* YANKEE GRANDMOTHER, LUNA*'s 84-year-old grandparent. She is a New England woman seated in a simple wooden chair next to* LUNA. *She cannot move her legs and cannot see well. She sees through her skin.*)

YANKEE GRANDMOTHER. Having been brought up in a typical,
country, Yankee country family,
with two generations living in the same house,
I had that background of always having to do my part,
never occurred to me
that I had any choice.

And as I got through school,
the job I took,
which was teaching,
I was a special teacher
at Clarke School for the Deaf in Northampton,
for six years,
and there again,
I had a great deal of responsibility,
it never occurred to me to question any of the responsibility
which I was given,
and which I accepted,
and I did more than I was asked to do many times,
because I LOVED what I was doing.
And then I was married, in 1935,
and there again, it didn't occur to me, or to my...
husband...
that we had any choice
other
than to accept the responsibility which we were given.
It seems to me
that some of the trouble that is in the world today
is because people haven't been taught
that they can do what they want to do
which may or may not go along with the morals
that we've been taught for so many years,
but there are consequences, and
if they're willing to accept the consequences, or,
if they are given to understand what the consequences
of not paying their bills, of not, eh,
not helping around their family's home, of,
if they take drugs, there are things that happen,
if they, uh, indulge in sexual behavior, which is in...
for which they're not really old enough...

they're not giv…they don't understand the responsibility
that goes with it, it seems to me,
that the big problem seems to be,
that somewhere along the line,
we have not been able to impart to the next generation,
and this happens gradually, from generation to generation, I
guess, that there is responsibility that goes with everything that
we do and we have to…somebody has to pay for it.
We know, if we jump off a cliff,
we're going to fall down,
but we think that's an exaggerated thing.
But, every single thing we do in our life has a consequence.
We make friends with somebody…
once you are…
meet somebody, and relate in any way to them…
you are,
you are…a part,
you become somehow responsible for that relationship.
You may not think it amounts to anything, but it does.
We are a part of everyone we meet.
Whether we know it or not.

> (LIGHT *becomes* GENIE *and* DAD, *who watch
> from the outskirts of the space. The beam
> of light falls off of* LUNA *and travels across
> the space, passing over them, and then out
> of the space altogether, leaving a ripe twi-
> light haze.*)

GENIE. (*Speaking to* LUNA) I wondered what you looked like while
you were inside of me. I had a dream that I had twin boys.
They were adorable. Black. Much darker than your father. I
woke up wondering. I wanted very much to have a boy. Both
times. And I did. People said all different things: you would be

somewhere between Dad and I. Some said oh, no it could be a flashback to anybody in either family—which on both sides could be scary. So, I wondered and imagined all sorts of faces and fingers and tummies. When you came you looked right. When they brought you to me, you didn't cry. You just looked up at me as if to say, okay, what's next?

> (LUNA *moves through the space, regarding the chalk-drawings, looking at the people gathered. Looking them in the eye. He is older. This is a future self, looking back.*)

LUNA. So, I'm sitting in this minority graduate student get-to-know-you gathering, and I'm talking to these med student types who are talking about their GRE scores, and I'm all…"I'm an artist," so they ask me my opinion of affirmative action. There's dip and these little baked things that smell like they have meat in them, so I am fixing to leave and find myself a salad, when… yellow light smacks my face…and…rush by…leopard print… lemon smell…locks popping all out…red dirt laughter pulls me up outta my seat to the corner over there where she's talking to the dean and the Black English professor with the bow in her hair and I never do this put out my hand, "Hi, I'm an artist." "Hi, I'm a playwright, I'm having a garage sale tomorrow, why don't you come by," so I do, and did I mention that she wears horn-rimmed tortoise shell glasses? We go upstairs afterwards for lunch that she prepared, kale with lemon—she's from Georgia, guacamole with garlic and cayenne, and Jiffy cornbread. "I'm a lesbian, I think I should get that on the table right off." "That's cool," I say, "I dig boys. What are your plays about?" And I'm eating this plate of greens and bread and I'm feeling filled up with good food and we're talking and laughing and I notice the altar and the photographs of those who came before and I say…thank you…and she says, why? And I say for making me feel at home, and she says, no problem, and grabs a bowl of chips and the rest of the guacamole, goes into the living room, "I just had cable installed, so we've got CNN, BET and *The Young and the Restless* at our fingertips."

DAD. Next.

> (*Footlights on the moon snap on.* LUNA *climbs up and embodies* JOSEPHINE BAKER *standing on crescent's edge.*)

LUNA. Left like Lena in the field, to sense and face the rising.
    I am a smile, a breath, a cotton shirt on the line, and stepping.
    "Oh, I see," and this picture here to mark it.
    Woke me up all early; not even no time to rouse the tiny lie.
    Breathe. Smile.
    Arms like ten, from my cotton shirt; hands at the end.
    "Oh, I see."
    Begin. You'll figure what to do with your hands.

> (LUNA's *back is to us, as though we were standing behind Josephine Baker on a stage, like flies on a wall, looking out over her shoulder to an audience of stars. The bright light allows us to see only the edge of* LUNA—*the rest, like the darkside of the moon, is obscured.*)

LIGHT.
    You live inside a solitude so vast, it has become sky.
    Shifting constantly, darkening, storming,
    clearing, whispering, ever present.
    This is the story of a boy.
    The creation story of a boy.
    Made for the darkness, under the lights…

(LUNA *dances, reaching into the light as it slowly fades. Moon waning into the sea of roaring stars. The dance becomes a testimony in growing shadow. Bright silver flash. Darkness.*)

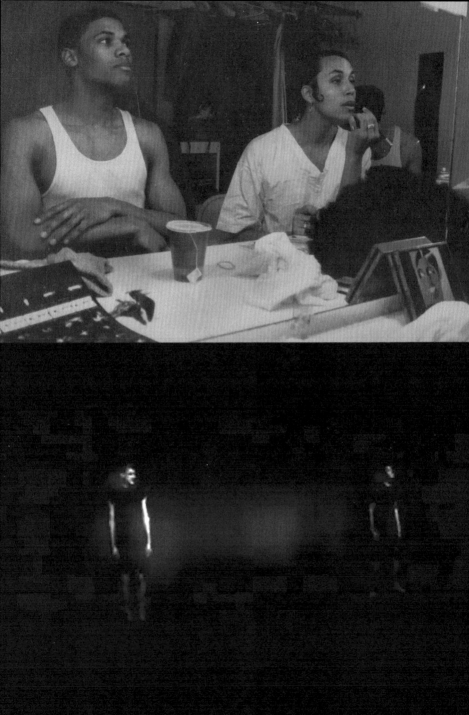

Phoenix Fabrik

for the unsung

FOREWORD

In the title *Phoenix Fabrik*, DAJ invokes the German term for factory, and if it is not bricks or cars or bullets or mouthwash but phoenix after phoenix that is manufactured within it, then he has created a theatrical location where we rebuild the dead into the flying free, again and again. The form DAJ develops to hold his characters and their words is a ring play based on the shout circle where we move through the corporeal death of our own dear ones, transmute the living death by which our bodies are subsequently threatened, become light and invincible. But we gotta get clean to join the circle. And we gotta knock three times. There is such humor in how this painful play proceeds. Even with unending hunger and humiliation, ghosts floating in the river of doll dresses—everyone has a crooked hip to lean into. It's set in 1945, and reckoning with the war's destruction starts with allowing the dead to talk. *Phoenix Fabrik* is a place to sing your burdens down, a thrilling rhythmic game, an emptiness into whose space we give over what hurts.

– Eisa Davis

ALTAR NOTES

Some histories must be exhumed, brought into the light, and then carefully returned to the dirt.

Phoenix Fabrik haunted me for years until I completed it. I pushed against it, ran from it, pulled the covers over my head, and otherwise did all I could to avoid the repulsive images that kept rising, in a nightmarish repetition, and the sadness that welled up like a flood from under my feet. Every night they were there waiting in the corner of the room when I turned the lights out: Eleanor, Inga, Mother Dixon, and the strange, smelly, nameless Boy. At one point Sharon Bridgforth, who had graciously agreed to be the primary dramaturg for the piece, wholesale had to lock me up in my apartment and threaten me not to run any longer. "They're gonna get you, Man, one way or the other!" Not long after that, Eleanor began musing about a black cat, and sure enough a black cat showed up outside my apartment and meowed and meowed until I let it in. It came every evening until I finished the draft. No lie. Several nauseating things that welled up in the dark hours of the night threaded back to historical facts I uncovered well after the fact of the writing.

As we built, the haunting was ropy, and it felt like none of our hands would ever come clean. The piece took the proverbial pound of flesh each time it was done. And it is the one piece of mine for which I'd offer a cautionary note: should you choose to explore it in performance, be deliberate about the process of entering and exiting the work, and find your way to honor the intensity that arises both within and outside the frame. The ring play was revealed as the medicine we needed and the more deliberate I was about utilizing it at all levels of the work, the more it became a conduit through which the most exacting emotions could move. Indeed, I came to understand the ring play as the necessary ritual form. In its traditional use the ring play could so directly and deftly relay a clear-eyed witness of harsh history that you might have to listen back and say, "Hold up, did I just hear what I *thought* I heard?"

o

I first worked with Leilah Stewart as a designer when I directed Erik Ehn's play *Heavenly Shades of Night Are Falling* in 1999. A prodigious artist and long time core member of Rude Mechs, Leilah's body of work spans a range of aesthetics, but is unified by her attention to detail, her interest in tactility, and her consistent collaboration with light. When we did the production of *Phoenix Fabrik* at Pillsbury House Theatre in Minneapolis, Leilah flew up to create the set. She designed and was extremely hands-on with the implementation. Cutting through the center of the space, the hallmark was a river of hundreds of doll dresses that she had carefully sewn. Leilah's set proposed the altar as a reliquary. The objects (doll eyes, hair, needle and thread, clay pipe, and a tin box among them) dwelled in the room with unmistakable magnetism, waiting for living hands to release their mysteries, and for the element of light to reveal their dark resonance. Mike Wangen once again worked his singular magic, creating a low-slung, undulating field of *sunlight-into-moonlight-into-shadow* complemented by saturated membranes of color that crawled ghostlike through the space, bruising all the surfaces they touched. Mike's lighting always had a comprehensive presence that animated each imagined world with a forceful intelligence every bit the equal of the actors. He arranged light like Gil Evans or Quincy Jones might music, having carefully catalogued all of the project's bones, and having listened with incomparable patience to the energetic longings connecting them. His light was the medium through which the soul of the piece came into view.

– DAJ

Phoenix Fabrik
Premiered at Pillsbury House Theatre
Minneapolis, MN
June 2006

Produced by Faye Price and Noel Raymond
Directed by Daniel Alexander Jones
Dramaturgy by Sharon Bridgforth and Abi Basch
Set Design by Leilah Stewart
Lighting Design by Mike Wangen
Costume Design by Heidi Hunter-Batz
Sound Design by Anton Jones

FEATURING:
Vinie Burrows as MOTHER DIXON
Barbara Duchow as INGA
Rhonda Ross as ELEANOR
Namir Smallwood as THE BOY
Aimee Bryant as understudy for ELEANOR

Phoenix Fabrik received a second production in 2007 at Todd Mountain Theater Project in Arkville, NY. It was produced by Suzanne Pred Bass and directed by Daniel Alexander Jones. Duchow and Smallwood returned to their roles as Inga and The Boy, Sonja Perryman played Eleanor, and Robbie McCauley played Mother Dixon.

Four players become these figures:

ELEANOR
INGA
MOTHER DIXON
THE BOY

Make a circle in the middle. This is where the players will play. Around the circle seat the people. Let them look upon the circle *and* one another as the play is played. Surround the circle with the witnessing trees.

The actors charge all objects with purpose and effect all necessary transformations themselves. The design may be spare or lush—but it should always guide our attention back to the breathing, pulsing bodies of the players.

Some shifts in time and place are called forth in the "playing"; others are subtle, internal—always they are meant to be immediate.

Fabrik is the German word for "factory" and is pronounced "fah-*breek*."

RING ONE

*(The four enter the space and begin play-
ing—they meet the eyes of audience members, their gazes linger, sometimes a smile,
sometimes not. They move about the room
and speak the world into existence. One
or more of them might take a line; if it's
two, the lines are not spoken in unison, but
rather sounded in a complementary way.
For each line, there is a gestural phrase
that may be echoed by the others, subtly. A
shared language for a shared act of remembrance.)*

ALL. South Carolina. 1945.

The valley, its red dirt, its trees, its boneyard.

The doll factory wall, and its window—a wide white mouth.
The window becomes a porthole in a Trans-Atlantic steamer.
Mother Dixon's prayer tent is a candle in the valley.

At the lip of the whole, a river flows. Dark, steady, relentless.

Shout!

*(They move in a circle, clapping the ring
play rhythms.)*

ALL. Soap, soap, 5 cents a cake! Soap, soap, 5 cents a cake!

ELEANOR. The boy lies by the river.

INGA. Mother Dixon comes upon him.

*(INGA and ELEANOR recede to watch.
MOTHER DIXON comes upon THE BOY.)*

MOTHER DIXON. Wake now.

THE BOY. How?! Who? Who?

MOTHER DIXON. You're 'cross my path.

THE BOY. No call to poke at someone, Aunty.

MOTHER DIXON. Sleep by the river ain't safe. Trouble come quick. Cottonmouth or cracker.

THE BOY. Cold. (*Breath, breath, breath.*)

MOTHER DIXON. Colder still, you don't dry off. You crossing the river or washing?

THE BOY. Crossing.

MOTHER DIXON. Sure weren't washing. Smelled you 'fore I seen you. Selling soap. 5 cents. Lather up good in this river water.

THE BOY. What's the time?

MOTHER DIXON. Still hot on the road. But dusk coming.

THE BOY. I'm late.

MOTHER DIXON. All the time in the world.

THE BOY. I'll lose the light.

MOTHER DIXON. All the light in the world, you spend your time right.

THE BOY. Humph.

MOTHER DIXON. Plenty of cures in my tent. Cures for the body. Fixing for the soul.

(THE BOY *takes her soap.*)

MOTHER DIXON. Cold hands. Got a tonic for that.

THE BOY. Petals, lye, tallow ... and something else ... can't put my finger ... How you put your cures together?

MOTHER DIXON. How they put together is one thing. How they work is another. You buying my soap or not?

THE BOY. "Mother Dixon's Angel Soap."

(THE BOY *gives the soap back.*)

MOTHER DIXON. You ever in need, I move about.

THE BOY. Walk the river alone don't sound much safer, Old Granny.

MOTHER DIXON. I'm mindful how I spend my time.

THE BOY. Walk by the boneyard that way. You not spooked?

MOTHER DIXON. (*She gestures to his bundle*) Branch or kindling, you got there?

THE BOY. Need it all.

MOTHER DIXON. Need my soap. I'll make a trade.

THE BOY. Not worth my wood.

MOTHER DIXON: (*Clucks tongue three times.*)

THE BOY. Some other time.

MOTHER DIXON. All the time in the world. Soap, soap. 5 cents a cake.

(MOTHER DIXON *moves off.* THE BOY *stands and watches, listens. Then a shift. The players regroup.* ELEANOR *and* INGA *now speak the tale of Shumann's dolls, further casting the details of the world. This is our method of moving in and out of the scenes.*)

ELEANOR & INGA. Shumann's dolls are prized for their tenderness. Their weight. The blush of their skins. And above all ... the bright color of their eyes. You will hold them and you will learn how to hold a real baby. You will hold them and your muscles and bones will bend and curve to coddle them. You will coo and gurgle for them. You will make space for them to breathe. You will not mash them. You will hold them tender to your nipple to suckle them and their tiny cold mouth will dime itself around you and you will dream the milk trickle treacly pink milk river rushing rushing rush. Shumann's dolls are prized for their sweetness. They are strawberry sweetie dolls. Cherry-ripe cherubs. Lemonade piss and syrup spit. Other dolls will curdle dreams. Never Shumann's!

MOTHER DIXON. Mother Dixon's Angel Soap!

ELEANOR & INGA. Shumann's dolls bring sweet cream dreams.

MOTHER DIXON. Scrub your skin!

ELEANOR & INGA. Tender butter tongue dreams.

MOTHER DIXON. Wash your soul.

ELEANOR. Tender smooth baked bun dreams.

MOTHER DIXON. Clear your eyes.

ELEANOR. Sleeping ...

INGA. Sleeping ...

ELEANOR. ...nuzzle ...

INGA. ...snoozing ...

ELEANOR. ...snoozing lips ...

INGA. ...Liebchen.

MOTHER DIXON. 5 cents a cake!

>*(All the players stop. They shake off the game. Look around. Nod at one another. The rules of play now demonstrated, the players restart the ring, set the stage anew.)*

ALL. Play? Play. Play? Play!

INGA. Mother Dixon in the boneyard.

THE BOY. Sunflowers in hand!

ELEANOR. Eleanor in the factory.

MOTHER DIXON. Making dolls!

ALL. Play!

MOTHER DIXON. Shaz. Shaz. Brought you something.

ELEANOR. Legs to the torso.

MOTHER DIXON. Little little suns. For my Shaz.

ELEANOR. Arms to the side.

MOTHER DIXON. Your cornbread and your clabber milk. Your sorghum syrup—just a taste.

ELEANOR. String the neck, then thread it through. Hook it, tighten, then release.

MOTHER DIXON. *(She places sunflowers on his grave)* Hold him well. I haven't asked much ...but hold him well. Nothing but a lamb, hisself.

ELEANOR. Place the eyes, one at a time.

MOTHER DIXON. I still know you, child. I know you in my mind's eye.

ELEANOR. Polish bright.

MOTHER DIXON. Know you by the edge of your smile. Know you by the glint in your eyes. Know you by the shape of your hands, by your salty smell. By your chin held high.

ELEANOR. Comb the hair. Prepare the dress. Pretty Miss Mary almost done. Save one thing.

MOTHER DIXON. Shaz. Shaz. Shaz.

ELEANOR. Make a small cut. Put in the heart. Sew it shut.

MOTHER DIXON. My only one. My only one…Never you mind…

ELEANOR. (*Taps the doll's heart 3 times*) "Mary. Mary. Mary." There we go. Ready for sale.

MOTHER DIXON. The light soon come.

ALL. Mother Dixon leaves the grave…At the boneyard's edge she spits on the ground. Where she spits, a hand breaks through the soil.

> (*On cue,* THE BOY *leaps to the ground, rolls over and reaches his hand up and out.*)

ALL. Inga Shumann crosses the ocean…Peeks through the porthole in the wall.

INGA. I have seen the birth of an angel. When I am but your size, and can barely write my name, I ride on the airship in my purple dress. Two days we skim the clouds. Die Palmen. Die Pyramiden. Inga…the river Nile! We lower the ropes to men as black as coal in long white dresses. Our man Klaus climbs down to make the trade. There in the river—das Krokodil!

I press my nose to the glass as the crocodile slips from the river and shreds our man Klaus in its jaws. Rip, mash, the head.

Crunch, the hand, the arm, the shoulder. *Tear, tear!* The belly, the sparking blood, the shiny liver—gobbled fast as a flash. Klaus's bones jut up toward the sun.

THE BOY. (*Smelling the sunflowers*) "Shad-rack."

INGA. With one gunshot the croc shakes, shakes and falls dead...

THE BOY. (*Digging in the grave*) Tibia. Fibula. Tarsals.

INGA. At night I sneak into the stateroom where they've packed away the bits and pieces left of our Klaus...

THE BOY. Metatarsals. Patella. Femur. Clavicles. Sternum.

INGA. Heavy butcher's smell. And there, Margarethe...

THE BOY. Humerus.

INGA. ...born from the pile of Klaus's scraps...

THE BOY. Radius.

INGA. ...and hovering just above...

THE BOY. Ulna.

INGA. ...is an angel. A crocodile angel.

THE BOY. Sacrum.

INGA. Glowing with fire, it smells of lightning. It looks at me. I know it will not bite me. Not yet. In my belly, I know why it has come. For something magical and terrible.

THE BOY. Vertebrae. Ribs. Scapula.

INGA. What, you ask? So hungry for the secret, my sweet. The secret is the jelly in the middle. Patience...

THE BOY. Carpals. Metacarpals. Phalanges. Mandible.

INGA. Patience. All things in their time ...

THE BOY. (*Plucking the sunflower*) Cranium.

INGA. (*Sighs*) Squashing through this filthy water is not travel. Still, there is no time for tears—we must brace ourselves for adventure!

ELEANOR. (*Springing out to surprise* THE BOY) Play!

THE BOY. Play what?

ELEANOR. This game.

THE BOY. I'm walking.

ELEANOR. Where you going?

THE BOY. (*Catching on*) To ...the school.

ELEANOR. Too old for school.

THE BOY. Going to ...the Institute.

ELEANOR. Too old for that.

THE BOY. Not old, just late.

ELEANOR. Good!

THE BOY. Not good.

ELEANOR. Is so good! You can play.

THE BOY. How so?

ELEANOR. Already late. You can be later.

THE BOY. I'll get in trouble.

ELEANOR. Trouble with who?

THE BOY. Trouble with whom.

ELEANOR. Copycat, don't copy me.

THE BOY. Let me go.

ELEANOR. Come here, copycat!

THE BOY. On my way.

ELEANOR. Come here, copycat. Nice copycat.

THE BOY. Alright, alright.

ELEANOR. Act kindly, copycat.

THE BOY. What's this game?

ELEANOR. (*Laughs hard.*)

THE BOY. What's this game, girl?

ELEANOR: Go like this ...

> *Mr. Postman die.*
> *How'd he die?*
> *He die like a this ...*
> *He die like a this ...*
> *Mr. Postman livin'*
> *Where's he livin'?*
> *He livin' all outside Tennessee*
> *He got a short-short dress and a ball on his knee*
> *Hands up (Twisty Twisty Twisty Twist)*
> *Hands down (Twisty Twisty Twisty Twist)*
> *Turn around (Twisty Twisty Twisty Twist)*
> *Touch the ground (Twisty Twisty Twisty Twist)*
> *I never went to college*
> *I never went to school*

Whenever I boogle I boogle like a fool[1]

...like that.

THE BOY. You went too fast for me.

ELEANOR. Expect they go that fast at school. Go on copycat!

THE BOY.
The postman died.
How'd he die?
He died like this...
He died like this...

ELEANOR. (*Uncontrollable laughter*) That ain't even right! (*Even more laughter.*)

THE BOY. Bust wide open laughing like that. Expect that your liver's gonna fall right out.

ELEANOR. My liver!? I don't have no liver!

THE BOY. Yes you do. Liver makes bile.

ELEANOR. Where?

THE BOY. Filters the blood. Situated right here.

ELEANOR. That's my stomach. Ain't no liver. Feed liver to the cat.

THE BOY. And what's this here?

ELEANOR. My heart.

THE BOY. Then your heart's gonna jump out and tha-thump thump thump right on down the road.

ELEANOR. (*Laughter.*)

---

1 "Mr. Postman Die" is a traditional ring play.

THE BOY. Then that cat is gonna come and chase it down and eat it up.

ELEANOR. No it's not.

THE BOY. Yes, it is.

ELEANOR. No it's not. My heart could beat it running.

THE BOY. Not quicker than a cat, no-no.

ELEANOR. Yes, yes.

THE BOY. Cat's gonna chomp that heart and eat it down.

ELEANOR. Can't eat my heart.

THE BOY. Chew the meat, lick the blood.

ELEANOR. My heart would shake shake shake and break out its teeth.

THE BOY. Cat just grow some new ones and bite down harder.

ELEANOR. No it won't.

THE BOY. Yes it will.

ELEANOR. Take that back.

THE BOY. Can't do.

ELEANOR. Take that back.

THE BOY. Too late.

ELEANOR. Take that back!

THE BOY. ...

ELEANOR. Won't eat me!

THE BOY. ...

ELEANOR. Not one bite.

THE BOY. No more games.

ELEANOR. Ain't no game. "Shaz." Say that name.

THE BOY. Say "Shaz?"

ELEANOR. Say the whole name like it is the long way...Mister...

THE BOY. Mister...

ELEANOR. Shadrack...

THE BOY. Shadrack...

ELEANOR. Ambrose...

THE BOY. Ambrose...

ELEANOR. Dixon...

THE BOY. Dixon...

ELEANOR. Go on.

THE BOY. Mister Shadrack Ambrose Dixon. (*Drops the sunflower.*)

ELEANOR. (*Catches the sunflower.*) Careful! Trip and fall and break to
pieces. Be no use to anybody. (*Hands the sunflower back to* THE
BOY.) Mister Shadrack Ambrose Dixon. That's a pretty name.

THE BOY. Hard to say.

MOTHER DIXON. (*At the edge*) Branch or kindling, you got there?

THE BOY. Need it all.

MOTHER DIXON. Need my soap. I'll make a trade.

THE BOY. Not worth my wood.

MOTHER DIXON. (*Clucks tongue three times.*)

THE BOY. Some other time.

MOTHER DIXON. All the time in the world.

ELEANOR. Bye now. (*Giggles as* THE BOY *leaves.*) Mister Shadrack Ambrose Dixon. Mister Shadrack Ambrose Dixon. Mister ... and *Mrs.* Shadrack Ambrose Dixon.

(ALL *make the clapping rhythm.*)

ELEANOR.
What color flowers gonna be at the wedding?
Are you gonna have pink flowers at the wedding?
Not gonna be pink flowers at my wedding!
What color flowers gonna be at the wedding?
You gonna wear red flowers at the wedding?
Don't wanna see red flowers at my wedding!
What color flowers gonna be at the wedding?
Is it gonna be blue flowers at the wedding?
What you mean? Blue flowers at the wedding?!
I tell you what color's gonna be at the wedding.
Just yellow flowers gonna be at the wedding.
Sweet yellow flowers gonna be at my wedding.

MOTHER DIXON. Gal?

ELEANOR. Yes, Ma'am?

MOTHER DIXON. Watch this here.

ELEANOR. Yes, yes.

MOTHER DIXON. Who's that there?

ELEANOR. That there's Shaz.

MOTHER DIXON. He's a pretty old thing.

ELEANOR. He's my husband.

MOTHER DIXON. How's that so?

ELEANOR. Just is so.

MOTHER DIXON. You just little. He's all grown.

ELEANOR. Still is so. Someday soon.

MOTHER DIXON. How you know?

ELEANOR. Gave me a flower. Said that's for you.

MOTHER DIXON. What color was the flower?

ELEANOR. Yellow yellow.

MOTHER DIXON. Yellow mean friend.

ELEANOR. Yellow mean love.

MOTHER DIXON. Red mean that.

ELEANOR. He's my husband.

MOTHER DIXON. No he's not. He's sweet on Sally.

ELEANOR. Old Sally Jones? (*Sharp gesture.*)

MOTHER DIXON. What you doin'?

ELEANOR. Taking care of that.

MOTHER DIXON. Toting that axe?

ELEANOR. Taking care.

MOTHER DIXON. Axe bigger than you, and just as sharp.

ELEANOR. I'll teach her right.

MOTHER DIXON. Gonna chop her down?

ELEANOR. If. Need be.

MOTHER DIXON. Set that axe down.

ELEANOR. Chop her. Down.

MOTHER DIXON. You mustn't do.

ELEANOR. Yes Ma'am. I know. (*Release gesture.*)

MOTHER DIXON. Got a powerful love.

ELEANOR. Shining hard.

MOTHER DIXON. Act mighty grown.

ELEANOR. Have to do.

MOTHER DIXON. Gal? Gal?

ELEANOR. Yes ma'am, yes ma'am?

MOTHER DIXON. Watch this here.

ELEANOR. No, thank you.

MOTHER DIXON. What's that there?

ALL. *Amazing Stories Magazine.* The factory.

THE BOY. Venus. Mercury. Sun. Mars. Jupiter. Saturn. Uranus. Neptune. They called it Planet X. Now they're calling it Pluto. I liked Planet X better. The unknown factor.

ELEANOR. Pluto. What's that place?

THE BOY. Planet.

ELEANOR. I know that. What's that place?

THE BOY. Not a place. A God. Of the dead.

ELEANOR. Know that, too. Seem to me I heard of a place like that.

THE BOY. Depends on how you see it I guess.

ELEANOR. What else is new?

THE BOY. It could be a place to watch from, it seems to me. Go all the way out to the edge and turn around and look back and watch.

ELEANOR. Watch what? Us?

THE BOY. Tiny as a pinhead. Us.

ELEANOR. Time you get out there liable to be everything here all changed up.

THE BOY. That's what Dr. Einstein says.

ELEANOR. He in that?

THE BOY. Not directly.

ELEANOR. Give me. *Amazing Stories.* 25 cents?!!!

THE BOY. Give me.

ELEANOR. You paid 25 cents for this thing?

THE BOY. Give me.

ELEANOR. Give me 25 cents and I'll tell you an amazing story. Tell you two. One about a fool who paid 25 cents for a magazine with a flying white man on the cover and another about the bigger fool sitting up talking to him. Pluto.

THE BOY. Planet X.

ELEANOR. Pluto. Seem to me, it could be where all them demons my mama cast out gone to sit a spell. Demons get cast out got to live somewhere. Expect it must be cold in space. Pluto even colder—all the way out like you say. Demons would have to cool their heads.

THE BOY. They could stay warm. Just dig way down in the dirt.

ELEANOR. Pluto got dirt?

THE BOY. Right here on Earth you could just dig down and down and down and get to the middle. You know what you'd find?

ELEANOR. China.

THE BOY. You'd find ... well, you'd find a sort of furnace, and the heart of the Earth.

ELEANOR. The Earth got a heart?

THE BOY. Heart of stone. Hotter down there than the skin of the Sun.

ELEANOR. Too hot for me. I'd dig my way right back on up.

THE BOY. You talk too much.

ELEANOR. You don't know nothin', except what all you read in that magazine.

THE BOY. You talk anymore you're liable to have your jaw fall off.

ELEANOR. That don't sound so scientific of you. Sound more like an amazing story to me. "JAW FALLS OFF MAN AND FLIES TO OUTER SPACE. 25¢."

THE BOY. Very funny.

ELEANOR. I know. I could write for the radio. Be funnier than what they have up on there now.

THE BOY. That'll be the day.

ELEANOR. Probably ain't even in there. Probably you made it all up. Pluto.

THE BOY. Planet X. We're not that far. Meat. Bone. Fire. Make dust. Elemental. Elements.

ELEANOR. Why you not at college learning.

THE BOY. Will be.

ELEANOR. ...

THE BOY. Will be.

ELEANOR. That cost. You can't be spending 25 cents all over.

THE BOY. I earn my money. I got my way to do that. Elemental.

INGA. (*Imagines across time and space. She "becomes" Mister Shumann.*) Play?

THE BOY. (*Listening, then agreeing to "play" along.*) Play.

INGA. "Boy did you clean the back?"

THE BOY. I was just...

INGA. "You reading Boy."

THE BOY. Yes, Sir. I was.

INGA. "That's not your book."

THE BOY. No, Sir. The book just catch my eye is all.

INGA. "What book is that?"

THE BOY. You got more for me to do, Sir. I can get right to it. At your service, Sir.

INGA. "*Anatomical Resource Manual.* What on Earth does a boy like you want with this here book? Answer me, Boy."

THE BOY. I like knowing how things are put together...

INGA. "Go on."

THE BOY. The systems. How one bunch of things goes together. And then works with other…things…Like right here…you can see the bones…bones of the hand…and the muscles that move the fingers. Each finger has its own set of muscles to move it…like so…The names are in, uh…

INGA. "What?"

THE BOY. Latin…

INGA. "How do you come to know such things as this???"

THE BOY. I'm sorry, Sir, Mister Shumann. It won't happen again.

INGA. Read…

THE BOY. Musculi interossei manus, Musculus abductor pollicis brevis, Musculus flexor pollicis brevis, Musculus adductor pollicis, Musculus abductor digiti minimi…Like so…

INGA. "You've always been such a good boy."

THE BOY. It won't happen again, Sir…Mister Shumann…

INGA. "These skeletons don't put a fright in you?"

THE BOY. No. Just bones.

INGA. "You're not scared of spooks, huh?"

THE BOY. No, Sir.

INGA. "By rights I should put you in the circus and make a pretty penny."

THE BOY. (*Bristling*) Sir. I mean to attend the Institute. Someday.

INGA. "The spook that spoke Latin. Ah? Ah?"

THE BOY. (*Forced laugh.*)

INGA. "You've been a very good boy. I've another job for you. I put all sorts of things together to sell. Shumann's dolls are known the world over for their quality. But my skeletons are worth their weight in gold—precise placement of all 206 bones. This job is a secret, just between you and me. You dig. You gather. You bring to me. I compensate. We both make a pretty penny to save, you see? You're handy with a shovel, Boy?"

THE BOY. Yessiree.

ELEANOR. Five fingers on each pretty hand. Ten toes in all. Glass eyes of blue, brown and hazel, green and gold. And the hair! The finest hair, carefully cut and shipped from Germany. Curled to frame their little faces. Hair from real little girls. Red from Leah, the watchmaker's daughter. Chestnut from Yasmin, the florist's helper. Blonde from Gefen, the baker's girl. Brown from Hannah, the dairymaid. Now just your hearts and you're ready for sale.

THE BOY. Got something for you, Mister Shumann!

INGA. "Is it whole?"

THE BOY. Incomplete.

INGA. "Soundness?"

THE BOY. Broken ribs. Name was...

INGA. "No. We don't want the names."

THE BOY. No, Sir. No names.

INGA. "Broken ribs—two bits."

THE BOY. Two bits, two bits. Got something for you, Mister Shumann!

INGA. "Is it whole?"

THE BOY. Arm and torso.

INGA. "Soundness?"

THE BOY. Sound.

INGA. "Thirty cents."

THE BOY. Thirty cents. Got something for you, Mister Shumann.

INGA. "Is it whole?"

THE BOY. Full frame, no head.

INGA. "Soundness?"

THE BOY. Cracked femur.

INGA. "Eighty cents."

THE BOY. Eighty cents! Eighty cents! Got something for you, Mister Shumann.

INGA. "Is it whole?"

THE BOY. Whole.

INGA. "Soundness?"

THE BOY. Sound. Except for a hand.

INGA. "I've got a spare. Two dollars."

THE BOY. Two dollars! Thank you. Sir. Thank you.

(INGA *walks away. The game ends.*)

THE BOY. (*To the sunflower*) What was your name, my friend? Shh-hhhh? Shhhhhhh?

ELEANOR. (*Whispers*) Shadrack Ambrose Dixon.

ALL. Eleanor hides behind a tree. Mother Dixon. Mother Dixon comes upon the empty grave of her son, Shaz.

MOTHER DIXON. Rippers! First you sap—now you scavenge?! These rippers.

Oh! I know their way. Shaz, you was just barely born...yet, back by the factory, red-eyed and hazy, a ripper walked the edge, waiting for his whim. Forced me to the shadows. Barn straw. Cow dung. Warm piss and foul breath. Ripper licked my milk. He took my mouth last. Made me taste myself on him.

Listen and hear the truth! Can't shit, can't sit, can't stand for days. I chewed leaves to a paste to patch and mend. Can't sit, can't lie. Weeks and weeks. When I felt the swelling I rid that rat from my own belly and buried it in the dirt. The light of the lamb shines through! So it's not the dead. No. Never the dead. It's the living and the living and the living. What I know? These rippers, these rust lickers. Gut you alive every time. No mistake, no misgiving. And even come to cull your very bones. Shaz...What I know? You can patch. You can fix. What I make of this? Iron assurance. Sacrifice can be taken as sure as given. We pull white from the river again this night! Let the light of the Lamb pierce the dark and all will rise to meet it! All will rise!!! I say, bring me the ripper and I'll find the Lamb.

INGA. "Inga Shumann is the luckiest girl!"

MOTHER DIXON. We smooth our palms.

INGA. Inga Shumann is the luckiest one.

MOTHER DIXON. All comes red in the gutting.

INGA. All the dollies in the whole world.

MOTHER DIXON. Then rendered. Ashed. Tallow and lye.

INGA. Are mine to name and dream with!

MOTHER DIXON. Mixed and cooked and poured and cooled. Cakes cut. Boxed clean. Quiet.

INGA. Play!

THE BOY. Play. (THE BOY *"becomes" a soldier.*) "Inga Shumann is full of delight."

INGA. Full to bursting.

THE BOY. "Inga Shumann is full of light."

INGA. I am full of cream and berries.

THE BOY. "Inga Shumann is full."

INGA. I am full of crusty brown bread. I am full of pork and fat and casings. I eat all my dinner. I am full and ready to dream.

THE BOY. "Sweet dreams Inga Shumann?"

INGA. The sweetest. Enough! Will you happen to have a key to my box?

THE BOY. "No. Which dolly is that in your hands?"

INGA. Margarethe.

THE BOY. "Hello, Margarethe!"

INGA. Hush! You mustn't speak at her. She is newly born. Her ears are too mushy to hold your thick words.

THE BOY. "I am terribly sorry."

INGA. You should be. She is a delicate thing.

THE BOY. "Porcelain and paint, silk ribbons, bright glass eyes. Carefully made. A genuine Shumann."

INGA. Her belly presses soft if you use your finger.

THE BOY. "May I?"

INGA. No. No you are too rough, you are a stinky pig.

THE BOY. "You are right, Inga. I am terribly sorry."

INGA. You should be. Stinky stinky. One may only touch her belly if one is gentle. Sweet Margarethe has devoured her dinner and is now sleeping gently and there is bread and sausage and cabbage and a thimbleful of milk in her belly so one would have to use the lightest touch or her meal might spurt out all over her lovely blanket.

THE BOY. "I promise to be gentle."

INGA. I don't believe you.

THE BOY. "How may I prove my gentility to you, sweet Inga."

INGA. A fat gingerman. You can give me a fat crusty gingerman. With a long green ribbon of frosting. A gentle person should have such a thing.

THE BOY. "Aha. Is this the sort of treat you mean?"

INGA. Yes! (*She devours the gingerman.*) You may touch Margarethe's belly, I think.

THE BOY. "Mmm. Her belly is so smooth. Yes, Inga Shumann you are a very lucky girl to have such a dollie."

INGA. Margarethe is special.

THE BOY. "She is."

INGA. Very special. Her hair is springy and she is made in a secret way.

THE BOY. "You must tell me."

INGA. No.

THE BOY. "At very least may I see her face, Inga?"

INGA. No, that is even more a secret.

THE BOY. "Oh, Inga, secrets are torture."

INGA. I know.

THE BOY. "Please."

INGA. No.

THE BOY. "Please."

INGA. No.

THE BOY. "Please."

INGA. Alright alright alright alright.

(*Pause.*)

THE BOY. "Her face is burned. In the oven too long."

INGA. No. Her face is toasty brown. Perfectly so.

THE BOY. "Her face is of the lowest kind. Pitchy face. Dirty baby. A dirty baby for a dirty girl."

INGA. Give her to me.

THE BOY. "We must clean her first."

INGA. Give her back.

THE BOY. "We must clean her. We must clean you."

INGA. You must give her back.

THE BOY. "You will stay here and sit in a clean way."

INGA. Give her.

THE BOY. "And eat in a clean way."

INGA. Now.

THE BOY. "And sleep and dream in a clean way."

INGA. You must give Margarethe to me and give me the key to my box!!!

THE BOY. "Locked here. You shall remain, until your thoughts are clean. *Lilienmilch* thoughts. *Für zarte weisse Haut.*"

INGA. Margarethe! Margarethe!

THE BOY. Come in, Miss Shumann!

(*The factory.*)

THE BOY. Eleanor. This here Miss Shumann. She come all the way from Germany.

All that way. By herself in a steamer ship. She Mister Shumann niece. Mister Shumann been real good to us. He been real good to me. I been working here, and doing work out at his other properties for him, and he even gets me some work over to the college. Yesiree! Real good. This here Eleanor, Miss ... Miss Shumann. Eleanor been working here, and she know the ropes, yes, indeed, she know the ropes. Wellsuh, anything you need to know, you could ask her, and she tell you 'cause she know the ropes, Miss Shumann. And you could ask me too. Eleanor, Mister Shumann say Miss Shumann here, Miss Shumann gonna be workin' with us for a spell. Ain't that nice?

ELEANOR. (*To* THE BOY) You smile any harder, your teeth gonna crack off.

THE BOY. She a funny one, Miss Shumann. Always playing games.

ELEANOR. Ain't no game.

INGA. Good day!

THE BOY. Good day!!!

ELEANOR. She working…what she gonna do?

INGA. Can you get into my box?

THE BOY. Excuse me, Miss Shumann?

INGA. There is brown bread and cheese in my box.

THE BOY. Well, now. We got to wait for Mister Shumann to open that there box.

He open all the boxes that come from over there in Germany. That's his business.

INGA. It is *my* box.

ELEANOR. You barking up the wrong tree, Miss. He one to follow the rules.

INGA. You will help me?

ELEANOR. I said, what she gonna do?

THE BOY. I'm gonna go check on that there box, Miss Shumann. Just you set tight.

Don't let this old gal worry you one bit.

ELEANOR. I'm gonna worry you, you don't find out what she's supposed to be doing up in here.

INGA.
Crocodile angel. Angel mine.

Shine your pointy teeth. Blink your jelly eyes. Crocodile angel.
Angel mine.
Before our little hearts and after the sun.
You're coming to gather us in your mouth. To fly us away.
Crocodile angel. Angel mine.

(*To* ELEANOR:)

All I have had is a gingerman. Have you anything salty?

(ELEANOR *assembles, paying no mind to*
INGA. *Eye. Eye. Dress. Eye. Eye. And so on.*)

INGA. I have seen "Manhattan Island." From the eyes of the airship, it's a spiny crocodile. We cast a fat shadow, gliding over. I go to the edge of the corridor and hide. It's cold there and you feel the wind lick the windows. The roar goes in your bones it shivers your belly and your lips buzz. *This is what gets remembered...* At night when my father sleeps, the soldier presses Mother in the shadows. She pulls down her skirt and he presses his meat between her legs, lifting. They lean to one side and their knuckles turn white from squeezing the rail while he presses her. Rocking and rocking and rocking. Hot salt breath. She smiles with all her teeth. I see this whole thing and don't think much of it. *Love is yellow. This future is metal.*

ELEANOR. You don't speak English?

INGA. Only if there is something to say.

ELEANOR. This model is Katinka. (*Places a tiny piece of chocolate in Katinka's hand.*)

"Katinka goes to the chocolate festival. She eats and eats and eats."

INGA. Fat dirty baby. (*Snatches and eats Katinka's chocolate.*)

ELEANOR. What are you doing? Leave that be! That's for the dolls.

INGA. Mmmmmmmmm!

ELEANOR. Give it! Each doll gets a chocolate. It's thirty dolls we're making. It's thirty pieces of chocolate.

> (INGA *grabs the tin of chocolates.*)

ELEANOR. You can't do that!

INGA. There is chocolate in my box. You help me open the box. There is chocolate there.

> (*No luck. She devours the chocolate reciting a poem as she does so.*)

The linden flowers open their mouths...
Their thousand tiny eyes, gold and cream.
They smell of honey.
Giddy honey things.

Mine mine mine mine MINE!!!

ELEANOR. How it can be, that you can be grown as you are, and still you can be a baby?

INGA. How can it be, that you can be a little girl, and yet you know that you are old?

ELEANOR. How it can be, that you can be who you are, and you can get under somebody skin? How that can be?

> (INGA *stuffs and chews chocolate. It dribbles down her chin.*)

ELEANOR. You gonna make yourself sick.

INGA. Good.

ELEANOR. Girl, you so simple. Simple. You simple, girl!

> (INGA *places a chocolate next to* ELEANOR.)

ELEANOR. Oh, no. You not catching me up in this mess.

> (INGA *waits.* ELEANOR *succumbs.*)

ELEANOR. Good. It's so good!

INGA. Only the best chocolate for greedy Katinka. These are Neger Küsse.

ELEANOR. What?

INGA. Neger Küsse.

ELEANOR. What's that mean.

INGA. (*Finger at* ELEANOR's *lips.*) Ne-ger Küs-se.

> (MOTHER DIXON *claps her hands.*)

ELEANOR. Shaz?

MOTHER DIXON. Gal?

ELEANOR. Yes ma'am, yes ma'am?

MOTHER DIXON. Watch this here.

ELEANOR. No, thank you.

MOTHER DIXON. What's that there?

ELEANOR. Don't recall.

MOTHER DIXON. Yes you do.

ELEANOR. Don't know at all.

MOTHER DIXON. Yes you do.

ELEANOR. I'd rather get going. Let morning come.

MOTHER DIXON. What's that there, gal?

ELEANOR. The fire they use.

MOTHER DIXON. How's that go?

ELEANOR. Gonna string him first. Gonna burn him last.

MOTHER DIXON. And what between?

ELEANOR. Shouts and hits.

MOTHER DIXON. Why is that?

ELEANOR. I don't recall.

MOTHER DIXON. He look too wild?

ELEANOR. I don't recall.

MOTHER DIXON. His chin too high?

ELEANOR. I don't recall.

MOTHER DIXON. He look too long?

ELEANOR. Hurts my eyes.

MOTHER DIXON. What's all that?

ELEANOR. Camera flash.

MOTHER DIXON. They make a picture.

ELEANOR. Picture to pass.

MOTHER DIXON. They smiling so.

ELEANOR. Pick them a nigger.

MOTHER DIXON. Good hats and dresses.

ELEANOR. Field hand or doctor. Pick them a nig.

MOTHER DIXON. Pickles and pie.

ELEANOR. They pick my Shaz.

MOTHER DIXON. Send it to their family. Send it to their friends.

ELEANOR. Yes ma'am, yes ma'am.

MOTHER DIXON. "Wish you was here."

ELEANOR. ...

MOTHER DIXON. Ella. Ella.

ELEANOR. Yes Ma'am.

MOTHER DIXON. What's that there?

ELEANOR. That there is Shaz.

MOTHER DIXON. Is not.

ELEANOR. Yes Ma'am it is.

MOTHER DIXON. That burnt up meat?

ELEANOR. Yes ma'am, yes ma'am.

MOTHER DIXON. That blackened bone?

ELEANOR. Yes sir, yes sir.

MOTHER DIXON. Where's his face.

ELEANOR. They picked it clean.

MOTHER DIXON. All the men?

ELEANOR. All those birds.

MOTHER DIXON. That you Ella?

ELEANOR. Is that me where?

MOTHER DIXON. Waiting in the night?

ELEANOR. Please ...don't hear.

MOTHER DIXON. Climbing that tree.

ELEANOR. Got to get him down.

MOTHER DIXON. What you'll use.

ELEANOR. Just my hands.

MOTHER DIXON. What? No axe?

ELEANOR. My own bare hands.

MOTHER DIXON. Your hands are stained.

ELEANOR. Where's he go?

MOTHER DIXON. We'll bury the meat.

ELEANOR. Where's he go?

MOTHER DIXON. We'll bury the bone.

ELEANOR. His precious bones.

MOTHER DIXON. They got his bones.

ELEANOR. What about his soul? How he gonna rise?

MOTHER DIXON. His precious soul.

ELEANOR. Never you mind. I make him back.

MOTHER DIXON. No such thing.

ELEANOR. Fashion his bones. Conjure his blood.

MOTHER DIXON. No, Gal. Catch the light.

ELEANOR. Catch the light?

MOTHER DIXON. The light of the Lamb. All answers in that light.

INGA. Neger Küsse. Some favor a lemony treat. I think chocolate is best. Dark and sticky, it goes right from your mouth to the heart of your bones. Nigger's Kiss. Chocolaty sweet secret.

> *Green, green, the crab apple tree.*
> *Where the grass grows so deep.*
> *Miss Ella, Miss Ella, your true lover is dead.*
> *He wrote you a letter to turn back your head.*

> > (*A ring play forms. One by one the players exit, leaving* ELEANOR *alone onstage.*)

ALL.

> *Green, green, the crab apple tree.*
> *Where the grass grows so deep.*
> *Miss Ella, Miss Ella, your true lover is dead.*
> *He wrote you a letter to turn back your head.*

ELEANOR.

> *Green, green the crab apple tree.*
> *Where the grass grows so deep.*
> *Miss Ella, Miss Ella, your true lover is dead.*
> *He wrote you a letter to turn back your head.*

> > (*End of Ring One.*)

RING TWO

(Dawn. The factory. ELEANOR *steals mate-rials. She works secretly on her own proj-ect—a doll of Shaz. Unlike Shumann's dolls, its center is formed of found objects—branches, bark, shells. The stolen materials are binding, dressing.)*

ELEANOR.

> *Shout shout*
> *Make you new*
> *Shout shout*
> *That branch bone*
> *Shout shout*
> *That cotton meat*
> *Shout shout*
> *New penny blood*
> *Shout shout*
> *That burlap skin*
> *Shout shout*
> *Dry corn teeth*
> *Shout shout*
> *What you put for his heart?*
> *Shout shout*
> *A big red stone*
> *Shout shout*
> *What you put for his eyes?*
> *Shout shout*
> *You'll see, you'll see…*
> *Shout shout*
> *Need lots of thread*
> *Shout shout*
> *Knit it tight*
> *Shout shout*
> *Piece by piece*

Shout shout
Shaz, Shaz
Shout shout
Make you back
Shout shout
Then wait for the light
Shout shout
Wait for the light
Shout shout!

> (ELEANOR's *ring play ends. She brims, open-eyed.* THE BOY *sits and watches* ELEANOR. *Suspicious.*)

ELEANOR. It's a cat comes here lately. Black cat. Claws, too. Come right over there to that window.

THE BOY. Does not.

ELEANOR. Does so.

THE BOY. Too high.

ELEANOR. I *said* claws.

THE BOY. I'd see it. I'd know.

ELEANOR. You don't know.

THE BOY. Hear it, too.

ELEANOR. You too busy talking to hear much. Plus. Didn't say it made all kinds of noise. Just said it come here to that window. Look, see.

THE BOY. It's here?

ELEANOR. No.

THE BOY. No cat. You wastin' time.

ELEANOR. Could have left that open. Sticky…smelly.

THE BOY. No.

ELEANOR. Come in the other day. Sat right on my lap. Just as sweet.

THE BOY. What you know…sweet?

ELEANOR. Know what I know.

THE BOY. You need to work.

ELEANOR. Then quit talkin.' You wastin' time. Readin' that rag.

THE BOY. Now it's broke. Broke.

ELEANOR. And who's the one broke it?

THE BOY. You.

ELEANOR. Hush.

THE BOY. Your fault.

ELEANOR. That's how you gonna tell it, too. Just like that.

THE BOY. It's true.

ELEANOR. Probably not broke. Probably you just don't know how to put it back right.

THE BOY. Sit down.

ELEANOR. Move.

THE BOY. Sit down!

ELEANOR. See. Right here. This is right where it comes. To this part right here. Sweet. Sweet. Sweet. Sweet. Sweet. Sweet.

THE BOY. Sit down and work.

ELEANOR. All right.

THE BOY. You hear that?

ELEANOR. ...

THE BOY. Said you hear that!?

ELEANOR. Cat's not the only one that comes.

>   (*Outside, the sound of children playing.*)

INGA. The game they make. You make this game?

ELEANOR. Used to do.

INGA. It goes around and around.

ELEANOR. ...

INGA. I want to make this game.

ELEANOR. Just cooled off. Sit still.

INGA. Show me.

ELEANOR. Time to go.

INGA. ...

ELEANOR. ...

INGA. Around and around and around.

THE BOY. You done with the order?

ELEANOR. Been done.

THE BOY. Good. You can go.

ELEANOR. Was already going.

THE BOY. Good. Now you got permission.

INGA. Please show me the game.

ELEANOR. Ask him. He know how to dance.

THE BOY. Forget you.

ELEANOR. Please do.

THE BOY. 'Scuse us, Miss Shumann.

INGA. You know this game.

THE BOY. Ma'am?

INGA. ...

THE BOY. Just a ring play.

INGA. Herky jerky.

THE BOY. Rough as dirt. You like something sweeter.

INGA. ...

THE BOY. Pretty music where you come from.

INGA. ...

THE BOY. Great composers.

INGA. ...

THE BOY. Artists and engineers and men of science...

INGA. The game is pretty.

THE BOY. So many discoveries...You named the elements...Sauerstoff.

INGA. Oxygen.

THE BOY. Kohlendioxid.

INGA. Carbon dioxide. You know my country?

THE BOY. Only from books.

INGA. There was no more bread. The streets snapped like bones. The roof of our factory fell on our heads. My country.

THE BOY. Everything that rises must fall.

INGA. My father's face mashed dead.

THE BOY. I'm sorry.

INGA. I'm not.

THE BOY. …

INGA. They stop the game.

THE BOY. Night falling.

INGA. She always has things to eat.

THE BOY. She won't like you going through that.

INGA. Her cornbread.

> (INGA *devours* ELEANOR's *pan of cornbread.*)

INGA. It is my factory. Mmmmm…mine, mine, mine…oh, salty!

THE BOY. Cooling down.

INGA. …

THE BOY. Goes like this…

INGA. So?

THE BOY. No, no. Slower. Slower. Here like…may I?

INGA. Yes.

THE BOY. Here. Like so.

INGA. Yes and then spinning, spinning, spinning...

THE BOY. Like the Earth.

INGA. Like the Moon.

THE BOY. Like Mars.

INGA. Jupiter.

THE BOY. Jupiter.

INGA. Saturn.

THE BOY. Neptune.

INGA. Uranus.

THE BOY. Pluto.

INGA. Pluto, Pluto, Pluto! Oh, I am dizzy.

THE BOY. Pluto. That's where I'll go. Build myself a rocket to go there, fast as light.

INGA. Dance!

THE BOY. You watch.

INGA. Dance!!

THE BOY. Miss Shumann?

INGA. You are not so smart to build a rocket. Just words words words from a book.

THE BOY. Ma'am?

INGA. You are hardly smart enough to make the dolls. Silly one. Close your eyes and shake your bones and wiggle and spring and shine your teeth. Close your eyes and dance, dance to Pluto.

THE BOY. Yes Ma'am, Miss Shumann.

INGA. Oh! Oh! Oh!...Inga Shumann is the luckiest girl.

THE BOY. ...

INGA. Inga Shumann is full.

THE BOY. Full of tasty bread.

INGA. I am stuffed full like a giant egg.

THE BOY. Egg, Miss Shumann? An Easter egg?

INGA. (*Laughter.*)

THE BOY. A robin egg?

INGA. A crocodile egg. A crocodile angel egg.

THE BOY. What's this riddle, Miss Shumann?

INGA. Big fat crocodile angel egg. Disgustingly full. I will swell and swell and then my skin will burst and the crocodile angel will spread its feathers, take my bones and those of sweet Margarethe in its mouth and fly them away.

> (INGA *spins off.* THE BOY *regards his palms, curling them into fists, unfolding them, covering his eyes. His words are as ripe as prayer.*)

THE BOY.
> *Away Away*
> *Pluto, Pluto*

Away Away
Demon boy
Away Away
The pitch black dark
Away Away
The pitch black dark

ALL. To Mother Dixon's tent.

> *(They sing. The audience is invited into the song. Perhaps they have all received the words, like a page torn from a hymnal.)*

Candle in the valley
Angels on the wing
Light in the darkness
Come ye and sing
In this old world
The light of the Lamb
The star in the East
Come walk hand in hand
Into the valley
Lilies and rain
Come lay down your burden
Come release your pain
Step lively step right
Through the clutch of night
Follow the music
Follow the light
Candle in the valley
Angels on the wing
Light in the darkness
Come ye and sing

> (ELEANOR *knocks.*)

MOTHER DIXON. You knock three times old gal?

> (THE BOY *listens, outside, in the shadows.*
> *Oh so quietly, he hears the claps and slaps*
> *and caresses happening inside the tent and*
> *echoes them with his body, learning them,*
> *as though holding them on his tongue*
> *to taste them—then lets them go. Inside,*
> MOTHER DIXON *puffs on her clay pipe in*
> *silhouette, as all our eyes adjust. Flickering*
> *kerosene light.*)

ELEANOR. Yes, Ma'am.

MOTHER DIXON. You come for a healing?

ELEANOR. Not my own.

MOTHER DIXON. Wash your hands in the water. Go on.

ELEANOR. Yes, Ma'am.

MOTHER DIXON. See you in my mind's eye. Seem to me I know you.

ELEANOR. Don't know.

MOTHER DIXON. You been to this tent?

ELEANOR. No.

MOTHER DIXON. (*Knee slap—ha!*) I seen you with Henrietta Pastor.
    Yes, yes.

ELEANOR. That's my mama.

MOTHER DIXON. She a mighty healer.

ELEANOR. She dead.

MOTHER DIXON. ....Child, what business you got with me?

ELEANOR. I been to many a tent. Working revival. My mama'd call them in: "Come on, children, come on! Walk through the eye of a needle!"

MOTHER DIXON. "Sweet salvation! We on our way! We on our way! All the many mansions! It's a balm in the upper room! Come on, children, come on!" Don't I know it.

ELEANOR. Clapping, kerosene and sweat. Blind Willie Morris stand in the back. Testify: "Was a voice come to me . . . !"

MOTHER DIXON. "Tempt me to gambling."

ELEANOR. "Tempt me to go with a wayward woman."

MOTHER DIXON. "Tempt me toward the drink."

ELEANOR. He moaning in the back repentant. Then he jerk. And his voice drop down low in a rumble. And he's leaning. And my mama shout:

MOTHER DIXON. "Willie Morris it's a demon got a hold to you!"

ELEANOR. My mama, Henrietta Pastor, call him up to the altar. And I'd be done run up ahead: "Let him through, let him through!" Blind Willie stumble and groan with his hands to his face. When he pull them down? His skin turn grey. And my mama, Henrietta Pastor, commence to casting out that old demon. Speaking all his old names from the Old Book. And just when the crowd starts to bring up that singing, Blind Willie choke and shudder, eyes rolled back in his head. My mama, Henrietta Pastor, done turned to tongues—slaps her palm on top his head and sure enough Blind Willie spits that demon up—sprays him out in a mess of blood all over my clean white dress.

MOTHER DIXON. The people just gasping.

ELEANOR. Screaming. Hands rising in the air. Blind Willie saying …

MOTHER DIXON. "Thank you, thank you, thank you, thank you."

ELEANOR. And my mama, Henrietta Pastor, saying ...

MOTHER DIXON. "Bear witness! No demon holds sway over the Light."

ELEANOR. Hands clap, coins drop in the basket. The next night a new town, a new dress: "Come on, children, come on!" Blind Willie with a new name for the new town, stand in the back. Fixin' to testify. Chicken blood and chalk and a empty basket for coins. So yes, Ma'am, I know all about casting out demons. I don't come for all that. What I come for? Real things. Things you know.

MOTHER DIXON. (*She puffs her pipe. She looks at* ELEANOR, *hard. Twists her mouth.*) You know the huck and the shimmer. What you want from me? Your eyes are old as dirt.

ELEANOR. Is it anything true about the light?

MOTHER DIXON. Depends.

ELEANOR. Stand at the edge of the valley, when that sun first tips on over. The way it press my eyes, lick my face, pull me up out my skin. All the flowers, all the trees, all the birds. All us leaning toward that sun. Seem like then, all that talk about the light ain't so far-fetched. The day the light come and folks be rising up whole out the dirt. Folk like Shaz. Tell me Ma'am. Tell me. True or not?

MOTHER DIXON. Oh, gal. You know.

ELEANOR. Don't know.

MOTHER DIXON. Remember back. You. Remember back, gal.

ELEANOR. I remember what they done.

MOTHER DIXON. You. You that little one. You that little one come around Shaz like butterflies. Always make a ring play. Dust flying up. That's you. True true?

Ella
Did you been to the wedding?
Did you get any cake?
How nice the taste?
Ella
Did you been to the wedding?
Did you get any wine?
How nice the drink?
Ella
Do you see my turkey?
Which side he go on?
Will you help me catch him?
Get ready let's go
Shoo turkey shoo
Shoo turkey shoo

That's you ...Remember. Back.

ELEANOR. Between me and that is what they done.

MOTHER DIXON. What's done. We can't hold. What's done. We give over. To the Lamb. Choose to. One way or another.

ELEANOR. You remember? What's done?

MOTHER DIXON. I see it everyday. I see it. I can't close my eyes but that I see it, I see it in front of my eyes right now. Every day.

ELEANOR. Now they got his bones. Ma'am ...the rising ...true or not?

MOTHER DIXON. (*Grunts ...then still ...then ...*) Truth be told? What has been fouled.

It can be turned back. Flesh on the soil, turned over and into. The red clay of this sweet Earth will cook it back into itself. Bring it down to salt and lime. Cooled by a river of ants and worms. Birds come. Pluck out the hairs to stuff their nest. Then the dead be halfway to flying ... That's as close to the light as we come, truth be told. What you carry? You got to set down. Give it over to the Lamb.

ELEANOR. Shaz. Shaz so pretty. All starry eyes, plum-colored and sweet.

MOTHER DIXON. That's your husband.

ELEANOR. I can't lay this down.

MOTHER DIXON. Lay it on the Lamb.

ELEANOR. It won't leave my bones. It's a fire in the heart of my bones.

MOTHER DIXON. What is foul is made pure again by sacrifice.

ELEANOR. What else I'm supposed to give? What else I got? Even his bones belong to them ...

MOTHER DIXON. Nothing belongs to them. NOTHING!

ELEANOR. This fire ain't gonna leave my bones.

MOTHER DIXON. Bring me my box.

ELEANOR. Ma'am?

MOTHER DIXON. My box. Bring it here! ...Everything they got they stole. Rippers!

They fly out together from between the trees. Thieves. They hunt in packs. Cover their faces, leave just their eyes. Silverfish slick in the pitch of night. Cowardly pack of dogs. But on the wing, above the trees and eye sharp as a blade, it's another hunter. She hunts alone. Circles and circles and circles. One will walk off by himself. On his way to the field, to the barn, to the outhouse. On they own they small as a mouse, as low to the ground and soft. This hunter? She fix them with her eye. She move quick, quick. So quick they don't feel the blade 'til too late. Land on they shoulders. Stuff they mouth with cotton while they squeal like a pig at the slaughter. They was on their way but…never come back. One at a time. Down to the river. Bleed them, gut them, render them, grind them. Down to ash. Surrendered clean unto the Lamb.

ELEANOR. You doing that leave you no better than them.

MOTHER DIXON. Tender thoughts. Where they leave you?

ELEANOR. …

MOTHER DIXON. You want truth. Here it is. Who the one tied the noose around our Shaz with his own nimble hands?

ELEANOR …

MOTHER DIXON. Old man Shumann. There's the truth. I told you the one way to do.

This be the other. (*She opens her box. Pulls out a bar of soap*) That new girl of Shumann's.

ELEANOR. Yes, ma'am? Yes, ma'am.

MOTHER DIXON. His little *pearl*?

ELEANOR. She not even from here.

MOTHER DIXON. Thief all the same. Tonight she'll walk the river, but won't come home.

ELEANOR. Your tree of life. That's all what's yours by rights.

MOTHER DIXON. I take what's mine by rights.

ELEANOR. I got my way. Make him back to me. My cornbread and honey. No more blood.

MOTHER DIXON. Always more blood. If not theirs, be yours soon enough.

(*Outside the tent.*)

THE BOY. Red heart. My pin-prick heart. Squirm in my sac. Red seed me. Drawn to the spark. Pulled to the scream. I root and turn. I halve and halve and halve again. My red heart. My pin-prick heart. Turn in my sac. My pitch black dark. Turn in my sac. My pitch black dark. Turn in my sac. My pitch black dark.

(*The factory.*)

THE BOY. This is the newest model. Miss Shumann? Mister Shumann want to know what you think we should call this doll. Want you to name it.

INGA. 'Inga.'

THE BOY. That's awful pretty. Eleanor. This the newest model, 'Inga.'

ELEANOR. Don't come up in here and think you know something cuz you don't.

THE BOY. This is the eye assembly chart.

ELEANOR. I know the ropes.

THE BOY. I could help you with this chart if I want…

ELEANOR. Don't mess with me…

THE BOY. …or not if I don't.

ELEANOR. …and I won't mess with you.

THE BOY. Fine. Here.

ELEANOR. How does this go?

THE BOY. You take ...

ELEANOR. Never mind.

THE BOY. You take the hook and you take the thread.

ELEANOR. I can see that. The rubber goes through and then you wrap it tight.

THE BOY. Mister Shumann always wraps the whole part, not just the top. That's what makes it quality.

ELEANOR. Then you take the hook and you put it up through the head and you put on the elastic and you pull it like so and then you take it and you ...

THE BOY. Hook it.

ELEANOR. Hook it onto the eye.

THE BOY. If you make a mark on the eye or on the face you ruin it. Rejected. And you've got to break the whole thing.

ELEANOR. What I know? You got to put it back gentle so there ain't no mark.

THE BOY. Did you wash your hands?

ELEANOR. How I'm gonna touch all on it ain't washed my hands.

THE BOY. Don't mess it up.

ELEANOR. Like this?

THE BOY. You just lucky this first time out.

ELEANOR. No mark.

THE BOY. Mmmmmm-hmmmmm.

ELEANOR. Lucky 'Inga.' Lucky me. Did you wash *your* hands?

THE BOY. Yes.

ELEANOR. Did you wash your*self*? That's what I should ask you. You stink like a dog.

THE BOY. Shut your mouth.

INGA. Stinky stinky.

THE BOY. Miss Shumann?

ELEANOR. She said it.

THE BOY. I'll be on my way, then. 'Inga' it is.

ELEANOR. And get me some thread.

THE BOY. What for?

ELEANOR. To sew your lips shut. What do you think for? I need it to put these legs on right. And while you at it, I could use some more muslin. And some pins and some raw cotton and also some wire.

THE BOY. You don't need all that.

ELEANOR. You want 'Inga' to come out one-legged and scrawny, we could play by your book. Matter of fact, I'll just sit here and wait for her to make herself.

THE BOY. Alright, quit batting your gums.

ELEANOR. How you expect somebody to do they work if they don't have what they need to do it?

THE BOY. I'll be back directly. It's a shipment supposed to come today.

I'll check with Mister Shumann, see if he thinks you need what you say you need, and we'll see if you get it.

ELEANOR. However you got to put that together in your mind. You go on ahead, just so long as I get my thread, and my muslin and my raw cotton and my wire.

THE BOY. You're real difficult.

(*He leaves.*)

ELEANOR. Tell me about it. Tell you what I know. I do what I have to do.

INGA. Inga can savor the weisswurst that sits in her box. Her box. Gingerman, sweet black kisses. Have you nothing salty?...The air is *pressing* her.

ELEANOR. Hot. Gets hotter still.

INGA. It presses through her dress. It wets her.

ELEANOR. Just heat.

INGA. We should make a thousand little fans for these thousand little dollies whose little dresses are wet and sticky.

ELEANOR. You could use this.

(ELEANOR *tosses her the eye assembly chart.*)

INGA. Inga you must take your nap.

(ELEANOR *sings a lullaby. It is something she has heard on the radio before, a romantic big band ballad feeling. She has found herself humming it from time to time. As she sings now, it becomes something else entirely.*)

ELEANOR.

> I'd like to make your dream come true
> There's nothing else I'd rather do
> Give you a magic carpet ride
> A thousand gold doubloons
> A snowstorm in July
> Atop a hundred red balloons
> I'd like to pluck the stars for you
> And lay them on your bedtime pillow
> Net a million butterflies
> To sing you lullabies
> Conduct a thousand honeybees
> To buzz buzz buzz a mellow cello
> Oh-oh but darling most of all
> When a teardrop falls
> I'll kiss it from your cheek
> And swallow all your sadness who-o-ole
> To make you smile again my dear
> I'll never leave you musn't fear
> I live for you and you alone
> There's nothing else I know
> So close your eyes and go to sleep
> I'd like to make your
> Dream
> Come true

> (*The air is full.* ELEANOR *works.* INGA,
> *moved, fans her doll.*)

ELEANOR. You gonna stir up all that air and wear out your arm and then you just gonna be hot all over again.

INGA. Where is the switch for that fan?

ELEANOR. Don't work.

INGA. Nothing works. We could walk to the river ...

ELEANOR. Sit by the window. Might catch a breeze.

INGA. Dead lights. Dead fan. Big black spider dead on its thread.

ELEANOR. How you see that?

INGA. Big spider fan.

ELEANOR. Spiders got eight legs.

INGA. Not always.

ELEANOR. Just stir up dust anyway.

INGA. In the heat it is appropriate to have a light picnic. A few favorites. Savories and sweets. Jellied meats, pickled eggs, potato salad, if there has been a roasting, tender slices of suckling pig. Plumcake, cherrycake, strawberry tart, blue flower coffee, schokoladenpudding mit crème ...

ELEANOR. Got my mouth watering.

INGA. I want my dinner.

ELEANOR. They don't feed you back in there?

INGA. ...

ELEANOR. I got a little something. Something sweet. (*Finds her cornbread missing.*) Where's my bread?

INGA. Uh-oh.

ELEANOR. You ate my bread?

INGA. I was hungry.

ELEANOR. You always damn hungry. You took it.

INGA. But it was so good.

ELEANOR. You leave my food alone.

INGA. I will trade you cakes from my box.

ELEANOR. It wasn't yours.

INGA. It was here. All night. Under the towel.

ELEANOR. That wasn't yours!!!

INGA. You leave the food and then get mad. You didn't want it.

ELEANOR. If I left it and it dried and turned to dust that's my business.

INGA. But even just now you were going to give it.

ELEANOR. Giving and taking is two different things.

INGA. I thought you are my friend.

ELEANOR. You a thief.

INGA. Like you...who takes my thread, who takes my pins, my cotton,
    who takes my wire? My factory!

ELEANOR. Fix it to you
        that's what I know
        start with the kindling
        gather from the yard
        say his name
        with each stick
        Shaz
        his name I call him
        like he calls me Ella
        and I call him
        and he call me
        kindling wood

stack em in
lit stick match
bottom of the stove
ashes scraped clean
Shaz
light em
Shaz
flame catch
pile the wood
one by one
shut the door
seen Mama do
I can too
bag of meal
dip three handfuls powder and salt
in the bowl
two fat eggs
from under the hen dip the buttermilk stir it good
lard in the skillet skillet on the eye sizzle and pop
just before I pour mix some honey
a fingerful
and a drop of spit turn it clockwise call his name
Shaz
Shaz
bake it till
it smell so sweet cool it on the porch
gonna walk it there walk it to him
tighten my plaits tie my ribbon
red and white revival dress
Shaz
Shaz
made it with my hands.
Sweet and mine.

You got all the dolls in the world.
But who you ever loved?!

INGA. Once I made a living doll.
    Behind Papa's factory
    a valley
    deep in the black night
    the tinkling of bells
    candles flicker
    in the valley
    wagons and horses
    Gypsies.
    Tin and glass and glittering eyes
    "They'll steal you Inga
    and make you into sausage!"
    Down the hill
    I creep
    night after night
    to the camp
    through the birches
    to the boy
    his long arms
    his black eyes
    his hair like a raven wet from the river
    he bids me
    hush
    like so
    he brings me
    a handful of beads
    a taste of spiced meat
    my belly full of fireflies
    my eyes full of his belly
    brown like leather with curly hairs
    my lips full of his honey

when he presses me
I ache and rock and rub
night after night after night after night.
Inga. Inga! Inga! INGA!
My father and his men swarm the valley.
Spiders on their arms.
They grab me and beat back the people.
The boy runs to me.
My father clubs him to the ground.
The next night.
Thick smoke smell.
I sneak from my room.
Down, down, down.
Their wagons burned to embers.
The Gypsies are gone.
On the ground.
Spiders.
...
I hold her once.
Pink as meat, shiny black hair.
In the pitch of night, my father takes her down to the river.
My living doll.
Drowned like kittens.

(*The tent.*)

MOTHER DIXON. Watchman surely pray. Blood in the air. That blood
of the Lamb.

(*Sings as she strops her knife.*)

Watchman, watchman see those eyes
Evil eyes, demon eyes
Watchman, watchman see those eyes
Watching you and me

Watchman, watchman see those eyes
Angel eyes, angel eyes
Watchman, watchman see those eyes
Watching you and me

(THE BOY *knocks.*)

MOTHER DIXON. You knock three times, Boy.

THE BOY. ...

MOTHER DIXON. You come for a healing?

THE BOY. Saw the light.

MOTHER DIXON. You been out this night?

THE BOY. Yes, Ma'am.

MOTHER DIXON. All kinds of things in the night, drawn toward the candle. Things that mean no good. Got to take care.

THE BOY. ...

MOTHER DIXON. What you come for, Boy?

THE BOY. ...

MOTHER DIXON. (*Clucks tongue*) Got that tonic for your hands. Two bits a bottle.

THE BOY. ...

MOTHER DIXON. You got two bits?

THE BOY. Got something better.

ALL. The Boy places a bundle by Mother Dixon's feet. She knows from the smell alone. Bones. Eleanor joins Inga by the river. She carries the doll she made of Shaz.

ELEANOR. Not safe to walk the river alone.

INGA. I am not long alone. The angel comes tonight.

MOTHER DIXON. Looking for my sweet Shaz…looking in the sweet brown soil for my only one…

THE BOY. …

MOTHER DIXON. …and what thing do I find?

INGA. Cotton meat. Branch bone. Burlap skin. Dry corn teeth…

ELEANOR. What should I put for the eyes?

INGA. I put the eyes. For a gift.

ELEANOR. No more blood.

MOTHER DIXON. By rights I should cut deep. Cut quick.

THE BOY. Yes, Ma'am.

MOTHER DIXON. You stink and slope, but you ain't no buzzard. Seem to me I know you, Boy. Who your people? What you called?

THE BOY. …

INGA. There! In the water. Under the skin.

ELEANOR. The light!

MOTHER DIXON. All them bones. All them names.

THE BOY. No names.

MOTHER DIXON. One at a time. We learn them back into ourselves.

THE BOY. He paid for the bones. He said no names.

MOTHER DIXON. Eleanor Simms. Aged 15. Died from drowning.

THE BOY. Eleanor Simms.

INGA. The crocodile angel. Its soul shines at the bottom of the river.

ELEANOR. Will it bite us?

INGA. Yes.

MOTHER DIXON. Inga Shumann. Aged 14. Died from drowning.

THE BOY. Inga Shumann.

INGA. The angel will hatch from our eyes…Fly us away. The prettiest eyes are angel eyes…

MOTHER DIXON. Shadrack Ambrose Dixon. Aged 17. Died from lynching.

ELEANOR. But, how will we see?

INGA. Our ears…

THE BOY. Shadrack.

INGA. Our mouths.

THE BOY. Ambrose.

INGA. Our hands.

THE BOY. Dixon.

ELEANOR. Wait.

MOTHER DIXON. Now you. What you called, boy?!

THE BOY. Veins pull salt
    And fat and sweet
    Plump my flesh
    My newly knitting bones
    You brewed hemlock

Added tansy
Stopped my heart with pennyroyal
You brought me down
To dirt, to dust
You slipped me down
To rot
You never gave *me* a name.

ELEANOR. Shaz. Shaz. Shaz. He needs his heart.

INGA. Ask the angel. It will bring you a heart, from the heart of the
Earth.

MOTHER DIXON. What's done, we can't hold. What's done, we give
over.

> (MOTHER DIXON *stares at him. Stoic. Clucks
> her tongue three times.*)

MOTHER DIXON. Pluto.

THE BOY. Pluto?

MOTHER DIXON. Your name. Pluto.

THE BOY. Ma'am. Wash my eyes.

ELEANOR. What will we see?

INGA. Sonnenblumen. Nur sonnenblumen in jedem mund in jeder
hand in jedem ohr. Die samen sind traenen. Glucklich wie glass.

MOTHER DIXON. Open your eyes. What do you see?

> (THE BOY *does so. Light falls on all of us.
> As though a veil has been pulled back, he
> moves toward us and studies our faces.*)

THE BOY. Sunflowers. Only sunflowers in every mouth, in every hand, in every ear.

MOTHER DIXON. The seeds are tears.

THE BOY. Happy as glass.

> (*Clap rhythm. As all the light leaves, the four circle. One by one,* ELEANOR, INGA *and then* THE BOY *separate and leave the space.* MOTHER DIXON *circles around the bundle on the ground; her hands trace lines in the air. Lights fade.*)
>
> (*End of Ring Two.*)

A CONVERSATION | faye price & daj

PRICE. What was the impulse for writing *Phoenix Fabrik*?

JONES. There are two impulses—one short, the other long.

Short—My romance with the traditional Black American form of the ring play. In particular, the recordings of such plays by the artist Bessie Jones, which I first heard 14 years ago when an intern at the Smithsonian Institution.

Long—Eight years ago, I was on tour in Charleston, South Carolina. I was excited to get to see South Carolina firsthand, as my paternal line came from there, and it had long occupied my imagination. I had come to love much of the so-called 'folk' art from there and the music of the Sea Islands shook my bones. Believing as I do that we carry the imprint of geography in our genes, I was curious to see if I would recognize the terrain, the way the light fell, etcetera. In Charleston, I did "recognize" it—in a way that escapes easy description. I had a lot of near-paranormal experiences in Charleston. I later learned that I'm not alone in experiencing it as a place where certain veils are lifted, if but for a moment.

Anyhow, I went with my buddy Helga Davis to tour a plantation on our day off. We found it exquisitely restored. The mill could grind corn into flour. The missus's silver was presented in fine polish. But, come to find, when we were searching for the slave graveyard, marked on the glossy brochure, we couldn't find it. We went back and forth and came to realize that it must be located in a grove wild with groundcover. Helga and I got down on our knees and dug, finally finding a corroded placard carrying the corresponding brochure number. There were no other visible markers. Unexpectedly we both started to weep. The feeling was "Still? Still? Still?"

So, flash forward a few years, and I am visiting my Black American émigré friend in Hamburg, Germany. He introduces me to all his German friends. Now, I had never had the desire to go to Germany, fully subsumed was I by the nightmarish stereotyping of the culture as inherently violent and cold and the idea that I would be utterly isolated in a visit there. I marvel, constantly, at the ways in which I call myself working for freedom from stereotypes, etc. but find myself jugged up in all kinds of colonized thinking—a common experience, I understand, more and more. So, I found myself at the Café Paris on the Rathausstrasse having a four-hour conversation with a 72-year-old man named Ulrich, whom I found willing to discuss everything having to do with history, race, fascism and US politics. I found—without exception—that the people I talked with (granted, people in a more 'liberal' German city and people connected in one way or another to the arts) were willing to talk quite transparently about the inheritance of their country's historical atrocities. And were willing to challenge me—as an American (not Black American or artist American, but straight-up American) about the hypocrisy of my country. When I would state, "Well, it's not me," I had to check myself. Where had I heard that statement before? I flashed back to Charleston as I walked those centuries-old streets and listened to the whispers in a language which cut my tongue as I tried to learn a few of its well worn words.

So, the impulse ... comes from a space of worrying/preoccupation about these questions: Can we ever be free as individuals if we don't face the violence in our (collective) pasts? How can we extend love and compassion when we have been deeply wounded? What was the strange story that came whispering up to me from the terrain I covered, and how could I tell it? A ring play, yes, that's the sound.

PRICE. What is the play about?

JONES. Eleanor works in Shumann's Doll Factory in South Carolina. It's 1945. Her beloved Shaz has been lynched. Inga, the orphaned German girl, comes to America to live with her uncle who runs the factory. She works alongside Eleanor. They make dolls. The story erupts from there.

Each time I arrive at the page or in the process of rehearsal, I have a new experience with *Phoenix Fabrik*. And, so, like any piece of so-called abstract art, I feel to a great degree that *Phoenix Fabrik* is about the experiences had by each individual audience member with its matrix of story, sound, movement, and image. My experience with it thus far leads me to feel—personally—that it is about finding the courage to stand in a space of radical empathy, an extension of the imagination beyond the self and into someone else's experience, a genuine willingness to walk in someone else's shoes and bear the consequences of that walk. Doing so is a messy, politically incorrect, psychically dangerous sort of thing—but it can result in something luminous rising from the "ashes" of personal and collective history. Love happens in spite of ourselves sometimes. It is an experience we have that overwhelms us—I don't know that we ever truly figure out what it is about.

Interestingly, I think the strength of the ring play is that it abstracts (as does much seminal Black music) crystal clear cultural and political analysis and political resistance. It invites participation in a radical act of transmutation that feels innocuous. One of Bessie Jones's recordings—a ring play *Way Go Lily*—is a contagious polyrhythmic piece that describes a slave/master reversal and the imagined retributions ... "gonna rule my ruler." Quite a radical message in a child's game. Similarly, I seek to find the music, the rhythm that houses the horror, but feels soft and seemingly innocent. The piece, I pray, moves in a lovely circle and entrances. The teeth are in the lingering, in the afterwards.

PRICE. What does it present, challenge, affirm, or examine?

JONES. It presents a theatrical ring play. If it challenges anything aesthetically, I believe it moves counter to the larger cultural slide toward historical erasure and simplicity in form and content. It is not easily digestible work; there are many tastes on the plate. Its narrative is unabashedly elliptical. I work in a tradition which has roots in the beginning of the last century—at least. I continue to challenge the willful ignorance of those who "forget" the Black avant-garde, by recognizing its artists as my direct forebears, and finding, in my work, new applications for the tools they so carefully honed, in addition to honing a few of my own.

PRICE. Where does the title come from?

JONES. *Phoenix Fabrik* = Phoenix Factory. The factory was one of the first images that came forward as I worked. What rises from ruin (personal, cultural, historical)? That was a core question.

PRICE. Is the play at all personal or from a personal experience? If so, how so?

JONES. In addition to the aforementioned story about South Carolina, I'd say that I work, fervently, to experience a personal connection to everything I write. There is, however, a fragment of family history in the piece—the retelling of a family member's lynching haunted me for years and found its way into the narrative in a prominent way.

PRICE. In the DAJ canon (you do have one, you know) where does this play lie? Is it new territory for you? If so, how so?

JONES. Each time it's a new world. I have actually been reviewing my work from the last 1 2 years getting ready to archive it on a website. I'm really happy with one thing—no two pieces look alike. There are certain themes that come forward I imagine (I'd leave that to the dramaturg). But I'm really interested in the arc of this interdisciplinary practice—I've cultivated work as a writer, a performer, and a director. I've increasingly come to understand that my strength as an artist comes when all those perspectives converge—*Phoenix Fabrik* is one of the projects where that happened—even though I am not now a performer in it, the characters came through my body with as much force as they would have if I were embodying them as an actor.

I don't know if you knew that I started out wanting to be a painter. I loved the depth of engagement—obsession even—with a project and the intensity of the compositional process. So this piece is new old territory in the sense that I am working like I did when I painted—conscious of everything in the frame. There is not a breath, a gesture or a word that I haven't sat with and wrestled with. Things have been crafted intuitively, vetted intellectually/critically and refined emotionally—much like the process of making a painting was for me.

PRICE. Talk to me about the experience of making this play. What was the process? Was this process different than what you usually practice?

JONES. It took a LOOOONG time. I do think it feels really "fresh" in the moment when it happens. But it is one of my most considered compositions. While researching, I read copiously about the period of history, about dollmaking, German Expressionist Aesthetics, Afro-German experiences, the Roma people, Josef

Mengele and the role of eyes in the horrifying eugenics experiments, the shared history between the US and Nazi Germany of racialized image-making, lynching postcards, etc ... I then went through a long period of absorption. During this time I also workshopped bits and pieces of material with collaborating performers Helga Davis, Barbara Duchow, Daniel Dodd Ellis, Vinie Burrows, Arrion Doss and Rhonda Ross. When the piece came out whole it was like a possession. I do not minimize the fact that there was a great deal of metaphysical work—this piece has a spiritual component. It holds stories that come from the ancestors—quite literally. In the rehearsal room, we are all aware of this energy and we must work carefully with it. I've done my best to craft the "house" for this energy—to honor the stories being told while also being conscious of the aesthetic choices being made.

BEL

CANTO

FOREWORD

When I met the utterly incomparable Daniel Alexander Jones on the first day of graduate school at Brown University in 1991, within moments I discovered that he was a singer, performer, actor, and writer. We read and commented on almost everything the other wrote during those graduate school years in late night sessions waiting for sweet potato pies to cool around midnight. His skills as a director and collaborator, his intellectual acumen, his gift for teaching, and his accomplishments as a community leader were revealed over time. It was when I read *Bel Canto* that his superpowers as a creative visionary became clear, and my response was deeply emotional. The title means beautiful singing in Italian, a style of operatic singing. Daniel has created a powerful work of beauty, great passion, and imagination.

Daniel's singular voice as a writer is in the tradition of theatrical jazz and improvisation rooted in his dedication to intellectual rigor, deep thought, and his deliberate and intentional creation of work that transcends his personal experience. In *Bel Canto*, realism is wed to surrealism and yet the play is grounded in the reality of what it means to be a teenager coming of age and the complexity of dealing with identity and race.

Set in 1978, 16-year-old Benjamin Turner is new to town. His father has disappeared, and his mother Bessie has moved them from Berkeley, California, to Springfield, Massachusetts, where he is terrorized by a small-minded school nurse, visited by the astral projection of Marian Anderson, energized by the music of Jimi Hendrix, educated by a passionate opera teacher, and drawn to explore new emotions of love with a new classmate, Terence, who himself has a deep secret. Carrying the weight of American history, 16-year-old Benjamin Turner is a young, bi-racial queer boy coming to terms with his racial, sexual, and creative identities. He and his new friend Terence are faced with making choices and decisions that will shape their manhood, and they are transformed by the unexpected force of love.

There is music in the structure of *Bel Canto*, and drama in the visual architecture, using the American flag as a powerful symbol. Research is married to imagination in this work that draws from Daniel's personal experience, history, and issues at the forefront of contemporary LGBTQIA life. *Bel Canto* amplifies voices seldom heard on the American stage. It's about time.

– Shay Youngblood

ALTAR NOTES

"If you can just get your mind together,
Then come on across to me.
We'll hold hands and then we'll watch the sun rise
From the bottom of the sea.
But first, are you experienced?
Have you ever been experienced?"

– Jimi Hendrix

Bel Canto is bound to the incredible moments of beauty and grace that visited it during its productions. Again and again, from within the company of players, and also from countless audience members who either approached me in person or wrote to me, I heard how important it was for them to see these people and these stories onstage, told in this way.

Bel Canto is also bound to the battles that surrounded its genesis. While certainly not the first time, nor the last time, we all had an especially rude experience of the pernicious realities of institutional racism and sexism. As often happens, the themes of the piece sounded themselves in "real" life. At every turn of its development, through its premiere, I centered the authority of Black women, and as a result, received outright disdain, dismissal, and in some cases wrath, from largely though not exclusively white men in positions of power. I was honored to work with Robbie McCauley as the director on the development and premiere, and I specifically invited the nuanced and pointed dramaturgical wisdom of the women who played in the various workshops and the premiere, including Lynda Gravatt, Ebony Jo-Ann, Vinie Burrows, Renita Martin, and the late, great Oni Faida Lampley.

Their presumption is that you are mistaken, and they must correct you. Sometimes that stance comes harshly with sharp-edged judgments, sometimes it comes wrapped in a warm paternal blanket. But either way, they know more than you about what you are doing. There is nothing more enervating to them than someone that does not regard them as superior, and to center the authority of those they have deemed marginal is salt in that wound. One renowned white male artistic director told me flat out that I needed a white man in the play. Since I had Marian Anderson in it, how about adding Benny Goodman. (For real, tho.) Some members of the technical staff of the premiere undermined our set and projection designer, the inspired Mirta Tocci (a long-time collaborator of Robbie's), by giving her faulty ground plans and then refusing to correct resulting errors in the construction of the set. But the pièce de résistance was the lighting designer of the premiere production, a white man, who boldly disregarded Robbie's direction by lighting (and therefore emphasizing) actors and moments that he deemed important, and throwing shade on those she wanted lit. When I arrived for the technical rehearsals, he pulled me aside to tell me in conspiratorial tones that Robbie (a celebrated artist) "didn't know what she was doing" and that he was going to "rescue" my play. He'd wholly disregarded the notes Robbie and Mirta had given him. When I shut him down about Robbie, he left and we all redid the entire design in one night. In the wee hours of the following morning, he snuck back into the theatre, restored *his* design, then absconded with the lighting board, leaving just the operating switch for the light op to page through his original cues. Some time later, Robbie recounted, one of the producers approached her at an event and confessed that we "were too sophisticated" and that, in the end, of course, they "had to have control." What became clear was not only that the piece was illegible to some, but that it was an affront to others, because of who it chose to center, and how it chose to explore the interactions among them. I, we, were "mistaken."

Bel Canto is bound to the theme of *experience*. The *experience* of stepping into your own right to tell the story in your way, and the fire of consequences for so doing. The *experience* of identifying your longings, and allowing your impulses toward utterance. The *experience* of feeling versus knowing your way. It was here especially that I marveled at Robbie as she guided the actors toward the power of their experience. In particular, I remember a moment among the original cast, when the actresses looked at Robbie and one said, "So, you mean, we get to be *all* of who we are?" after she invited them lovingly to stop "performing," i.e. to get anyone's gaze other than their own out of their minds. Robbie nodded matter-of-factly and kept on about the business of making the piece.

o

I spent a year listening almost exclusively to opera. Not having grown up around it, other than recordings of Caruso sounding out from my Italian neighbor's house, or the '70s child touchstone of the opera-singing orange on *Sesame Street*, I had a lot of work to do. I also devoured every narrative that I could find from Black American opera singers. It was fascinating to piece together the intersecting networks among the generations of singers whose lives overlapped with the subjects in the play. I paid close attention to the tensions in the singers' lives among their individual pursuits of artistic excellence and career longevity, and the sense of obligation to the Civil Rights Movement they either embraced or eschewed. In the writing, I invoked Marian Anderson—who was universally hailed for her personal conviction and her commitment to lifting up other singers. The character of Barbara Scarlatti, while fictional, contained genetic material from the lived experience of dozens of Black opera singers whose lives I studied, complete with their complicated dance with systems of measurement and worth borne from a system that would not recognize their full humanity.

As I researched, I reintroduced myself to the work of painter Jacob Lawrence. His formalism resonated with me, as did his ability to render the epic approachable, through a deceptively simple focus on the movement of often tender, vulnerable, quotidian "every-people." These folks navigated Lawrence's distinctive architecture, which often included multiple layers of time-space-history scaffolded under their feet. It felt like the inside, the lived side, of a saga. And it mirrored, for me, the trembling intimacy of an individual aria delivered within the grand sonic and visual sweep of the larger opera. And so, I embraced the most "operatic" symbol I could imagine given the content of the play—the United States flag. And I imagined the characters and their stories, all shaped by the wake of the country's history, playing in intimate, everyday relationships to one another within this epic visual architecture. Sometimes the meanings of the experiences we have are articulated in sync with the larger historical narrative of which we are a part. But often, what we experience unfolds within us in an ever-unfolding private matrix of meanings. When we give voice to the latter, the resulting song can be the thing we least expect to hear, and is often quiet, confessional, and finely nuanced, borne, as it is, from the lived side of life.

– DAJ

Bel Canto
Premiered as a co-production of The Theater Offensive & Wheelock
Family Theatre with support from the Rockefeller MAP Fund
Boston, MA
June 2003

Directed by Robbie McCauley

FEATURING:
Burl Moseley as BENJAMIN TURNER
Lynda Gravatt as BARBARA SCARLATTI
Renita Martin as BESSIE TURNER and DADDY VELVET
Merle Perkins as MARIAN ANDERSON
Jimonn Cole as TERENCE LONG
Maureen Brennan as MISS PAVA

Bel Canto received a second production in 2003 at Actor's Express
Theater in Atlanta under the direction of Jasson Minadakis and a
third production in 2004 at Pillsbury House Theatre in Minneapolis
under the direction of Stephen DiMenna.

Bel Canto was written during a National Endowment for the Arts/
Theatre Communications Group Playwriting Residency at Boston's
Theater Offensive. It was read in 2001 as part of the New Work
Now! Festival at The Joseph Papp Public Theater, and in 2002 at
New York Theatre Workshop under the direction of Robbie McCau-
ley. In 2002 the play was read as part of the Cornerstone New Play
Series at Penumbra Theatre Company, under the direction of Dr.
Omi Osun Joni L. Jones.

The play was developed at the 2002 Sundance Institute Theatre
Lab under the direction of Robbie McCauley with dramaturgy by
Elissa Adams.

the what

The set for *Bel Canto* is an American flag, mammoth in size and protean. This "flag" should be constructed with a combination of varied dimensional/sculptural elements and light. The white or red stripes can, for example, fuse to become a unified whole, thereby isolating a particular room in Barbara's house or the façade of an apartment building. The blue can fill the whole space, can brighten or dim to be either morning or nighttime sky. The stars can cluster to form a sun or moon, or can move through the space and hang like lanterns; one star can be a lamp or a streetlight. Nothing should be ordinary or clichéd about this unifying element; rather, the design should be searching and inspired. The works of painter Jacob Lawrence offer examples of different spatial possibilities. All the players are a part of the space—"painted" in. When they leave a scene, they should remain a part of the composition in some way. Benjamin should never leave the stage.

the who

BENJAMIN TURNER. Aged 16. Lanky.

BARBARA SCARLATTI. Early 60s. Tall. Dramatic.

BESSIE TURNER. Late 30s. Benjamin's mother. Short, natural hair.

TERENCE LONG. Aged 17. Wears glasses.

MARIAN ANDERSON. An astral projection of the famed contralto.

DADDY VELVET. Terence's father. (May be played by the actress who plays Bessie.)

MISS PAVA. Aged 50. School nurse. White.

the where

Springfield, Massachusetts. A small, working-class city in the western part of the Commonwealth.

the when

1978.

the how

Passionately.

the notation

/ indicates that the line immediately following should begin, over-lapping the line being spoken.

(++) indicates that a substantive musical rest should be taken.

ACT I

I sacri nomi di padre, d'amante
Né profferir poss'io, ne ricordar;
Per l'un, per l'altro confusa e tremante,
lo piangere vorrei, vorrei pregar.

Those sacred names of father, of lover,
I dare not utter or even recall;
for one, for the other, confused, trembling,
I would weep and pray.

– Aida

JANUARY 1978 (OVERTURE)

(*One. Two. Three stars flicker on in the distance. A fourth star becomes a streetlight and catches* BENJAMIN TURNER *in its spittle. He dances outside the front of the apartment building into which he and his mother* BESSIE *have just moved. Snow falls from passing clouds, gently.* BENJAMIN *allows himself to be anointed by the snowflakes. A constellation of stars blinks on. Unbeknownst to* BENJAMIN, MARIAN ANDERSON's *astral projection stands inside the constellation, looks down upon him and sings.*)

MARIAN ANDERSON.
How we wish
while drowning!
Though soft and silent
this fateful flood
holds no less danger.
Oh, so delicate—
each drop a sudden dream
sketched in unique symmetry.
We drown, nonetheless.
Filled by
brittle worlds
that melt into tears
at our touch.

(BENJAMIN *opens his jacket. He reveals the tattered tie-dyed tee shirt he is wearing. It is clearly not his own. He pulls on it a bit.*)

BENJAMIN. Come on, Dad.

> (BESSIE TURNER *appears at the doorway. She is lit from behind. We only see her silhouette throughout this scene. When he hears his mother's voice,* BENJAMIN *closes his jacket to hide the shirt.*)

BESSIE. Come inside, Benjamin.

BENJAMIN. It's too beautiful.

BESSIE. You'll catch your death.

BENJAMIN. Come and see.

BESSIE. I grew up with this. And it's not like you haven't seen it before.

BENJAMIN. This is different than home.

BESSIE. This is home.

BENJAMIN. Snows even harder up north. I bet.

BESSIE. Bet so.

BENJAMIN. Cold, too.

BESSIE. Bet so.

BENJAMIN. I think I can take it a little while longer.

BESSIE. I think you need to come inside.

BENJAMIN. Did you ever look and see things? Just see things. Like you never saw 'em before?

BESSIE. All the time. Come inside.

BENJAMIN. The light is funny.

BESSIE. Reflection.

BENJAMIN. Where's the moon?

BESSIE. It's there.

BENJAMIN. The stars?

BESSIE. Them, too.

BENJAMIN. Where do you think thoughts go ...?

BESSIE. (*A sigh*) Thoughts.

BENJAMIN. ...I think thoughts go out in all directions. Like the radio.

BESSIE. You're stalling, oh great philosophical one.

BENJAMIN. Yep.

BESSIE. Come inside.

BENJAMIN. What about wishes?

BESSIE. Oh, Benji. Come on.

BENJAMIN. Serious. Where do wishes go?

BESSIE. Remember what I used to tell you?

BENJAMIN. About wishes?

BESSIE. Find a point of light. A star. Planet. Point of light. Then send your wish there. Told you it was a window to heaven. "Wishes are straight-ahead things."

BENJAMIN. You told me that?

BESSIE. All the time.

BENJAMIN. Who told you that?

BESSIE. Your Dad.

BENJAMIN. Did you believe him?

BESSIE. I'm freezing, Benji.

BENJAMIN. What about now, when there are clouds?

BESSIE. I don't know. He didn't say anything about that. If he did,
I don't remember.

BENJAMIN. Oh.

BESSIE. I don't even know which box to pick, babe. Where to start
unpacking.

BENJAMIN. In a minute.

BESSIE. Pretty sure I know where some cocoa is.

BENJAMIN. Deal.

BESSIE. The light is pretty. Makes things look softer than they are.

BENJAMIN. Yeah.

BESSIE. One minute.

BENJAMIN. Mmmm-hmmm.

BESSIE. I'm counting.

> (BESSIE *exits.* BENJAMIN *opens his jacket
> and scans the sky.*)

BENJAMIN. That looks like a good window.

> (*He scrunches the tee shirt into his hands.
> Then, wishing hard...*)

BENJAMIN. *Come on . . .*

Come on . . .

> (*A soft blue pane of light falls next to* BEN-
> JAMIN. MARIAN ANDERSON *descends into
> the pane of light. She lights just above the
> ground and beams at* BENJAMIN. *She sings
> her lines to him.*)

MARIAN ANDERSON.
> *It does appear to be a good window, but we can never be certain
> at such a distance.*

BENJAMIN. Hello.

MARIAN ANDERSON.
> *What is your name?*

BENJAMIN. Benjamin.

MARIAN ANDERSON.
> *Benjamin.*

BENJAMIN. Are you an angel?

MARIAN ANDERSON.
> *We have been called an angel, among other things.*

BENJAMIN. I'll bet.

MARIAN ANDERSON.
> *And you?*

BENJAMIN. I'm no angel.

MARIAN ANDERSON.
> *Finding our right windows is tricky business. Being certain of
> our wishes is even more challenging.*

BENJAMIN. I'm certain. I know exactly what I want.

MARIAN ANDERSON.
> *We must offer caution, young man.*
> *Sometimes our wish flies in the face of destiny.*
> *Our will may block what is meant to come our way.*

BENJAMIN. But it's really important. It's not just for me.

MARIAN ANDERSON.
> *For every wish a price. And this you are willing to pay?*

BENJAMIN. How much?

MARIAN ANDERSON.
> *You must give of yourself, you will know how much. For now,*
> *word your wish with care and send it through your window.*

BENJAMIN. Just tell it?

MARIAN ANDERSON.
> *Give it.*

BENJAMIN. Here.

> (BENJAMIN *holds out his hands like a but-*
> *terfly to his window.* MARIAN ANDERSON
> *opens her hands, and reflects the gesture.*)

MARIAN ANDERSON.
> *What beautiful hands.*

BENJAMIN. Dad's.

MARIAN ANDERSON.
> *We are very brave to make that wish.*

BENJAMIN. We are?

MARIAN ANDERSON.
> *Uncommonly so.*

(MARIAN ANDERSON *begins to rise into the air.*)

BENJAMIN. Wait! What do "we" do now?

MARIAN ANDERSON.
> *Follow the signs.*
> *Be prepared to act.*

(MARIAN ANDERSON *ascends and the light flickers before going out.* BESSIE's *shadow reappears in the doorway.*)

BESSIE. Time's up, Benji. Don't give me a hard time tonight, babe.

(BENJAMIN *stares upward in wonder.*)

BESSIE. Benji?

(*Sound of a shower.*)

SHOWER

(BENJAMIN *stands at a changing bench in the Classical High School boy's locker room. He starts to take off his clothes. Standing at the opposite side of the changing bench is* TERENCE LONG. *They sneak glances at each other as they change. Terence wraps a towel around himself and goes into the shower. Voices echo out.*)

Here's your girlfriend.

Faggot.

Get your eyes off my shit, faggot.

(BENJAMIN *gets dressed.*)

Look at him. He's checking out your ass, Brian. He wants a piece of that.

Fuck you.

Look at him.

Fucking freak!

(*Sounds of a fight ensue.* BENJAMIN *walks into the shower. The fight gets deep.*)

Who the fuck are you?

What, nigga, that's your girlfriend?

(TERENCE *runs out, clutching his stomach, dripping wet. He falls on the floor.*)

Get off—get off my boy!!! Owww! Fuck you!

(BENJAMIN *cries out from the shower in pain.*)

Man, you're going to get suspended for that shit.

Fuck that! This mothafucka cut my lip. And let that bitch try and put me out this school. Even she want some of this shit.

(TERENCE *has hurriedly pulled his pants on and runs from the room.*)

IN WHICH MISS PAVA SPEAKS

> (*The Classical High School nurse's office.*
> BENJAMIN *is in severe pain.*)

MISS PAVA. Let's have a look there. Zikes, I'll bet that hurts.

BENJAMIN. Awwwwww!

MISS PAVA. Shhhhh. Can you wiggle your fingers?

BENJAMIN. It kills!

MISS PAVA. Whimpering won't take the pain away. Wiggle your fingers.

BENJAMIN. I can't. Auuuurrrrrgh!

MISS PAVA. Looks like a clean break to me.

BENJAMIN. *Please.*

MISS PAVA. You know, when I was your age, I had my wrist snapped by a rather aggressive gal with a medicine ball...

BENJAMIN. Can't you give me a pill or something?

MISS PAVA. For weeks, there were a thousand miniature blades, stabbing, stabbing. No codeine for me.

BENJAMIN. It's killing me!

MISS PAVA. Let's get this wrapped in a compress until your Mom gets here. Can't do anything else 'til then.

BENJAMIN. You didn't call her, did you?!

> (MISS PAVA *begins leafing through a sizable file.*)

MISS PAVA. Of course we called her.

BENJAMIN. She's in class. I don't want her to get worried. She's under a lot of stress right now...

MISS PAVA. (*Reading*) Benji Turner. I see you brought a 3.4 GPA with you from California.

BENJAMIN. They have that in my medical file?

MISS PAVA. I pulled the big file. "Our secret." I always peek—gives me a little more "insight."

(MISS PAVA *begins to apply a compress.*)

BENJAMIN. OUCH!

MISS PAVA. Down, horsey! 3.4 ... That's impressive, Benji.

BENJAMIN. OUUUUCH!

MISS PAVA. That's not too familiar, "Benji," is it? Good. I loved that movie. *Benji.* About the cute little dog who thwarts the kidnappers. Animals are good people.

BENJAMIN. Some people do a pretty good job as animals. (*She touches a particularly painful spot*) Grrruuuh!

(MISS PAVA *laughs awkwardly.*)

MISS PAVA. My goodness, you've got me laughing out of turn. Here's where my training kicks in. Anyone else would stop with the easy yack. But I know this wisecracking masks a deeper truth. Been hard "adjusting," hmm?

BENJAMIN. You're quick.

MISS PAVA. Thank you.

BENJAMIN. But I think it's the other way around. People at Classical are having a hard time "adjusting" to me.

MISS PAVA. There's pain under that smile. You can let that out here, Benji.

BENJAMIN. You're damn right there's pain.

MISS PAVA. Is there trouble on the old home front?

BENJAMIN. You really know how to turn a page. What's in that file anyway?

MISS PAVA. Private. Hmmm. Says "a little something" here about your Dad. Tell me, Ben. About your Dad. Confidential. Just between you and me.

BENJAMIN. Confidential...like the file?

MISS PAVA. No? I understand. Being abandoned by a parent is a painful thing.

BENJAMIN. He didn't *abandon* us.

MISS PAVA. Says here that he's somewhere singing "Oh, Canada," right about now.

BENJAMIN. You're pretty funny yourself.

MISS PAVA. I'm on the case, Benji; flattery will get you nowhere. Now. You and your mother, a Betty Turner...

BENJAMIN. Bessie.

MISS PAVA. "Bessie" it is... All that loose California handwriting. (*Flipping a page*) My *goodness*... Wait. Wait...

(MISS PAVA *turns his face up to the light.*)

MISS PAVA. Let me get a better look. Wow. It barely shows, but now

I can see it. I must say, even I was fooled. (*Excited*) The key was right in front of us and we didn't even know it.

BENJAMIN. The key to what?

MISS PAVA. The rage that triggered this fight! Hello! You'll never believe … I wrote about the cognitive development of mixed race children in college.

BENJAMIN. No.

MISS PAVA. (*So excited*) Can you believe! I did field research and everything. Up the road in Cambridge. No one would suspect the blood of the oppressor and the oppressed are clashing through your veins.

BENJAMIN. I don't know about all that…

MISS PAVA. Benji. This arm is an obvious cry for attention, a banner saying, "SEE ME, UNDERSTAND ME!" Hey kiddo, I'm with it. All teens want to be understood.

BENJAMIN. I don't need understanding. I need codeine.

MISS PAVA. Mr. Funny Bones. It's crystal clear that you have socially awkward tendencies, rooted in an irreconcilable racial identity. You're a sepia James Dean, stirring up tension and adverse reactions from everybody around you.

BENJAMIN. I was breaking up a fight! Not starting one! Why don't you pick on those guys?

MISS PAVA. UUUUPPP! Talking back may play in California but you're in Massachusetts now! Those boys are perfectly normal; boys will be boys and a good scrap is a good scrap. *You* on the other hand…

BENJAMIN. But *I* didn't do anything.

MISS PAVA. Benji, let me cut to the chase here. Socially awkward tendencies are a breeding ground for all sorts of bad characteristics. You already have the race thing to deal with, and the violent temper. Don't add to your troubles by fighting the people you should befriend, and protecting the people (*making a sissy gesture*) that would really only *add to the problem*. Do you catch my drift?

BENJAMIN. Do I ever.

MISS PAVA. Good guy. Good guy. But, hey, on the positive side, you're brave enough to get in the ring. Not like Dad, huh? I'm going to fill out this report and you can wait in the office until your mom gets here. Go home, watch some TV, eat some ice cream for a few days. Think about what I said.

(BESSIE *rushes into the office.*)

BESSIE. Benji! I was in class; I didn't get the message. Oh, God, are you alright?

MISS PAVA. He's fine.

BESSIE. And you are?

MISS PAVA. Peggy Pava. I'm the school nurse and (*winks at* BENJAMIN) part-time psychologist.

BESSIE. Did you do this?

MISS PAVA. Break his arm? No.

BESSIE. Put this compress on, lady.

MISS PAVA. Yes, that's my handiwork.

BESSIE. I didn't give permission for this to be done.

MISS PAVA. Permission. You signed a medical release form for the Massachusetts school...

BESSIE. I didn't give my permission. You should have waited.

BENJAMIN. Mom, it's okay.

MISS PAVA. It won't cost you anything, if that's what you're worried about. It happened on school property so...

BESSIE. The cost is not a factor here! It's your choice of therapy.

MISS PAVA. No need to get "angry."

BESSIE. I'm not...

MISS PAVA. We run a pretty good clinic here.

BENJAMIN. MOM! I'm okay. She did a good job.

MISS PAVA. It's okay, Benji. (*Scans* BESSIE'*s face.*) Your mom's only "protecting her young." You have a very handsome son. I see a little resemblance there around the eyes. (*Back to* BENJAMIN.) Bet he looks a lot more like his dad. There will be some paperwork for you, Ms. Turner, but we can just mail that on. I'll be in the office when you're ready.

BESSIE. What's *that* about?

> (*They share a look.* BENJAMIN *smiles through the pain.*)

BENJAMIN. COINTELPRO.

BESSIE. Benji. Your arm.

IN WHICH TERENCE WALKS HOME

> (TERENCE *walks home from school.* BENJAMIN *follows a few feet behind* TERENCE.)

BENJAMIN. Hey.

> (TERENCE *looks over his shoulder, and then he begins to walk faster.*)

BENJAMIN. Hey, man, wait up.

> (BENJAMIN *follows. They walk the stripes of the flag. Jimi Hendrix's "Fire" plays in the distance at first. The volume increases with each stripe* TERENCE *walks down. They arrive at* TERENCE'S *street.* TERENCE *pauses at his door. He looks around him, as though to get a breath of fresh air before going inside. He opens his front door and the Hendrix blares out. He steps in and shuts the door. The Hendrix song dissipates immediately. At the same moment* BARBARA SCARLATTI'S *door swings wide open.*)

IN WHICH BARBARA AND BENJAMIN MEET

> (BARBARA *executes three vicious sweeps.*)

BARBARA. Out! Out! Out! My good, sweet Lord! I've had to clean her hoof prints out of my house. I've only just got my babies quieted down. Why must I struggle so? *Signore, perque remu-*

neri cosi?! You would think that after all I've done I would be rewarded with better than *this*. Am I right?

BENJAMIN. Absolutely.

BARBARA. I've given a year to that … that *cow*! All the training I could muster. I walked her, hand-in-hand, through a series of lieder that would otherwise prove a minefield to someone as slow-witted as she. I practically spoon-fed Amneris to her, over and over and over, throughout this treacherous winter. I gave her secrets, priceless tricks of the trade, do you hear me?

BENJAMIN. Yes!

BARBARA. OH! I should have known. It's in the eyes. Her dim bovine eyes. I was projecting what I wanted to see. It's always the way! That heifer. Uggghhh, switching to that Shreck woman at this point will prove disastrous for her. Heifers both!!!

BENJAMIN. Help me out. This lady went to another teacher?

BARBARA. Shreck, a teacher? A true teacher? Hah! It's all manufacture. Cheap manufacture. She *calls herself* a singer. I could call myself a fairy princess and that wouldn't make me one. Do I look like a fairy princess?

BENJAMIN. Not at all.

BARBARA. Not at all!!! Shreck does not teach singing! Does not sing! She butchers voices!!! …*I* teach singing.

BENJAMIN. Of course you do.

BARBARA. To a select group that is. More select now than ever. I teach the old-fashioned way. The *true* Italian method. Bel canto.

BENJAMIN. I don't know what that is. Sorry.

BARBARA. Never say you're sorry. Ignorance is not a crime, unless it is celebrated. Then? It's a sin.

> (BARBARA *turns and begins walking back into her house.* BENJAMIN *stops her by speaking.*)

BENJAMIN. I like the sound of that. Bel can't-o.

BARBARA. Cahn-to.

BENJAMIN. Cahn-to.

BARBARA. Bel *canto*.

BENJAMIN. Bel *canto*.

BARBARA. *Bel canto!*

BENJAMIN. *Bel canto!*

BARBARA. A-hah! Baritone?

BENJAMIN. Hmm?

BARBARA. Your range. You *are* a singer, no?

BENJAMIN. I like to sing, yeah. / But, I'm not...

BARBARA. Well you *must* know your range. It's like knowing your name or your blood type. Rather essential.

BENJAMIN. You think I'm a "baritone?"

BARBARA. Hard to tell, the speaking voice can deceive. I'd have to hear the voice in flight. *Say.* You've come all this way.

BENJAMIN. I have?

BARBARA. *Here.* I'll fix you something warm to drink, and we'll see about this voice of yours.

BENJAMIN. I don't know.

BARBARA. Your choice. The facts just seem auspicious. You're walking down the street. I'm sweeping out my house. You want to sing. I'm a singing teacher. I've just had a space open up in my studio. A rather large, bovine-shaped space. There's more than enough room for someone as slightly built as you.

BENJAMIN. It'd be cool to know what kind of voice I have.

BARBARA. I'm…certain…you won't regret it! Really. This is for the best…"Benji."

BENJAMIN. How do you know my name?

BARBARA. It's on your bag. I'm Barbara. Barbara Scarlatti.

BENJAMIN. Benji Turner.

BARBARA. Such a *pleasure* to make your acquaintance, Benjamin. What would you like to drink?

BENJAMIN. Cocoa.

BARBARA. We'll have tea. Cocoa will cloud the voice. Now. Through that door, up the stairs to your left. Two floors. First room on the right.

> (BENJAMIN *enters the house.* BARBARA *smiles and sweeps the sidewalk up to the stairs. Sweeps up the stairs and sweeps the porch to the door. She steps in through the door and sweeps from the frame into the house. She then leans out the door frame, toward the street, and spits.*)

IN WHICH BARBARA TESTS THE VOICE

> (BENJAMIN *stands by the piano. He sniffs the air. Something is off. He touches the piles of dusty sheet music and books. He walks to the piano and begins to play three or four notes. They surprise him with their warmth. He looks around at the walls, which are covered in framed programs, articles, and photographs. A portrait of* MARIAN ANDERSON *is illuminated from behind for a moment.* BENJAMIN *leans toward the frame to read the name.*)

BENJAMIN. Marian Anderson.

> (BARBARA *enters with a flourish; the picture goes dim.* BENJAMIN *spins around, embarrassed to have been caught looking.*)

BARBARA. I see you've found your way ...

BENJAMIN. This house is huge. Do you live here all by yourself?

BARBARA. Of course. Do you live nearby?

BENJAMIN. Up the hill.

BARBARA. Stand just there.

BENJAMIN. My mom and I just came here from California.

BARBARA. I've never understood why anyone would want to live there. How fortunate for you that you've moved. We'll warm the voice. Just repeat after me. On "ah."

> (BARBARA *performs a simple vocalese.*)

"Ah-ah-ah-ah-ah-ah-ah-ah-ahhhhh."

BENJAMIN.
"Ah-ah-ah-ah-ah-ah-ah-ah-ahhhhh."

BARBARA. Now, now, now. First things first. Stand up straight. Chest out. Shoulders back. Chin up. A-aah! Not so far. There we are. Now, deep breath. Again. On "ah."

BENJAMIN.
"Ah-ah-ah-ah-ah-ah-ah-ah-ahhhhh."

BARBARA. Better. Well then. Tip-toeing up the stairs just slightly.

BENJAMIN.
"Ah-ah-ah-ah-ah-ah-ah-ah-ahhhhh."

BARBARA. Again, higher.

BENJAMIN.
"Ah-ah-ah-ah-ah-ah-ah-ah-ahhhhh."

BARBARA. And down again.

BENJAMIN.
"Ah-ah-ah-ah-ah-ah-ah-ah-ahhhhh."

BARBARA. There. Do you know any songs that we might sing?

BENJAMIN. I guess. It's hard to think on the spot. Umm… Do you know "Turn Your Lights Down Low" by Bob Marley?

BARBARA. I'm afraid not. You know Christmas carols, I assume?

BENJAMIN. Christmas carols? But it's February.

BARBARA. I'll tell you what. We won't be ashamed. We'll have a "devil may care" attitude—so what if it's February and we're singing Christmas carols, eh? / We're *artists*. This is the stance we take.

BENJAMIN. (*Laughs*) Okay.

BARBARA. Let's see ... Here we are. "We Three Kings" ...

(*They sing.*)

BARBARA & BENJAMIN.
> *We three kings of Orient are*
> *Bearing gifts we travel afar*
> *Field and fountain*
> *Moor and mountain*
> *Following yonder star*
> *Oh ...*

(BARBARA *drops out. She listens hungrily.*)

BARBARA. Keep going ...

BENJAMIN.
> *Star of wonder*
> *Star of might*
> *Star of royal beauty bright*
> *Westward leading*
> *Still proceeding*
> *Guide us to thy perfect light*

BARBARA. There, now. We'll rest the voice.

BENJAMIN. So?

BARBARA. Lemon with your tea?

BENJAMIN. Am I a baritone?

BARBARA. Mind your saucer. Like this.

(BARBARA *shows* BENJAMIN *the proper way to hold and sip the tea from the china cup.*)

BENJAMIN. Never did make chorus. I sound pretty crunchy, huh?

BARBARA. There is a sizable break in the voice.

BENJAMIN. That doesn't sound like a good sign.

BARBARA. Let us not be mistaken!!! There's work to be done. Breathing. Pitching. Attacking the phrase. Posture. Not to mention certain basics of etiquette.

BENJAMIN. Lot of work, huh? Well, thanks for, you know, listening to me howl.

BARBARA. You've no idea, do you? Benjamin, yours is the voice of an opera singer.

BENJAMIN. Are you serious?

BARBARA. Deadly *serious*. We must start right away. Saturday, it is.

BENJAMIN. Saturday. What time?

BARBARA. Nine A.M. We'll strike the voice unawares. We must set an aggressive schedule. Six days a week, minimum.

BENJAMIN. I don't know if I can do that.

BARBARA. Why ever not?

BENJAMIN. We don't ... I don't have any money.

BARBARA. Add mental attitude to the work list.

BENJAMIN. Not enough for six lessons, at least. Can I come once a week?

BARBARA. The study of voice demands a full commitment, young man. Where there's a will there's a way. You look to be able-bodied. Except of course for the cast. But you've one good arm. That will do.

BENJAMIN. Do what?

BARBARA. This house desperately needs repainting ... I would have to pay the painters a fortune. You will do the work for lessons. An old-fashioned exchange.

BENJAMIN. Painting?

BARBARA. You *do* know how to paint?

BENJAMIN. Yeah. Sure. I'm a painter from way back. But I've got school?

BARBARA. You'll sing first thing in the morning on your way, then come for a full lesson in the afternoon. Simple. Besides, you'll learn more of value here than there, I promise you.

BENJAMIN. This is a lot of music. I don't read music.

BARBARA. "I don't. I can't. But. But. But." Listen to yourself! Benjamin, we must wash this language out with soap.

BENJAMIN. You're right, you're right.

BARBARA. What a marvelous arrangement. What a fortuitous day. You'll do the room across the hall first.

> (*Suddenly, from every direction comes the wild barking and howling of dozens of dogs.* BENJAMIN *jumps.* BARBARA *seems unfazed.*)

BARBARA. Of course, there's the matter of the dogs. I'll move them, mop the floor down and all.

BENJAMIN. I thought I smelled dogs.

BARBARA. My babies.

(BARBARA *picks up a book and hands it to* BENJAMIN.)

An Introduction to the Italian Language. Start reading. Do you have a turntable?

BENJAMIN. I just unpacked it.

BARBARA. I know just the thing. Here. *Tosca!* Callas, conducted by de Sabata at La Scala, 1954. We start with the best. Guard it with your life. Listen to this and only this. When it's time I shall give you another.

BENJAMIN. This is great…you know, I think we've got some opera records… I mean, my dad has this huge record collection—opera, jazz, rock, everything…

BARBARA. You will bring me a list of the opera you have, the singers, the conductors, the date of issue. Then we will decide what is appropriate. "Everything" isn't appropriate for an impressionable voice.

BENJAMIN. Never thought of it like that. But, hey. Okay.

BARBARA. Benjamin Turner. Here, I'll see you down.

(BARBARA *leaves.* BESSIE *crosses with a box of old clothes. The Turner apartment.*)

STUFF

(BENJAMIN *looks for records.* BESSIE *is cleaning.*)

BENJAMIN. There's stuff missing.

BESSIE. There's too much stuff in this closet.

BENJAMIN. I can't find all the records.

BESSIE. God, this dress is hideous. And you need to go through your closet again, too. I've got a new bag going to give away.

BENJAMIN. Mom, where did you move the records that Dad had, like the opera ones?

BESSIE. The Salvation Army.

BENJAMIN. Come on. Really. Where are they? I need some of them.

BESSIE. I'm serious. Took them down to Sally two days ago along with a whole bag of your father's stuff.

BENJAMIN. Wait a minute! What stuff?

BESSIE. That old busted radio, some shirts, tie-dyed and moth-eaten...

BENJAMIN. Those were in my room!

BESSIE. And?

BENJAMIN. It was my *private* stuff.

BESSIE. No, it was his old junk.

BENJAMIN. And those records, he always had those records... I mean... WHAT THE HELL DID YOU DO THAT FOR?

BESSIE. Lower your voice!

BENJAMIN. Where!? What Salvation Army is it?

BESSIE. What on *Earth* is wrong with you?

BENJAMIN. Fine, I'll just go and find it and tell them you made a mistake.

(BENJAMIN *moves to walk outside.*)

BESSIE. Benjamin, no you won't.

BENJAMIN. You can't do this! You have no right!

BESSIE. I have no right to throw junk out of my own house?

BENJAMIN. He's my father!

BESSIE. Okay. He's my goddamned husband. Let's get clear about that.

BENJAMIN. I'm clear that I am on his side since you're not.

BESSIE. Don't you start acting like a rowdy little white boy on me, now, Benji.

BENJAMIN. (*Confronting*) What are you going to do?

BESSIE. I'm going to start by standing here and telling you that I am astonished / and confused here...

BENJAMIN. Nothing. Like usual.

BESSIE. Ooooh, no you won't bring this drama. Move.

> (BESSIE *starts to chuckle and gets back to sorting as* BENJAMIN *speaks.*)

BENJAMIN. Why are you laughing? Well, I'm not sorry. I don't apologize this time. You're wrong. I said, why are you laughing?

BESSIE. I am laughing because I didn't just beat your behind.

BENJAMIN. Oh, that's real funny.

BESSIE. Quit poking your lips out. I guess it's true.

BENJAMIN. What's true?

BESSIE. Your Nana, as one of her *hundred* reasons why I shouldn't have married your dad, told me that I would spare the rod and spoil the child. Marrying him would compromise my ability to be a *legitimate* Black mother. Old woman's been riding me since I walked back up in this city. She was right about the rod, at least.

BENJAMIN. This isn't funny at all.

BESSIE. Oh, but it is. Benji. I'm…going to take my ugly dress. I am going to take any of my husband's remaining belongings. I am throwing them out because they don't match *this* new reality here in Massachusetts…here…today…where we are *now*. And whenever I see something that I decide doesn't belong to this place, this life, right now, I am going to get rid of it.

BENJAMIN. I guess Nana was right. You're awfully white all of a sudden. Dad was more Black than you.

BESSIE. You'll have to come better than that.

BENJAMIN. All you say about the struggle and the people. He's staying free.

BESSIE. Get out of my way. *Underground* is not free.

BENJAMIN. *Underground* for what he believes in, and when the going gets tough you just want to throw him away and run back here to hide. You just couldn't take the heat and you had to drag me with you. You want to do it all the easy way.

BESSIE. Easy way? Easy way?

BENJAMIN. That's why we came here.

BESSIE. We came here to start clean. And I'm fit'na clean house for real right about now. *You want this?* It's *on*! Closets for starters!

(BESSIE *pokes back into the closet and snatches out some choice items.*)

BESSIE. One red velvet jacket. One pair Birkenstock sandals...

BENJAMIN. That's his Hendrix jacket!

BESSIE. ...Get out of the way! GIVE IT HERE! Now, out the window!

(*She opens the window and chucks the things outside. She doesn't stop. She throws.*)

BENJAMIN. Stop! I'm sorry!

BESSIE. Naw, Mama's on a roll...
Collected Works of Mahatma Gandhi...
To Kill a Mockingbird... Out!
Martin Luther King's *Letter from Birmingham Jail*...
Five Smooth Stones...

BENJAMIN. PLEASE STOP!

BESSIE. My Lord, my Lord...
The Family of Man...

BENJAMIN. OKAY, I'M SORRY.

BESSIE. *Autobiography of Malcolm X*...that stays.

BENJAMIN. WHAT'S WRONG WITH YOU?

BESSIE. Pete Seeger
Joan Baez
Peter, Paul, and goddamned Miss Mary—

BENJAMIN. He's coming back!

BESSIE. Jimi Hendrix Experience...

(BENJAMIN *grabs the record and he and*
BESSIE *face off*.)

BENJAMIN. Mom, he's coming back!!! I swear he is!!!

(BESSIE *stares at him.*)

BESSIE. Benjamin Turner, come back to reality. We sat in front of
that television...

BENJAMIN. Don't start that again.

BESSIE. You sat in front of that TV with me when Jimmy Carter /
came on...

BENJAMIN. Yeah, yeah, yeah! Jimmy Carter. Amnesty. WHATEVER!!!
He could have gotten caught already.

BESSIE. No.

BENJAMIN. He could be in trouble... FBI...what if he tried to find us?

BESSIE. Mail is forwarded.

BENJAMIN. He wouldn't know where to look.

BESSIE. I sent letters to each of the safe houses. All our people in
Berkeley know where to find us. It's deeper than all that and
you know it.

BENJAMIN. I. KNOW. HE. IS. COMING!

BESSIE. I *don't*. (*Long beat.*) Shut that window.

(BENJAMIN *doesn't.* BESSIE *does.*)

It's cold as hell in here. Benjamin, Benji, look at me. Look at
me. We've got to face some facts here. This thing is no piece of
cake for either of us. But...bottom line? We've both got school
in the morning.

BENJAMIN. I promise he is ...

BESSIE. My GOD you get to me! Look at that. (*She surveys the mess she's made on the ground below*) There goes the neighborhood, hmmm?

BENJAMIN. Mom.

BESSIE. No, this is due time. I just can't believe I carted that junk across the country in the first place.

BENJAMIN. I promise.

BESSIE. Get right to me.

(*A bell rings. School.*)

IN WHICH TERENCE AND BENJAMIN TALK FOR THE FIRST TIME

> (TERENCE *sits on the floor, against a wall inside the high school, outside the cafeteria. Sounds from the cafeteria ricochet through the space.* BENJAMIN *sneaks in and tries to peek at what* TERENCE *is drawing.*)

BENJAMIN. What are you doing?

> (TERENCE, *slightly startled, closes his sketch-pad.*)

BENJAMIN. I just want to know what you're doing, that's all.

> (TERENCE *picks up his bag and pencil.*)

TERENCE. I'm leaving.

BENJAMIN. Calm down. I didn't mean to scare you.

TERENCE. You didn't.

BENJAMIN. What were you doing? Come on.

TERENCE. I was ... um ... It's really rough. It's this ... Look. About what happened. You shouldn't have done that.

BENJAMIN. You shouldn't let people pick on you like that.

TERENCE. I didn't let them or not let them. It just happens.

BENJAMIN. Getting beat up does not "just happen."

TERENCE. It was ... Brian thought I was looking at him and I was but I wasn't really *looking*-looking at him. I was trying to see his planes refract.

BENJAMIN. His what?

TERENCE. Skin. Light. Water. Planes. It wasn't personal.

BENJAMIN. So that's a good excuse for them to call you a faggot and jump on you?

TERENCE. You're not from here are you?

BENJAMIN. I'm Benji. Turner.

TERENCE. Hi.

BENJAMIN. And you are?

TERENCE. Um. I'm sorry. Terence.

BENJAMIN. Terence?

TERENCE. Terence Long. Where are you from?

BENJAMIN. Not from here. Berkeley. California. Ever been to California?

TERENCE. No. No, I haven't.

BENJAMIN. That's okay. It's not a crime. *I guess.*

TERENCE. I have cousins though who are out there. They sometimes send oranges and avocados at Christmastime.

BENJAMIN. You'd like it there.

TERENCE. It's not gray like this, I bet.

BENJAMIN. It's gray sometimes. Just different gray, that's all. The sky is... all...

>   (BENJAMIN *gestures with his hands.*)

TERENCE. It catches the light differently.

BENJAMIN. Yeah. It catches the light differently.

TERENCE. I get it.

BENJAMIN. God that sounds weird, "catches the light."

TERENCE. Yeah.

BENJAMIN. I like it there, anyway. I miss it already.

TERENCE. Why did you move here, if you like it so much in Berkeley? Not that you shouldn't have, I mean it's great that you're here ... I mean, I don't even know you, but ...well, welcome, you know ...um, God ...

BENJAMIN. It's cool. I like the snow.

TERENCE. That'll wear off.

BENJAMIN. My mom says the same thing. She grew up here.

TERENCE. For real?

BENJAMIN. She used to have all kinds of family here and the whole nine. Now it's just us, though. She's enrolled at nursing school. In Holyoke.

TERENCE. Wow.

BENJAMIN. She wanted to do something with her hands.

TERENCE. Why not try gardening, or something like that?

BENJAMIN. Yeah. I guess. Kinda hard in the snow, though.

TERENCE. I hear that.

BENJAMIN. You're gonna have to show me around Springfield, cuz I really don't know which way is up.

TERENCE. Yeah. No. I mean. Well, there's not a whole lot to see... Ben?

BENJAMIN. Benji.

TERENCE. I should probably warn you, Benji. I'm not too popular around.

BENJAMIN. Neither am I, now.

TERENCE. They won't pick on you though. They think you're crazy.

BENJAMIN. (*Intrigued*) They do?

TERENCE. Yeah. Cuz you jumped them like that. They don't think twice when they talk about me, it's always "faggot" this and "he wants to suck your dick" and "look at your girlfriend" and stuff like that. But you, they think you're *mental*, like you'll snap or something. That's what they're saying.

BENJAMIN. Really?

TERENCE. You're not crazy are you?

BENJAMIN. Do I seem like I'm crazy to you?

TERENCE. Well. Kinda. I mean. Anybody who would jump into a fight like that for no reason? Yeah.

BENJAMIN. I had a reason. So what were you drawing? I'm assuming you were drawing.

TERENCE. I'm not going to show you.

BENJAMIN. Well... What else do you like? You do sports?

TERENCE. I like to watch tennis.

BENJAMIN. I do martial arts.

TERENCE. Real Bruce Lee stuff?

BENJAMIN. Hardly. I studied karate in Berkeley. My mom's big into self-defense. But I never practiced in a shower. If we were outside when that happened? Man, they wouldn't have known what hit 'em.

TERENCE. God. I'm really sorry. (++)

> (BENJAMIN *shifts his weight, moving ever so slightly closer.*)

BENJAMIN. So...how long have you known?

TERENCE. Known what?

BENJAMIN. *Known*, known.

TERENCE. (*Tensing up*) Look...Uhmmm. You know what? I'm going in there now.

BENJAMIN. I was just asking.

(*Beat.*)

TERENCE. It's that obvious?

BENJAMIN. It was the tennis. Dead giveaway.

TERENCE. Oh. My. God. You really are crazy.

BENJAMIN. Now can I see what you were drawing?

TERENCE. Not right now. It's really rough.

BENJAMIN. Come on.

TERENCE. No.

BENJAMIN. Don't make me have to take it from you. One-arm-*Enter-the-Dragon*-style.

TERENCE. That's not fair. I thought you were trying to protect me.

BENJAMIN. Who said that was my reason? But I did take a hit for you—and you booked out of the room. It's the least you could do.

TERENCE. You'll get mad. You'll snap again.

BENJAMIN. Come on.

TERENCE. It's abstract. You won't get it.

> (BENJAMIN *looks at the sketchpad. He moves himself around a little to "feel" the drawing in his body as he observes it.*)

BENJAMIN. That's me.

TERENCE. (*Surprised*) You got it.

BENJAMIN. That's outta sight.

TERENCE. How'd you get it? I mean it's...

BENJAMIN. I don't know. I guess, well the lines are all...like this... in here and...then they go...

TERENCE. ...up and over and up again and kind of leaning...then *out!* Like... (*Catches himself, embarrassed*) I wasn't trying to... I just sketch people...

BENJAMIN. I like them.

TERENCE. You do?

BENJAMIN. I think you should do another one of me though. I'll pose. Look. I'm thirsty, I'm gonna go back in and get a drink before lunch is over. You want to come?

TERENCE. With you?

BENJAMIN. Yeah.

TERENCE. Okay. If you're sure.

BENJAMIN. Come on.

TERENCE. You must have a death wish.

BENJAMIN. They won't dare. They think I'm crazy, right?

(*Orchestral music surges.*)

IN WHICH TOSCA IS PLAYED

(BENJAMIN *listens to* Tosca. BESSIE, *curious, reads from the concordance. Without meaning to do so, they begin to inhabit the*

crucial scene between Tosca and Scarpia.
BENJAMIN *is Tosca and* BESSIE *is Scarpia.*
They play together. Big. Dramatic. New.

Scarpia stands at his desk, and signs the pass for Mario as Tosca wrings her hands in anxiety, knowing what Scarpia wants.

Seeing a letter opener on his table, she grabs it up and hides it behind her back.

Scarpia turns to her and with a cry of "Tosca, finalmente mia!" he advances amorously toward her.

Tosca rushes him and plunges the opener deep into his abdomen. He recoils as the life swiftly leaves him. Tosca glares and gesticulates as he collapses, commanding him to die.

On the ground, Scarpia lets out a final groan. Tosca puts her ear to his face and asks, "Are you dead?" When it is clear he is, she raises her hands to the heavens and flees the chamber.

BESSIE *raises up from the floor and grabs* BENJAMIN. *They laugh in an embrace. The lights snap on in* BARBARA'S *music room.*)

IN WHICH BENJAMIN RECEIVES HIS FIRST LESSON

(BARBARA *stands behind the piano as* BEN-JAMIN *moves to its side.*)

BARBARA. Your first lesson! This is a remarkable event, Benjamin; you will recall it, and me, with indescribable sentiment each time that velvet curtain rises and falls, rises and falls.

BENJAMIN. I'm excited.

BARBARA. You should be!

BENJAMIN. I listened to *Tosca* again and again.

BARBARA. Tell me, tell me!

BENJAMIN. It was... It was... Wow!

(*They laugh in tandem. Excitement.*)

I mean I couldn't understand any of the words...

BARBARA. You will, you will...

BENJAMIN. But I felt them...

BARBARA. You felt them!

BENJAMIN. I read the story from the liner notes... And I followed along with the words for a while, but then something else kind of took over...it was like I could see it just from hearing it...

BARBARA. All the colors! All the scenery, no?

BENJAMIN. WOW!

BARBARA. The music?

BENJAMIN. The voices. The guy...

BARBARA. Gobbi.

BENJAMIN. He was all ... (*Sings a few menacing notes*) *yah-la-la-dah*, you know ...and Callas!

BARBARA. Callas!

BENJAMIN. Her voice ...

BARBARA. The best. Some have critiqued it.

BENJAMIN. How could you?

BARBARA. No matter. Those who critique? Would that *they* would go to sing, all that would fall from their mouths would be a pile of green teeth.

BENJAMIN. Is she still singing?

BARBARA. No, my dear. She passed last year.

BENJAMIN. She died?

BARBARA. Of a broken heart. Overwhelmed by loss and death. But, you see, those depths of feeling also gave her peerless interpretation.

BENJAMIN. I'll say.

BARBARA. The opera will ask much of you, Benjamin. And you must be ready to give.

BENJAMIN. That's beautiful.

BARBARA. Such pearls of wisdom are to be yours in abundance. (*With a flourish*) They are my humble gifts.

BENJAMIN. I'm ready. Let's go.

BARBARA. We start with the old songs. Here. I bought it for you at the music store yesterday. This is to become your Bible, young man. *Twenty-Four Italian Songs and Arias.* Turn to page seventy-four.

BENJAMIN. "Guy-yah..." /

BARBARA. "Gia il Sole dal Gange." Gia... Gi-a... "eeeee," "aaaah" one tone to the front of the face... "eeee" ...

BENJAMIN. Eeee.

BARBARA. The other out the back of the head "aaaah" ...

BENJAMIN. Aaaah.

BARBARA. You'll hear when we sing.

BENJAMIN. How do I do it? I don't know how to read music.

BARBARA. It will come. For now, you'll make like Pavarotti and learn by listening.

BENJAMIN. That's the big guy with the beard, right?

BARBARA. ...Yes.

BENJAMIN. I thought all opera singers had to know how to read music?

BARBARA. Orrechiante. Earers. You learn by hearing. All singers do at first. Some just get stuck. Alas, in his case, perhaps, the bigger the body, the smaller the brain. Like the dinosaurs, my dear. We can only imagine what delicious tones they made.

> (*Dogs start barking.* BARBARA *begins to play.*)

IN WHICH BENJAMIN PAINTS WITH SCARLATTI RED

BARBARA. Here we are! Here we are! Not a tail in sight.

BENJAMIN. This is a big room.

BARBARA. Let's shed more light ...

BENJAMIN. Whew. I've never seen such a red-red before.

BARBARA. "Scarlatti Red!"

BENJAMIN. What color are we going to paint over it?

BARBARA. Why red of course. "Scarlatti Red." This room and every other room in this house. I want passionate walls.

BENJAMIN. But they are already.

BARBARA. They're not fresh. Passion must be fed, Benjamin.

BENJAMIN. You can call me Benji, if you want.

BARBARA. I don't. Benji is a dog's name. Not a man. Benjamin. That's a man's name. I suggest you make the change. Ah! I almost forgot! A new sling for my painter! (*She moves to place it over his cast*) Wouldn't want you to get drips all over your names ... Why, Benjamin!

BENJAMIN. What?

BARBARA. You haven't any names.

BENJAMIN. No. I guess I don't have so many friends, yet.

BARBARA. It's for the best. "So many friends?" Pshaw. You see, you're like I was at your age. Focused. Serious. When other children would come around with their sticky faces and foul hands, I looked upon them with disdain. A waste of my precious time.

BENJAMIN. Have you always been that serious?

BARBARA. Always! I was surrounded by adults when I was a child, thank God! I didn't utter a word until I was five years old; I was quiet as a stone. When I did open my mouth? I spoke in full sentences.

BENJAMIN. That's impressive.

BARBARA. No baby talk for Barbara.

> (BARBARA *reaches down, picks a small brush from the can of brushes on the floor, dips it in the red paint, and with swirling strokes, paints her name on* BENJAMIN's *cast. She smiles.*)

BARBARA. Better to have one good friend. Someone who sees the great artist you are destined to become.

BENJAMIN. Thank you.

> (*Dogs bark from below.*)

BARBARA. *Mama's coming*! Now, I've washed down the floors and gotten the cobwebs out. And here, fine sir, are the tools of your trade! Drop cloths, masking tape, stepladder and, of course, several brushes from which to choose. Which do you prefer?

BENJAMIN. Um...

BARBARA. Your choice.

BENJAMIN. This one.

BARBARA. *Just* the one I would have chosen. Now, I've set up a record for you to work with as you paint. The most important words come first. Get used to them. They'll come up often in the music.

(Dogs bark from below.)

BARBARA. The little ones are hungry. I'll be back.

ITALIAN RECORD. Vivo—alive.

BENJAMIN. Vivo.

ITALIAN RECORD. Vivo!

BENJAMIN. Vivo!

ITALIAN RECORD. Morire—to die.

BENJAMIN. Morire—to die.

ITALIAN RECORD. Amore—love.

BENJAMIN. Amore—love.

ITALIAN RECORD. Nevicare—to snow.

BENJAMIN. Nevicare—to snow.

ITALIAN RECORD. Sangue—blood.

BENJAMIN. Sangue—blood.

ITALIAN RECORD. Doloroso—painful.

BENJAMIN. Doloroso…

> *(The record catches on the following word.)*

ITALIAN RECORD. Fuoco—fire.
Fuoco—fire.
Fuoco—fire.

> *(The red wall parts like a curtain revealing*
> MARIAN ANDERSON, *dressed in a beautiful,*
> *sensual gown of bronze. She speaks to* BEN-

JAMIN, *who is slightly taken aback, but not frightened.*)

MARIAN ANDERSON. Fuoco!

BENJAMIN. Fuoco!

MARIAN ANDERSON. (*Singing a line from* Tosca)
"*Ed io venivo a lui tutta dogliosa per dirgli: invan stasera, il ciel s'infosca…*"

BENJAMIN. I don't have a clue what that means.

MARIAN ANDERSON. A new language must be stuck to the tongue with honey. Its tones will only deepen with longing for that first sweetness.

BENJAMIN. That's what you said in Italian?

MARIAN ANDERSON. (*To the record player*) Repeat.

ITALIAN RECORD. Vivo!

MARIAN ANDERSON. Alive. When we stand on the stage in Leningrad and press our knees together to keep from falling as God enters our throat and floods the crowd with sound. Vivo.

ITALIAN RECORD. Amore!

BENJAMIN. Love. When we stand in the crowd and Mom holds up the sign that says "PEACE ONLY PEACE," and Dad holds her from behind and I stand between their legs and we sing… Amore.

ITALIAN RECORD. Nevicare!

MARIAN ANDERSON. To snow. When the train rolls toward Stockholm and the snow bounces light through the car, as my secret love kneels in front of me and blesses me with his kisses en français and touches en español. Nevicare.

ITALIAN RECORD. Morire!

BENJAMIN. To die. Run for the mail—see the letter I sent him stamped "Return to Sender." All the way to Canada and back. I wrote, "You can come home now, it's safe." I tear it up and put it in the trash. Morire.

ITALIAN RECORD. Sangue!

MARIAN ANDERSON. Blood. The taste that fills my mouth when I am asked to set aside my program of Strauss and Meyerbeer to sing folk music at the White House for the King of England. *Sangue.*

ITALIAN RECORD. Doloroso!

BENJAMIN. Doloroso...

BENJAMIN. Pain. When I run into the bathroom and catch him with the needle. Shhhh, he says. Don't tell Mommy. And I don't. Ever.

MARIAN ANDERSON. Doloroso...

> (*The record catches on the following word.*)

ITALIAN RECORD. Fuoco-Fuoco-Fuoco...

> (BENJAMIN *paints the word "fuoco" on the wall.* MARIAN *smiles in approval then steps forward out of the wall.*)

MARIAN ANDERSON. Go home, young man,
I see it. Your wish is coming true...

> (BENJAMIN *puts down the brush and rushes home.*)

MARIAN ANDERSON. ...true in all its wonder and terror.
"And I came sadly here to tell him
that in vain, tonight, the sky will darken."

ASHES AND DUST

(BENJAMIN *rushes into the apartment.*)

BENJAMIN. Mom!?

(BESSIE *turns to* BENJAMIN. *He stops dead in his tracks.*)

BESSIE. Benji
Benji
Benji
Benji
Benji...

BENJAMIN. Don't, Mom.

BESSIE. Benji, come here.

BENJAMIN. Mom, you're scaring me. Stop.

BESSIE. He's coming home, babe.

BENJAMIN. "Dear Mrs. Turner, it is with profound regret that we inform you of the death of... / Percy was a gentle, wonderful man. He came to us a year ago and I am pleased to say that his dependence was no longer an issue when he passed. We begged him to contact his family, but respected his privacy and are only doing so now out of duty. Please contact us as soon as you receive this letter. You may reverse the charges if need be. We were forced to cremate... / and sincerely hope that this would not have gone against any religious preference. We hold his ashes and will arrange for their transfer immediately upon hearing from you. I enclose this photograph, which, next to an old driver's license and seven Canadian dollars, was found in his wallet. He showed it to me when he first arrived. 'This is my family,' he said."

BESSIE. (*So softly*) Benji...

BENJAMIN. "Sincerely,
Inez Bartlett
Toronto African Methodist Episcopal Church"

>   (*The sound of sweeping. Everything fades away except* BENJAMIN *and the ash, falling gently. A small piece of light traces the sky; it carries* BENJAMIN'S *eyes with it. Lights down. Sweeping continues.*)

>   (*End of Act One.*)

ACT II

THE MOON AND THE STARS IN HIS HANDS

> (MARIAN ANDERSON *sings "He's Got the Whole World in His Hands."* BENJAMIN *stands outside looking down at his hands. He digs his shoes into the snow, mixing it with dirt.*)

MARIAN ANDERSON.
> *He's got you and me, brother, in his hands.*

BENJAMIN. Where is the moon?

MARIAN ANDERSON.
> *He's got you and me, sister, in his hands.*

BENJAMIN. Where are the stars?

MARIAN ANDERSON.
> *He's got you and me, brother, in his hands.*

BENJAMIN. Thoughts?

MARIAN ANDERSON.
> *He's got the whole world in his hands.*

> (BENJAMIN *makes half the butterfly gesture. One hand is still in the cast. The half-hand lingers. He turns his face up to* MARIAN ANDERSON.)

BENJAMIN. And wishes?
> My wish
> slam
> cut
> *come on*
> *come on*

twisted
snapped
slipped
burned.
Wishes aren't straight-ahead things at all.

>(MARIAN ANDERSON *looks at* BENJAMIN *and speaks.*)

MARIAN ANDERSON. When my first major tour was confirmed I walked into the department store where my mother worked as a cleaning woman on her hands and knees scrubbing the corners as though the sun, moon, and stars depended upon it, day after day—and how I had wished that she would not have to do such work. I walked to her employer's office and I told her that my mother would not be in to work again. Sometimes wishes are made for you.

>(BENJAMIN *glares at* MARIAN ANDERSON *and with the fever of a tantrum opens his mouth and bleats out an ugly, agressive open tone. She turns her head toward* BARBARA's *studio, where the lights snap on.*)

BENJAMIN.
 A-a-aaaa-aaaa-aaah!

IN WHICH "VITTORIO, MIO CORE!" IS SUNG

BARBARA. Stop. *Stop*! Benjamin. We want the tone of a bell—chiming at dawn.

BENJAMIN. What does it sound like now?

BARBARA. A bell—lodged in a mud pit at midnight.

BENJAMIN. I'm standing right and I'm using my diaphragm.

BARBARA. Effort misdirected is effort wasted. Your tone is ponderous and dusty and I'm afraid, Benjamin, you sing this song as though it were a punishment.

BENJAMIN. What am I doing wrong?

BARBARA. Close your eyes. As we ascend the scale, what do you envision?

BENJAMIN. I hadn't really thought about it...

BARBARA. Close your eyes. What do you see as you sing?

BENJAMIN. It's a bookshelf...

BARBARA. A bookshelf?

BENJAMIN. Yeah. When I sing *a-a-a-a-ahh*, those notes, they're like the books I can reach out and touch right here... Then *a-a-a-a-aaaah*, those I have to reach down like this and pull them up, and *a-a-a-a-a-aaaaaaaaah*, those I have to get up on tiptoe to reach.

BARBARA. I *hear* you stretching on tiptoe toward the high "books" and it's not pretty. How does someone as young as you get such a dull image in his mind? The notes, Benjamin, are *within* you, not on a shelf.

(BENJAMIN *sighs, discouraged.*)

BENJAMIN. I'm not really feeling the song.

BARBARA. "Victorious, victorious, my heart! I shall cry no more..." Is this all so dry to you?

BENJAMIN. My heart doesn't feel so victorious today.

(BENJAMIN *takes a photograph from his book of music. He hands it to* BARBARA.)

BENJAMIN. That's him.

BARBARA. You favor him.

BENJAMIN. I don't know.

BARBARA. I see why the words are challenging. A contradiction.

(BARBARA *hands the photograph back to* BENJAMIN.)

BARBARA. We must use the feelings we do have and transform them.

(BARBARA *sings "Vittorio, mio core!" The notes tremble in the air and the walls blush to a deep, passionate red. At the completion,* BARBARA *rises and goes to a pile of books and begins to rummage through.*)

BENJAMIN. Your voice is incredible.

BARBARA. A fraction of its former majesty.

(BARBARA *hands a photograph album to* BENJAMIN. *As he turns the pages, the images he sees—beautiful studio photographs, Brownie snapshots with their edges muted, programs from various operas and recitals—vibrate along the red stripes of the flag.*)

BENJAMIN. This is you?

BARBARA. Who else could be so cunning?

BENJAMIN. This?

BARBARA. My mother. Who else could have such a sour face?

BENJAMIN. Wow. This guy's really handsome.

BARBARA. That is *my* father. Niccolò Scarlatti. The cellist.

BENJAMIN. So Scarlatti's not a "stage name."

BARBARA. "Stage name?" My love for music, and food, is in the blood!

BENJAMIN. Is this your brother?

BARBARA. I had no brother.

BENJAMIN. He looks just like you.

BARBARA. "He" *is* me, Benjamin.

BENJAMIN. You used to be a man?

BARBARA. I'm fascinating, Benjamin. But not *that* fascinating. This is, however, the picture I want you to see.

BENJAMIN. The light, you're both squinting. Where are you?

BARBARA. Standing outside La Scala in Milan.

BENJAMIN. *"La Scala"* La Scala?

BARBARA. My father
was a mystery to me for most of my childhood.
I only knew he was a musician, *Italiano*, and he'd never been
able to honor my mother with marriage...
money was sent,
notes with no return address at Christmas...etcetera,
a gripping tale for another day.
Now! In March of...I'll spare you the year,
he arrived in Washington,
quietly,

much to our great surprise.
I was sworn to silence.
He stayed inside the house and
I was sent to play while he and my mother
went about their re-acquaintance, so to speak …
—he was terribly handsome—
two days later …
The eve of my tenth birthday
I was awakened in the still of the night
by my father standing over my bed.
He got me up, he dressed me quickly
in strange new clothes, *boy's* clothes,
and hid my hair under a cap.
Within hours we were on a train,
in a private sleeping car, in the white section.
With his smooth, precise hands, he snipped away my hair.
Henceforth, he introduced me as his "boy."
And this was our arrangement for the next two years.

BENJAMIN. You weren't scared at all, were you?

BARBARA. I was no sissy, Benjamin. This is what I had *prayed* for *each and every night*! To be released from her silent stares. To be rescued from that awful Colored cage.

BENJAMIN. Where did he take you?

BARBARA. Everywhere. *Everywhere*! We sail the Atlantic on the White Star Line. Oh, Benjamin. We rush headlong into sites I'd only dreamed about over tattered books from the Colored library. Istanbul, Alexandria, Athens, Venice. I hear majestic symphonies; see spinning Sufi, snakes in baskets; learn the names of the finest concerti; and eat figs off the tree. He puts me in charge of the care of his cello. I carry it from place to place, rub the resin on the bow … (*Sniffs the air*) still … *Milano.*

(BENJAMIN *reads the inscription below the photograph.*)

BENJAMIN. "Twelfth birthday. La Scala. Barbara. Niccolò."

BARBARA. In Milano I find my destiny. He takes me to the opera. *Tosca.* I sit on his shoulders in the back. From the first note, I know I will never be the same again. When at last Floria hurls herself off the parapet, "Oh Scarpia, avanti a Dio!" As though *Tosca* were the key and my heart was locked, I am opened. In an instant, I have found my destiny. And then, young man, there, in La Scala, atop my father's shoulders, amidst the thunderous applause. My first blood comes.

BENJAMIN. My God, that's so dramatic!

BARBARA. And rather messy, I'm afraid, my father's fine shirt, ruined. We both knew a choice was at hand. Soon my body would change more dramatically, and it would be futile to keep up our pretense. "Mia figlia adorata. My beloved daughter. La più bella del mondo." (*to* BENJAMIN) "La più..."

BENJAMIN. "La più..."

BARBARA. "La più bella del mondo."

BENJAMIN. "La più bella del mondo." The most beautiful in all the world?

BARBARA. Grazie.

(*Pause.*)

BENJAMIN. Did he bring you back home then?

BARBARA. No, Niccolò Scarlatti returned alone.

BENJAMIN. How long was it 'til you saw him again?

BARBARA. Never again did I see that man.

BENJAMIN. Niccolò.

BARBARA. He wanted me to see the world, Benjamin. He wanted to free me from this ... (*Gestures*) and he did. After that night, he knew the music was in my blood. Our blood. My father left me in Milan for a year. He paid a large sum of money to a woman named Dona Lazzi. She took me in. I scrubbed her floors, she taught me piano and voice.

BENJAMIN. "An old fashioned exchange."

BARBARA. Much more to my history of course—my début, my triumphs in Europe, my recordings, my loves, my cars ... but that night reigns on the throne of passion. Passion, Benjamin. Passion alone must drive you.

> (BARBARA *takes the scrapbook from* BENJAMIN *and quickly places it atop the piano.*)

BARBARA. *Stand up!* When I sing? From where do I sing?

BENJAMIN. From your diaphragm, / with support from all your ...

BARBARA. No! I sing from here!

> (BARBARA *grabs* BENJAMIN'*s crotch.*)

BENJAMIN. YOW!!!

BARBARA. The music must spring from the very core of you. You are creating beauty. It is the force of life you reckon with. Now! Face that bookshelf head-on, young man. Fix it in your gaze.

> (BARBARA *releases him and returns to the piano.*)

BENJAMIN. Yes, ma'am!

BARBARA. Now dismiss it. Out loud! You are no longer reaching for its dusty contents ...

BENJAMIN. I don't need you, shelf!

BARBARA. Notes! Notes bubble between your legs, dance up through your belly, buzz about your chest ...

BENJAMIN. I've got the notes!

BARBARA. Turn your attention to a space above the bookshelf, slightly behind it. There's a little window there. A bright, open window. The sky is clear and blue. A Roman sunrise.

BENJAMIN. I see it.

BARBARA. Now!

(BENJAMIN *begins to sing freely, lushly.*)

BENJAMIN.
Vittoria, vittoria ...

BARBARA. Again! Brighter.
Lighter.

BENJAMIN.
Vittoria, vittoria mio core ...

BARBARA. And squeeze!

BENJAMIN.
Non lagrimar più, non lagrimar più,
ascolta d'amore la servitù ...
Asco-o-olta d'amore la se-er-vi-tu!

BARBARA. Yes!!!! Well, then! What do you see?

BENJAMIN. I'm floating in the sky.

BARBARA. No more bookshelf?

BENJAMIN. I'm on fire. Fuoco! I want... I want... Barbara?

BARBARA. Yes?

BENJAMIN. Let's feed the fire. Something else, another song...

BARBARA. Well, then. We shall sing our song about light. The sun god! "Gia il sole dal Gange"!

BENJAMIN. "Gia il sole dal Gange"!!!

BARBARA. One benefit to this song? It's fast. Can't hit a moving target! Benjamin, Benjamin, Benjamin!

IN WHICH BENJAMIN LEARNS HOW TO DRAW LIPS

(BENJAMIN *holds out his cast to* TERENCE.)

BENJAMIN. Terence, you have to sign it.

TERENCE. And then you'll sit still?

BENJAMIN. I want my friend's name on my cast.

TERENCE. You're weird.

BENJAMIN. You got it.

TERENCE. Any particular place...hey now—"Barbara" kind of took up a lot of space.

BENJAMIN. She kinda does.

TERENCE. She goes here?

BENJAMIN. She's my singing teacher.

TERENCE. Singing and karate? And you get me on tennis?

BENJAMIN. You could do it right in here.

> (TERENCE *leans in close to sign the cast.*)

BENJAMIN. You smell good.

> (TERENCE *moves away quickly and begins
> setting up his pad and pencils.* BENJAMIN
> *sits.* TERENCE *sits somewhat close.* TERENCE
> *draws* BENJAMIN.)

BENJAMIN. Where do you start?

TERENCE. Usually where I tend to look first when I look at the person. Where my eye gets caught.

BENJAMIN. Caught?

TERENCE. Like if I was drawing Carly Simon I would start with her teeth.

BENJAMIN. Gotcha. It's sorta chilly.

TERENCE. Mmm-hmm.

BENJAMIN. How come we couldn't just go to your house?

TERENCE. Lift your face up back where it was.

> (TERENCE *draws.*)

BENJAMIN. Are you going to draw my cast for posterity?

TERENCE. Shh.

BENJAMIN. Do you always start in the same place whenever you draw the same person?

TERENCE. Shhhhh.

BENJAMIN. Sorry.

TERENCE. Depends on who I'm drawing.

BENJAMIN. With me.

TERENCE. Your lips.

BENJAMIN. My lips.

TERENCE. Always.

BENJAMIN. That's where I would start, too.

TERENCE. Start what?

BENJAMIN. Drawing you.

> (TERENCE *drops his pencil and erasers.* BENJAMIN *and* TERENCE *bend down to pick them up. On the way up* BENJAMIN *kisses* TERENCE *full on the mouth.*)

BENJAMIN. With the lips. For sure.

> (TERENCE *takes his pad and pencils and runs off.* BENJAMIN *smiles to himself.*)

BENJAMIN. Passion.

IN WHICH BESSIE OPENS A PACKAGE

> (BENJAMIN *walks toward* BESSIE, *two boxes and bills in hand. He sets the boxes down and "sorts" the mail.*)

BENJAMIN. Bessie Turner ... Bell Telephone
Bessie Turner ... New England Gas Company
Bessie Turner ... Master Charge

BESSIE. You can keep the bills. Give me the boxes.

> (BENJAMIN *reaches down to pick up one of the boxes.*)

BENJAMIN. Miss Bessie ... Land's End.

BESSIE. Oooh, our turtlenecks.

BENJAMIN. Turtlenecks? Mrs. Percy Turner ...

BESSIE. Hunter green for you ...

BENJAMIN. Mom.

BESSIE. Magenta for me ...

BENJAMIN. Canada.

BESSIE. What?

BENJAMIN. Mom ... Is this it?

BESSIE. Here. Here.

BENJAMIN. I forgot it was coming.

BESSIE. Easy babe.

BENJAMIN. Look at it.

BESSIE. In a cardboard box with stamps.
Percy. Percy Turner.
Hush.
The way the sun fell off the lip of the sky. The beach is our bed
is the outstretched palm holding just you and me in that blue

light falling off the lip of the sky. Everything stretched thin and wide and you thrust inside me and me wrapped around you and wishing so much it breaks like a wave in our chests and shimmers through our eyes and our close salt-cleansed skin sweet cool in that first blue light falling off the lip of the sky and the birds calling look, calling look, calling look. God, look at the love you made glinting out of these two silly springs in the palm of your hand in the sidelong rush of the blue light falling off your lips!

And this is what I get?

And this
is what
I get?

> (BESSIE *laughs. She can't wrap her head around it. She opens the box, expecting an urn, but finds just a bag of ash. She opens the bag, matter-of-factly. Then, suddenly, surprising even herself, she scatters ashes around the room. She grunts and breathes and is covered in ash. She stands still.* BEN-JAMIN *immediately tries to gather the ash from the air, from the ground. He slaps the air, then himself, then his head. He stands up and runs…*)

IN WHICH BENJAMIN MEETS DADDY VELVET

> (*…to* TERENCE's *house. Up and down the stripes. The opening guitar riffs of Jimi*

Hendrix's "Voodoo Child" are played. It stops and repeats, as though someone were working it out. The front door is ajar; BENJAMIN *steps through.*)

BENJAMIN. Terence! Terence!

(*A guitar wails.* DADDY VELVET, TERENCE'S *father, is seated in a deep chair, with his back to the audience. Throughout the scene we only see his silhouette. The guitar underscores his speech.*)

DADDY VELVET. You always bust into somebody's house without knocking?

BENJAMIN. I'm sorry. I need to talk to Terence.

DADDY VELVET. Get shot doing that. Understand?

BENJAMIN. Yes, sir...

DADDY VELVET. Understand?

BENJAMIN. Is Terence...?

DADDY VELVET. At the store. Shut the fucking door? Please.

BENJAMIN. Sorry.

DADDY VELVET. Cold as shit. Cut the lights on for yourself.

BENJAMIN. I'm alright. Unless you need them?

(DADDY VELVET *chuckles to himself. Then he sings and plays.*)

DADDY VELVET.
Angel came down from heaven yesterday

She stayed with me
Just long enough to rescue me
And she told me a story, yesterday…

(BENJAMIN *joins in singing with him.*)

BENJAMIN & DADDY VELVET.
…About the sweet love between
The moon and the deep blue sea…

BENJAMIN. You like Hendrix?

DADDY VELVET. That's a dumb-ass question.

BENJAMIN. I grew up on Hendrix.

DADDY VELVET. You and me both.

BENJAMIN. Not supposed to be singing anything like that now though.

DADDY VELVET. Why the hell not?

BENJAMIN. My singing teacher. Got a list. He's not on it…

DADDY VELVET. Anybody tells you not to sing Hendrix is full of shit. You got to be the one Terence talking about. Ben, right?

BENJAMIN. Benjamin.

DADDY VELVET. You his friend, huh? From California?

BENJAMIN. Yes, sir.

DADDY VELVET. You don't *sound* like no sissy.

BENJAMIN. No.

DADDY VELVET. Uh-huh. *I get by with a little help from my friends.* You like that shit?

BENJAMIN. Mmm-hmm.

DADDY VELVET. "Mmm-hmm." *I* like that shit. Don't get scared. I know about California. Stationed out there before my first tour of duty.

BENJAMIN. I was born in Berkeley.

DADDY VELVET. I been through Berkeley, alright. All the peaceniks.

BENJAMIN. Lot more than that. You'll have to go back and see it.

DADDY VELVET. I ain't gonna see shit. Get me my lighter.

BENJAMIN. Where is it?

DADDY VELVET. Over there. Where I was sitting earlier.

BENJAMIN. Here.

DADDY VELVET. Had one going. But you know.

BENJAMIN. Could you tell Terence...

DADDY VELVET. *I* ain't telling Terence shit. You tell him. He's at the store. He'll be back. Just sit your ass there.

BENJAMIN. That's alright. I'll come back. Thanks.

> (BENJAMIN *gets up to leave.* TERENCE *walks in through the door.*)

DADDY VELVET. Close the door behind you.

TERENCE. What are you doing here?

DADDY VELVET. Terence?

> (BENJAMIN *watches* TERENCE *and* DADDY VELVET *hungrily.*)

TERENCE. Yeah.

DADDY VELVET. You get them?

TERENCE. Hold on.

DADDY VELVET. Come on, now.

TERENCE. Let me get some water.

DADDY VELVET. Come on, now.

TERENCE. Here.

> (TERENCE *hands* DADDY VELVET *his pills.*)

DADDY VELVET. Somebody came by looking for you. I think I scared him off.

TERENCE. That's okay. You want some juice?

DADDY VELVET. Nah. Just let me sit right now.

TERENCE. Okay. You should really have this down a little bit. It's only gonna make your head worse.

DADDY VELVET. It helps me, baby.

TERENCE. That's what you always say. Then you get a headache.

DADDY VELVET. That's what you always say. Then you give me a pill.

TERENCE. They took a long time. It was a new guy at the drugstore...

DADDY VELVET. Motherfuckers. Like they the ones own the pills. What I tell you?

TERENCE & DADDY VELVET.
Money make the world go round.

TERENCE. I'm turning this down.

DADDY VELVET. Alright, little man.

TERENCE. I'm upstairs.

> (TERENCE *gestures for* BENJAMIN *to be quiet. They walk through the space.* DADDY VELVET *strums softly on the guitar.*)

TERENCE. You know you should really just leave well enough alone.

BENJAMIN. Is he okay?

TERENCE. He just needed his stuff.

BENJAMIN. Cuz my mom's a …well, she's …

TERENCE. Look …

BENJAMIN. I bet she could take a look at him.

TERENCE. What gives you the right to come swinging up in my house … and everything else?

BENJAMIN. Terence. It's a mess in here.

TERENCE. Just get out of here.

BENJAMIN. No.

TERENCE. Just go, alright. Just go!

> (TERENCE *begins to pick stuff up off the floor.*)

BENJAMIN. I want to help you.

TERENCE. We don't need charity.

BENJAMIN. I'm not trying to give you charity. I'll help you clean up and stuff. I'm real good at that.

TERENCE. Me and him. We're all we've got.

BENJAMIN. Now you've got me.

(TERENCE *starts to laugh.*)

BENJAMIN. What's funny about that?

TERENCE. (*Confronting*) I've got you? And who have you got?

BENJAMIN. You.

TERENCE. You. Don't. Know. Me.

BENJAMIN. Yes, I do.

TERENCE. You couldn't. Cuz you can't see yourself.

BENJAMIN. Oh, and you do?

TERENCE. Every curve, every crack.

BENJAMIN. So, I don't know you, but you know me?

TERENCE. No, I don't. I just *see* you. You are all about yourself.

BENJAMIN. How can you say that, / when I'm offering ...

TERENCE. Walk all up in my house like you've got the right to the world. Like nothing scares you. Like you're not just as much a mess as you think I am.

BENJAMIN. That's not why I came here. I didn't mean ...

TERENCE. Yes you did! Yes you do. You are just another kind of bully. They want to close me down at all costs.

BENJAMIN. I don't want to close you down!

TERENCE. You want to open me up but you are clueless about *what that costs*. And all you've got to give me are some corny words ...

BENJAMIN. Corny!?

TERENCE. "Now you've got me." Who *says* stuff like that?

BENJAMIN. That hurts.

TERENCE. He feels.

BENJAMIN. I just...you're...you...that...Terence...it's this...
you make me...
feel...
and
believe it or not
I came here
Because... I...
I am scared of not feeling
I want to feel
and you make me.

(*Long pause.*)

TERENCE. Well what about what I want?

BENJAMIN. What do you want?

> (TERENCE *walks over to him. Pause.* BEN-
> JAMIN *kisses him once, very tenderly. Then
> again, more deeply.* TERENCE *pulls away. He
> shares the story simply, filling* BENJAMIN *in.*)

TERENCE. He was in a bomber
got shot down
woke up
there were these kids
their grandmother
in bamboo hats. He said
they smiled.
His buddies, K.C. and Jack came
they didn't

they thought
so they, you know.
Shot them.
The last thing he saw.
A Red Cross truck
Then blind.

BENJAMIN. I'm sorry.

TERENCE. What about your dad? Does he have war stories?

BENJAMIN. He didn't go.

> (*Jimi Hendrix's "Castles Made of Sand"
> rises like heat from downstairs.*)

BENJAMIN. "Castles Made of Sand?"

TERENCE. The Hendrix helps.
He
says it sounds like inside…um
the inside of his head.

BENJAMIN. My dad, too.

IN WHICH A CAST IS REMOVED

BARBARA. Ahhhh! Let me see, let me see! Liberated at last!

BENJAMIN. It feels so strange. It's like my arm is filled with air; it's
so light.

> (BENJAMIN *pulls the cast out of the bag.*)

BARBARA. I can only imagine.

BENJAMIN. They sawed right through you and Terence. See?

BARBARA. Terence?

BENJAMIN. Terence.

BARBARA. And who, pray tell, is Terence?

BENJAMIN. My friend. From school.

BARBARA. Terence. Terence. I've had many friends, but none has given me what the music has given me.

BENJAMIN. I tried to get them to cut around your names, but they said that would be too much trouble.

BARBARA. What would you want with an old dull cast? My name is written on your heart. Scarlatti. Repeat. Scarlatti.

BENJAMIN. Scarlatti.

BARBARA. Lazzi.

BENJAMIN. Lazzi.

BARBARA. Santuzzo.

BENJAMIN. Santuzzo.

BARBARA. Berteletti.

BENJAMIN. Berteletti.

BARBARA. Zannettacci.

BENJAMIN. Zannettacci.

BARBARA. Corigliano.

BENJAMIN. Corigliano.

BARBARA. Together.

BENJAMIN. Scarlatti.
Lazzi.
Santuzzo.
Berteletti.
Corigliano.

BARBARA. Zannettacci!

BENJAMIN. Scarlatti.
Lazzi.
Santuzzo.
Berteletti.
Zannettacci.
Corigliano.
Scarlatti.
Lazzi…?

BARBARA. Dona Lazzi.

BENJAMIN. Your teacher. The others are teachers, too.

BARBARA. When they ask your origin, Benjamin, you will not say Springfield, nor will you say Berkeley. You will immediately name the source. Corigliano is the source, you see. You can, I can, *we* can trace our teachers back to the first generation of great teachers. This is our "pedigree." Now we shall sing something in recognition. Let's see…

(*They start looking through sheet music.*)

BARBARA. Methinks "Lasciatemi Morire." Your upper register seems so comfortable, I want to try the high voice version…

BENJAMIN. How about this!?

BARBARA. Eh?

(BENJAMIN *holds up the music for her to see.*)

BARBARA. A Negro spiritual, indeed.

BENJAMIN. Well, it is a day of emancipation.

BARBARA. Really, Benjamin! I'd rather focus on your repertoire.

BENJAMIN. Please!!!

BARBARA. *De little chillun gwine dis, de little chillun gwine dat.* All they want to hear. If you *knew* how I had to fight, how we all had to fight to be respected as singers of serious music you would understand why I resist.

BENJAMIN. But I listened to a record of spirituals that Leontyne Price did...

BARBARA. That was *not* on the list I gave you...

BENJAMIN. I know. I saw it at the library... They're beautiful.

BARBARA. I'm not disputing their particular beauty.

BENJAMIN. Just as beautiful as...

BARBARA. It's all well and good for Leontyne Price to sing a record full of spirituals, for she can pick and choose. Besides, your vocal timbre is just not suited...

BENJAMIN. But I want to put something of myself in my repertoire...

BARBARA. Oh, really! Something of yourself?

BENJAMIN. Yeah, myself. And it's not just Leontyne Price. I got out records by Paul Robeson and Roland Hayes / and (*indicating* MARIAN ANDERSON) *her*...

BARBARA. Benjamin, no one, *no one* is going to take one look at you and expect "Deep River" to fall from your lips. And believe me, as quiet as it's kept, that is to your benefit. When I've finished with your voice, you will be able to sing any role. Transform yourself into any character without any hindrance. Any barrier.

BENJAMIN. I don't want to hide my ...who I am, if that's what you mean.

BARBARA. I think you've been around too many red walls. My goodness. We ought to put this fire to good use while singing "Lasciatemi Morire..."

> (BENJAMIN *points to the picture of* MARIAN ANDERSON *on the wall.*)

BENJAMIN. *She* was *famous* for spirituals...

BARBARA. Outside the States she was equally famous for her lieder...

BENJAMIN. Touché.

BARBARA. You may sing one. *One.* And nothing with the word "gwine," for God's sake.

BENJAMIN. Here.

> (BARBARA *plays the accompaniment as* BENJAMIN *sings. At the end of the song, she joins him, harmonizing.*)

BENJAMIN.
> *Sweet little Jesus boy*
> *They made you be born in a manger*
> *Sweet little holy child*
> *Didn't know who you was*
> *Didn't know you'd come to save us, Lord*
> *To take our sins away*
> *Our eyes was blind*

We couldn't see
We didn't know who you was
Long time ago
You was born
Born in a manger, Lord
Sweet little Jesus boy
World treat you mean, Lord
Treat me mean, too
But that's how things is
Down here
We don't know who you is
Just seem like we can't do right
Look how we treated you
But please forgive us, Lord
We didn't know 'twas you
Sweet little Jesus boy
Born long time ago
Sweet little holy child
And we didn't know who you was…

> (*A long, comfortable pause.* BARBARA *stares off.* BENJAMIN *is shaking slightly, both with the resolution of their confrontation, and with the excitement of having sung together.*)

BARBARA. You should finish the sitting room, now.

BENJAMIN. We can do "Lasciatemi Morire" if you want.

BARBARA. Another time. Painting should be easier without the cast.

> (BENJAMIN *leaves the room. Slightly confused.* BARBARA *stands.*)

BARBARA. Touché.

(Lights dim, the picture of MARIAN ANDER-SON *glows slightly, then out. Dogs bark.)*

IN WHICH LOVE LESSONS ARE PRACTICED

*(*BENJAMIN *and* TERENCE *lit by the light of fifty twinkling stars. They trade these lessons like breath and kisses. This is their own tiny opera.)*

Lesson One: Lips

Ripe lips swell with nectar.
Handle with utmost care.
Hold in your mouth.
Caress awake with a tender tongue.

Lesson Two: Necks

Necks are caramel skin
over bundled feathers
and electric cables.
Stroke warm necks
or nibble lightly.
Strong sweet coffee
beads up at the nape—
lick with abandon.
Biting the neck,
while altogether right,
runs the risk of shock.

Lesson Three: The Breath

Breath sweeps
coiled heat
soaring bone
expands,
deepens,
engages
abdomen.
Mold your skin to his
attune
expand
contract
your bodies.
Vascular rush
arterial pulse
immediately
audibly
in response
in wave formation.
Feel that
feel that
feel that
dizzy feel
emit red sounds:
you
are
on
the
right
track
Jack.

Lesson Four: Vulnerable

After rubbing

After pressing
After unbuttoning
After unzipping
After pulling off
After pulling down
After seeing him all
After hands go there
After letting him stroke you
After shameless tastes
After friction
After back tooth candy crunch
After can let please that more
After desperate
After rampant
After inhale
After clutch
After lift
After refract
After you two remember you two again
Comes vulnerable

IN WHICH BESSIE SMELLS SOMETHING

(BESSIE *jumps on* BENJAMIN's *bed.*)

BESSIE. Well, well, what's that smell?

BENJAMIN. I just took a bath; leave me alone.

BESSIE. This is an inside-out smell.

BENJAMIN. Quit.

BESSIE. Ouch, it's strong, too.

BENJAMIN. Get off me.

BESSIE. I thought so.

BENJAMIN. How come you always get all in my stuff?

BESSIE. I *could* say it's because I'm your mother.

BENJAMIN. Yeah.

BESSIE. I could take the "carried you for nine painful months, while you siphoned my dreams and my blood..." line of argument.

BENJAMIN. Won't be the first time.

BESSIE. Or the last.

BENJAMIN. It's that obvious?

BESSIE. Not at all. You've done a very good job of hiding it. Too good.

BENJAMIN. So how'd you guess?

BESSIE. Didn't guess. Knew. When I fell in love with your father I smelled just like you do.

BENJAMIN. Smell like what?

BESSIE. Smell like green. Silly. Heady. Funky. Anxious. Molasses. Plus, you have that look.

BENJAMIN. Blissed out.

BESSIE. We can leave it at that, yes.

BENJAMIN. Is it possible to be in love with everything?

BESSIE. Thank God it is.

BENJAMIN. It kind of hurts.

BESSIE. Where?

BENJAMIN. When I finish thinking about him. When I get ready to think about him. All. Here.

BESSIE. This is worse than with little Airhead.

BENJAMIN. His name was Ariel. And besides I was just a kid.

BESSIE. That was last year!

BENJAMIN. The year before!

BESSIE. Just thank your lucky stars I'm your mother. You'll appreciate me when I'm gone.

BENJAMIN. I'll sing at the funeral, *She was so open minded and patient and couldn't keep her nose out of her son's business...*

BESSIE. Oooooh, this is much different than Airhead. Look at your face. You're ruint.

BENJAMIN. I am not.

BESSIE. Yes you are and you'd better be grateful for it. It's a family tradition. The day Nana pointed that finger at me and told me I was ruint, I knew I had arrived.

BENJAMIN. Dad?

BESSIE. Mmmm. He was a later chapter. Let's just say ...your Dad happened upon the ruins and recognized their timeless beauty.

BENJAMIN. Well, *alright.*

BESSIE. Don't get any ideas.

BENJAMIN. I know how you Hippies were.

BESSIE. You wouldn't know a Hippie if one bit you.

BENJAMIN. Stop! That tickles.

BESSIE. Look at your pale little arm. We ought to put it under a lamp like the plants.

BENJAMIN. Why you treat me so mean?

BESSIE. It's fun.

> *(A flicker of concern flashes across* BESSIE's *brow.)*

BENJAMIN. What?

> (BESSIE *shakes her head "never mind."*)

BENJAMIN. What?

> *(Pause.)*

BESSIE. I hate myself for saying this, but be careful, baby.

BENJAMIN. Mom, he's...

BESSIE. Shush. Shush. Shush. I'm talking about *out there*. Not in here. Out there, little man.

BENJAMIN. Is that what they told you?

BESSIE. They were right.

BENJAMIN. And so were you.

BESSIE. And so were we. And so are you. But, this kind of open smells strong. It scares people, baby.

BENJAMIN. I don't care.

BESSIE. I know you don't. You have a right not to. We *raised* you not to. But it ...well, it smells out there, too. Something off. Something changing.

BENJAMIN. You're not thinking about leaving again? This's how you were talking in Berkeley.

BESSIE. Is it?

BENJAMIN. You're not happy *here*, either. I can tell.

BESSIE. I'm happy with you.

BENJAMIN. That's avoiding.

BESSIE. That's true. I'm happy with you. It's the truest thing I know right now. And I think we're doing it, Benji. The rest is gonna come. Whatever it looks like. We're not going anywhere. Not like you could travel in this condition anyway, all ruint up.

BENJAMIN. We. It feels so. All.

BESSIE. Good. That's yours. Everything you feel inside. You pray it exists in the other person, you know? But, you *never* know for sure.

BENJAMIN. *You* knew it existed.

BESSIE. We didn't know a goddamned thing existed, my sweet fool. All we could do was practice the possibility that it did.

(*Pause.*)

BENJAMIN. Buona notte, signorina.

BESSIE. Goodnight, sir.

> (BESSIE *leaves as* BENJAMIN *picks up his Italian book. He opens it randomly.*)

BENJAMIN. "La conosco." I know her. "Non lo conosco." I don't know him anymore.

> (*He flips pages, randomly.*)

"La finestra era troppo piccola. In caso d'emergenza non si potrebbe nemmeno usarla!" "The window is too small. In case of emergency one could not even use it."

(BENJAMIN *closes his book.*)

IN WHICH AN EASTER LILY IS GIVEN

> (BENJAMIN *puts the ladder aside and checks a picture, which he has draped in cloth. He tidies somehow, somewhat nervous.*)

BARBARA. Here I am!

BENJAMIN. Eyes closed.

BARBARA. Yes, sir.

BENJAMIN. Hold on. Don't peek.

BARBARA. I won't.

> (*He stands behind her, puts his hands over her eyes. She reaches her hands up and covers his. He leads her into the center of the room.*)

BENJAMIN. Here.

> (*Hands down.*)

BARBARA. It's beautiful!

BENJAMIN. Thank you.

BARBARA. Just beautiful. Not a drip in sight. You would most definitely have to be a painter, if you weren't destined to be an opera star. Transformation!

> (BARBARA *suddenly grabs* BENJAMIN'*s arms and dances him around the room.*)

BENJAMIN. Is this a waltz?

BARBARA. Soon enough. Up. Up. A-ha! Better.

> (*They laugh.*)

BARBARA. I hated the dances, until I learned that they were an extension of the dramatic line.

BENJAMIN. Everyone watches you.

BARBARA. And that, my dear, is how I came to *love* them!

> (*They stop dancing.*)

BARBARA. As you will. Everyone will watch you. Everyone will listen.

BENJAMIN. We can move the piano in here and the music will go along that wall ...and Barbara, I had an idea.

> (BENJAMIN *takes the cloth off the picture—a newly framed image of* MARIAN ANDERSON.)

We can call this The Marian Anderson Music Room.

> (BARBARA *is quiet. She walks away from the picture.*)

BARBARA. 1939. Easter Sunday.
There were thousands of us, Benjamin.
Endless clusters of faces and hands
leaning toward those high marble steps,
awkward together in this

sudden wonderment.

> (*As* BARBARA *tells this story, the room frac-
> tures and re-forms itself into a modified
> flag with vertical stripes and a horizontal
> bar of blue and stars. This should happen
> silently, magically.*)

Her entrance was the shock of
pure radiance.
She walked down the steps
to the wide bank of microphones
Her face...you see, light streamed forth from her face...
She opened her mouth...
And the wave of sound,
the rolling luminous wave...
Oh! we barely *breathed*
and *this child* decided that the sun itself had been humbled
had drawn the clouds to its face
and we...we all stood in her presence...
bowed
transfixed
lifted
our hot tears stung our cheeks—
for, on that day, that woman, Benjamin, that great lady from
Philadelphia, belonged to something far greater than anything
we could rightly name...

> (*Amidst the clustering stars, the silhouette
> of* MARIAN ANDERSON *appears.*)

At the conclusion,
I ran past the people;
I dashed up the steps
as Ms. Anderson ascended with her entourage...

and ...
I reached out my hand to touch her coat.
She turned *that face* down to mine.
She met my gaze.
"*Yes ...*"
she said to me.
Not a question. A *statement*.
Then she took a single lily from the bunch she carried
and handed it to me before floating away.
Its lush scent softened my knees.
I stood trembling on those steps
listening to the lap and roar of the crowd.
I heard ...
I turned
over my shoulder, I looked
up and back
to a crowd of well-known musicians,
who were busy
discussing the import of the day,
and there among them
as plain as day
was my father.
Without even thinking,
I cried out
Pappo! Pappo!
I ran further up the steps,
he turned his face toward me
and a look of clear terror flashed across it.
I tripped and fell,
rolling back and down,
tearing my stockings,
bloodying my hands, my knees,
cutting my lip.

I stood
turned back
He looked down, and
for an incredible instant
this child saw through him … Benjamin …
The way you can see through me right now …
My father. *All that time.*
He was afraid that people would
discover that he in fact was a colored man.
My mouth filled with salt.
The man who called himself Niccolò Scarlatti
turned his face from me
and receded into the Memorial
with the other musicians.
Crushed and bloody
my lily
dropped to the steps.

> (BARBARA *stands, head bowed. Tears.*)

BENJAMIN. Barbara. (++)

> (BENJAMIN *takes* BARBARA's *hands. He comforts her.*)

BENJAMIN. Barbara, c'mon. Sometimes people …they just get weak. It's not like they don't love you. They just. Don't know how. They can't stay through the hard parts. He still loved you … He still loved you … He still loved you … He still loved you … He still loved you …

> (BENJAMIN *matches her, breath for breath.*)

"Mia figlia adorata. La più bella del mondo. La più bella del mondo."

(BARBARA *turns her face to* BENJAMIN. *Suddenly, softly. She kisses his lips. He pulls away. He shakes his head. The dogs howl.* BENJAMIN *runs from the room.*)

IN WHICH THEY FEEL BIGGER

(*Nighttime.* BARBARA *stands outside her house and whispers the words from* Aida *as she sweeps.* MARIAN ANDERSON *sings softly underneath the dialogue. As this occurs,* BENJAMIN *is modeling for* TERENCE, *who is putting the finishing touches on a huge drawing.* MARIAN ANDERSON *participates, altering something here or there. She is amused. The scenes should flow as one.*)

BARBARA.
I sacri nomi di padre, d'amante
Nè proferir po'ssio, nè ricordar.
Per lun, per l'altro, confusa, tremante,

TERENCE. Your eyes are bigger.

BARBARA.
Io piangere vorrei pregar
Ma la mia prece in bestemmia si muta,
Delitto è il pianto a me, colpa il sospir
In notte cupa la mente è perduta,

TERENCE. Lips too. Bigger.

BARBARA.

> *E nell'ansia crudel vorrei morir.*
> *Numi, pieta del mio soffrir!*
> *Spemi non v'ha pel mio dolor.*

BENJAMIN. And my teeth?

TERENCE. Your hands. Your chest. You're bigger than your skin, bigger than your bones.

> BARBARA.
> *Amor fatal, tremendo amor*
> *Spezzami il cor, fammi morir!*

BENJAMIN. How am I going to fit on your paper.

TERENCE. You don't.

BENJAMIN. Let me see.

> MARIAN ANDERSON.
> *Those sacred names of father, of lover,*
> *I dare not utter or even recall;*
> *for one, for the other, confused, trembling,*
> *I would weep and pray.*
> *But my prayers seem turned to blasphemy;*
> *to weep is a crime, dark sin to sigh*
> *in deep night my soul is lost,*
> *in this anguish I would die.*
> *Gods have mercy on my suffering!*

> (TERENCE *turns* BENJAMIN *around to see the piece. It is a mass of violent lines and patches of roughly textured color.*)

BENJAMIN. It's. Different. Than your other ones.

> (TERENCE *nods his head.*)

BENJAMIN. Where am I?

TERENCE. You can't tell?

BENJAMIN. But ... I don't look like that. It's all ...

TERENCE. Different.

BENJAMIN. I mean I like it, I just don't see myself.

TERENCE. It's you. But different.

BENJAMIN. It's not.

> (TERENCE *is quiet.*)

BENJAMIN. It's a mess, man. I mean, it's ...look. Let's do another one.

TERENCE. I shouldn't have shown it to you.

BENJAMIN. No. No. I. I just. I just have to ...(++)

> (BENJAMIN *sits and looks at it for a minute. He holds himself a bit.*)

BENJAMIN. What are you gonna call it?

TERENCE. *Berkeley Springfield Map Home.*

BENJAMIN. How can you see that, and I can't feel that?

TERENCE. I just drew what I saw. I didn't mean to upset you.

BENJAMIN. Don't say that. Don't start acting crazy on me.

> (BENJAMIN *tries to hold* TERENCE. TERENCE *pulls away from him.*)

BENJAMIN. Terence.

TERENCE. It's a weird day.

BENJAMIN. Don't do this.

TERENCE. I'm not doing anything.

BENJAMIN. Yes you are. (++)

TERENCE. You don't fit this anymore.

BENJAMIN. I still fit you.

> (TERENCE *hands the drawing to* BENJAMIN.)

BENJAMIN. Right?

TERENCE. Here.

> (TERENCE *rests his head on* BENJAMIN'*s shoulder. They breathe there for a beat.*)

BENJAMIN. I don't know how to do this.

TERENCE. I just gave you a map, stupid.

BENJAMIN. I've got to go.

TERENCE. Okay.

BENJAMIN. See you tomorrow?

> (TERENCE *stares at him. Silence.* BENJAMIN *exits.*)

BARBARA. (*Sweeps. Looks.*)

MARIAN ANDERSON.
  Pity these tears hopelessly shed.

BARBARA. (*Sweeps... Looks...*)

MARIAN ANDERSON.
  Love, fatal and dreadful,

break my weak heart,

BARBARA. (*Sweeps...*)

MARIAN ANDERSON.
Let me die.

YES

> (BARBARA *sweeps to her doorway. She stops and stands... sensing...* BENJAMIN *walks to the stoop. She keeps her back to him initially.*)

BENJAMIN. I'm sorry.

BARBARA. Never say you're sorry.

BENJAMIN. I'm ready for the lesson. I prepared.

BARBARA. No.

BENJAMIN. I'll just get to work then. I can put away the ladders and stuff...

> (BARBARA *turns to face him.*)

BARBARA. No more lessons.

BENJAMIN. What?

BARBARA. We're done.

BENJAMIN. You can't just say that. You're teaching me.

BARBARA. We had an exchange. You've finished your painting. Our arrangement is concluded.

BENJAMIN. But I did everything you said. You promised ...

BARBARA. I promised nothing.

BENJAMIN. Look. What you said to me ... and what happened ... it was a lot to handle.

BARBARA. A lot to handle, indeed. Benjamin. A true artist runs toward fire—embraces contradiction with open arms.

BENJAMIN. That's exactly what I did! It's what I do. It's what I always fucking do. And every time it's like I get punished for it. Slammed. And this was the only place since coming here where I wasn't. You have no right to stop me. I'm right here and I'm ready to sing. I want to sing, Barbara. I need to sing. It's the only thing that's ... It's the only place I know anything anymore. I need to sing!

BARBARA. And you will, Benjamin. You will sing. But not with me.

BENJAMIN. WHY!

BARBARA. Everything is not appropriate for an impressionable voice.

BENJAMIN. This isn't fair!

BARBARA. It has been a pleasure, young man.

BENJAMIN. No.

BARBARA. (*Sweep, whisper*) Out.

BENJAMIN. Stop!

BARBARA. Out. (*Sweep.*)

BENJAMIN. Barbara, NO!

BARBARA. (*Barely audible*) Out.

(BARBARA *shuts her door. Her silhouette slowly, faintly appears behind it, shrouded in red, as the scene continues.* BENJAMIN *balls up the drawing* TERENCE *gave him and throws it against the door. He sinks to the stoop. Cracked.*)

BENJAMIN. Please…

(MARIAN ANDERSON *walks down the street. Her feet don't touch the ground. She stands next to* BENJAMIN.)

BENJAMIN. You are definitely not an angel.

MARIAN ANDERSON. Neither are you.

BENJAMIN. I told you that upfront. You're just a ghost. Always bad news.

MARIAN ANDERSON. Not a ghost.

BENJAMIN. Evil ghost, mean death. How did you die?

MARIAN ANDERSON. We are very much alive. And not evil. At all.

(*Pause.*)

BENJAMIN. All of it's broken. Falling apart.

MARIAN ANDERSON. Falling away. There's a sizable difference in interpretation.

BENJAMIN. I don't know what to do. It's *all* different.

MARIAN ANDERSON. It's what you chose.

BENJAMIN. I didn't choose any of this. It all fell in my lap.

MARIAN ANDERSON. Gifts. So many gifts. A salmon as long as my arm from Sibelius. Shiny. A wrought iron cage with two tufted white birds no bigger than my thumbs. Money in the collection plate to fund my first lessons with Maestro Boghetti. But the greatest gift ... At the foothills of the Himalayas. Dharamsala. The sitting man with the silvery eyes. He has requested our presence. We have traveled in the carriage up the long road. Butter lamps. Juniper. Jasmine. Sandalwood. In the blush of twilight, he teaches us. The greatest gift. We've kept it secret. And here we are, sitting with you.

BENJAMIN. I thought you chose me. Like a vision.

MARIAN ANDERSON. We *saw* you. Dancing in the snow. We saw the wish around you. We came and listened. Curious.

BENJAMIN. You *saw* the wish?

MARIAN ANDERSON. He helped *us* our first time.
　　　　　The sitting man started by telling us to sit comfortably.

　　　　　　　　　　　　(MARIAN ANDERSON *sits next to* BENJAMIN,
　　　　　　　　　　　　hovering just above the ground.)

Like so.
We were told to close our eyes (++)
We were told to breathe from the deepest part (++)
We were made to still our thoughts (++)
We were asked to turn our gaze upward
To a tiny window
At the top (++)
Waiting (++)
Waiting (++)
Waiting (++)
And then
In the stillness (++)

(MARIAN ANDERSON *touches* BENJAMIN's *head.* MARIAN ANDERSON *and* BENJAMIN *ascend—become points of light, moving.* BARBARA's *silhouette is clearly defined. She sings softly, contrapuntally in the melodic line of Amneris's final words in* Aida.)

We lift.

BARBARA.
Pace, t'imploro, mio adorato ragazzo ...

MARIAN ANDERSON. Benjamin?

BARBARA.
Isi placata, ti schiuda il ciel.

BENJAMIN. What are all those lights?

MARIAN ANDERSON. Thoughts. Trails of experience.

BENJAMIN. So many.

MARIAN ANDERSON. So many had.

BENJAMIN. So many to have.

MARIAN ANDERSON. And around us.

BENJAMIN. That's me.

MARIAN ANDERSON. And there?

BENJAMIN. Mom.

MARIAN ANDERSON. And there?

BENJAMIN. Barbara.

MARIAN ANDERSON. And that, right there?

BENJAMIN. I see it.

MARIAN ANDERSON. Do you recognize it, Benjamin? It's a wish. From a son to his father.

BENJAMIN. Mine.

MARIAN ANDERSON. And that. Over there.

BENJAMIN. Another ... wish.

MARIAN ANDERSON. From a father to his son.

> BARBARA.
> *Pace ...*

BENJAMIN. What is it?

> BARBARA.
> *Pace ...*

MARIAN ANDERSON. Listen. Do you hear?

BENJAMIN. Yes.

> (BENJAMIN *begins to laugh. Full, blue and uncontrollably. Lights. Stars. Black. Laughter.*)

The moon and the stars in his
hands.

FOREWORD

We made a prayer. We departed from the all-too-familiar patriarchy and invited the divine feminine to guide our fragmented hearts through the vestibule to a new tomorrow. Were our prayers answered? Well, ask yourself...

"How is your heart?"

Daniel wears many a hat for many a folk. To the colleges and universities where he has taught, he is a professor. New York knows him as a "multidisciplinary" artist. To Springfield, Massachusetts, he is a brother and a son. Our tribe regards him as a healer. Additionally, I would call him an activist, maybe with a side gig as a medium. Anybody that has interacted with Daniel, even in passing, can recall the exact time and place of contact. One thing is for sure: we have never known Daniel as a stranger.

Evoking the energy of any script is a holy act. Spreading space like wild seeds across time ...cosmic tethers uniting us all. Moving the movement in the name of those that came before. Paving the path for those still yet to arrive.

What we made then is no longer. Where there is water, there is flow.

So much hurt. So much sorrow. So much loss. Much of this moment in history is painted with a numbing pain. Proto-martial law helicopters beat their wings on our doorsteps, discriminately threatening our lives in exchange for being born. Illusions and distortions of the truth trick us into betraying even our most basic loving inclinations. And yet, somewhere, somehow, somebody has already cracked open the seed that will change our world for the better. Unprecedented leaps for freedom with a list of demands, unambiguously calling for the total extinction of chains that bind.

"How is your heart?"

The incantation is startling. Suddenly, we are invited to explore what it means to hold space. What it means to tremble in fear and excitement at once, to fight and to dance, to laugh in the dark like a flower in bloom.

Welcome to the crossroads.

DUAT.

– Jacques Colimon

ALTAR NOTES | feeling in the dark

Lena Horne sat in an interview with the noted television interlocutor Dick Cavett in 1981. Flush with the impact of her victorious show, *The Lady and Her Music*, Horne spoke with candor when Cavett referred to old perceptions of her as a "cultured introvert" in contrast with the ferocity of her persona in her show, and in the room that night. "I was a late bloomer," she said, "I didn't 'un-introvert' until I was fifty...I was behind a mask that I thought would *not* make me seem stereotypical...I went way back and got some kind of mask that just erased everything...an unknown category, I could not be reached. I would not give myself easily because of my hangups, racially and otherwise...But I found that some of them were creating a block in me artistically." She went on to discuss the impact of hearing the voice of Aretha Franklin, a voice she called, "an ultimate free sound." Franklin's voice broke her heart open. And it became a model for her, not to emulate stylistically, but to understand emotionally, spiritually, and psychologically. "I was very icy for many years, and I could not be at ease with you, with many people. Because of the ice that society had put around my heart."

We live in heartbreaking times. Our individual proximity to the burning eyes of violent destruction is determined by a number of factors, including privilege (or lack thereof) on the one hand and chance on the other. In the United States, there are particular new cycles of violence rooted in old, poisonous, and systemic scripts that prey upon us because of the bodies we are in, the rights we assert, the culture we embody, and the transformations we enact. The cost of courageous confrontation is grave. The codes for access to comfort and relative safety may be updated, but they are not new; and there is definitely no guarantee that your deal with the devil will be worth the skin it was written on this time around. The impact of that violence will reach everyone, eventually, for that violence is irreparably damaging our Earth. As the old spiritual says, *"the rock cried out—no hiding place."* The ice caps are melting fast.

I always felt a kinship with Horne's iciness. It was hauntingly familiar. I would sometimes stare at her face, a face that many folks said my own resembled. I could *feel* her brilliance, and also her unambiguous decision to be in charge of who did, and who did *not* have access to the inside. While she was a peerless luminary in the pantheon of great Black stars, and I was just a little kid from a working-class neighborhood in a small, fading, northeastern city, I felt some resonance between macro and micro. From a young age, I had developed my own distance and reserve as a way of disrupting the caging and distorting projections, and deflecting the barely veiled attacks from folks within the strange world I'd entered, so different from my own home and neighborhood. That home was a so-called interracial household; that neighborhood was a diverse, close-knit, predominantly Black, working-class enclave. That strange world was a predominantly white public school system. I was, in the 1970s and 1980s, an integrator. Part of a generation that came of age in the wake of the Civil Rights Movement, who boarded yellow buses to make our way away from our neighborhoods to receive a complicated education. We were meant to embody and enact the sunny side of the ideals espoused; but we also navigated the shadow side of pernicious resistance, silent retreat, and gradual yet persistent reversal. Buoyed by a crystal clear combination of a) the unwavering assumption of our capacity for excellence, instilled in us by family and community, and b) their unerring faith in us, my friends and I experienced an odd prescience that we were entering something far more complicated than just "going to school," but that we were not only equal to it, but were expected to stay on top of, and ahead of it. Whatever "it" was.

Years later, I would come to understand that "it" included a tightrope dance over a treacherous terrain of absorptive and erasing white supremacy at worst, cultural chauvinism at best, as well as patriarchy, misogyny, and just plain old meanness. Those are not descriptors that would resonate for a bus full of elementary school students; but I assert that while we couldn't name "it," we could sure as hell *feel* "it." And we could sense the harrowing damage it wrought, sometimes slowly, sometimes swiftly, as we grew in macrocosmic and microcosmic ways further away from original intentions; one way that integration failed. There was no halcyon time. No idyllic, CHIC-soaked roller-skating haven immune to the shadow side. But, there were real people, in community, with all of their complexities and contradictions, who made a go of it and practiced a way of becoming based on a kind of radical if quotidian vulnerability. A fragile web of actions rooted in a desire to enact equality, hold space for difference, make room for people to stretch out beyond the habits of their identities, and act with some measure of intentional kindness; one way integration succeeded, however briefly.

"And I said God, let me open up myself," Horne continued, recounting Franklin's impact on her self-described icy heart. "When she … and things that happened to me, of course, broke my heart, I realized I wasn't ice. I was very fragile, very human, and a woman who had been this way for protection, so I loved it that she made me cry. Because I wouldn't cry for years."

It's a joke my friends are very familiar with: "I don't cry; I don't drink enough water to make tears." Partially true, it has been my way of deflecting attention—others', yes, but largely my own—away from the ice around my own heart. I haven't cried, because the water was not in liquid form. Now, the peculiar algebra of navigating a post-integration United States landscape, while trying to keep hold of integrity and while seeking some measure of civic possibility (that is dynamically inclusive, egalitarian, and aggressively anti-colonial) is nothing unique; it is a well-worn story of trusting hearts face-to-face with a fundamentally untrustworthy proposal. And that there has been something braced, coiled, rigid, sentinel, and ready-for-the-other-shoe-to-drop-as-a-signal-that-it's-time-to-rumble in the core of me, too, is nothing unique. I don't think my experiences are "special," or that I am somehow divorced from a larger context. But I begin with my testimony because it is my melody, and it is a truthful point of departure—in it remain insights only revealed through the playing, and with it I can call to others to put their hands on their own melodies, as we move, together, into a particular experience of the larger contexts within and without. My heart pierced by the accelerated, unspeakable violence and loss I have witnessed these last few years, I have wept. My heart breaking open, from within, in a sustained unstable wail for the irreparable and irreversible damage being done, macro- and microcosmically. Throughout, I have been visited by fragments of memory, flashes of emotion and insight flowering forth from the past. Evidence.

I sense that my personal struggle, and the greater, more pointed struggle of many others, is in part a struggle against the erasure of potential, against the winnowing and constraining of the breadth of life and expression, against the wholesale assault on the *imagination*. The urgency at the core of me, and the connected urgency of many others, is to voice that potential both in terms of what gets imagined and in terms of what gets remembered. We manifest what we imagine. My forebears imagined freedoms they did not, themselves, experience. And by so doing became architects of a trans-temporal reality. I have felt a block in me—a block of ice. I am sure I cannot articulate all the reasons why it exists. But I can say without question that the block has to go. And I can say with certainty that most people I encounter, on the real, are contending with some version of this block, regardless of whatever elements comprise their own. I understand that we need to be fully available to imagine beyond the boundaries of this current experience. Heart in hand, I consider the evidence. My heart has surged with a profound, unambiguous love for the beauty and bravery of all those who face this abyss and keep breathing, moving, seeking, cultivating expansion in the midst of harrowing reduction, even erasure. A community of feeling in the dark.

And so, this work began as an impulse to explore a ritual of deliberate undoing and transformation that felt at once future and ancient. I asked for inspiration and information from both those temporal spheres. I relied on the words of the late Alice Coltrane, "They'll be there. They'll be moving in a translinear path." Within the Black American autobiographical tradition, there is an implicit relationship between "I" and "we"; the first person narration is specific, yet part of a congregation of experiences that are familiar, it is hoped in the fullest sense of that word. Testimony is a call and witness is a response intended to arouse an affective experience, for which each individual has particular vantage points. We share space.

In the belly of Duat, Osiris sits back to back with the god Atum. It is a space devoid of anything save the structure upon which Osiris sits. There is no light, no sound, no movement of air. He is aware of the sentience of Atum, but that awareness alerts him even more keenly to his ultimate isolation. Osiris is alone. After the death of his "self," he is other than, yet housed among, the ruptured (phantom?) fragments of that dismembered self; he is beyond that which was remembered then released by those who loved him. Nothing stirs. The crucible of his own thoughts, regrets, longings, and fears grows ever more intense. With no marker, he cannot tell if he has sat there for a moment or a century. In desperation he cries out, "Will I be here forever?" The answer comes back—"Yes."

In the tradition of mythic conundrums, this rates pretty high up there. For the soul's journey through Duat is beset by doubts and demons, riddles and lies, distortions and derangements, and, too, cues and clues. The imprint of the seed, does it remain long after germination?

of us was in the dark, does that person, that aspect of ourselves, in part, remain, tethered? Does that person give way to our transformation, to our becoming, like the hull of a seed gives way to the plant within? Spoiler alert: Osiris makes it out. But he is changed. He has been killed, dismembered, remembered, and resurrected, and then "dies" to the living world to live in the eternal world of the dead (an alternate dimension of the gods in the sky above us). Is the fear of willing myself out of the icy dark not in fact connected to the visceral knowledge that I will be irrevocably changed when I do? Pain awaits. That thing which breaks open in me could destroy or renew me; but it will shed the life I've been living in the process either way. Easier to hang back in an "unknown category," a windowless, airless, still fortress of solitude. Easier, 'til you can't no more.

I commit this to you: I will offer you my real heart through *Duat* (no ice). Indeed, my work and the work of my collaborators has been to stay in the heat of that realness. Some aspects of that realness are revealed in oblique ways, since there are spirits in the corner that you can only spy through your peripheral vision. So sometimes we conjure abstractly. Other aspects of that realness must be offered directly. No distractions or attempts to prettify. Uncut. There is a conscious dance between familiar and unknown, set and improvised. This text, for example, is like a chart in music—a point of departure into a lived experience. *Duat* is an *experience* into which you are invited.

If myths are narrativized symbol sets, then deep within the symbols themselves lie urgent desire to recollect the pieces of experience, to remember them in the chambers of the heart, and then to communicate them, inviting others to imagine their way beyond caging habits of reduction and into the wide, pulsing *feeling* of life.

– DAJ

Duat
Premiered as a production of Soho Rep at the Connelly Theatre
New York, New York
October 2016

Directed by Will Davis
Music direction by Truth Bachman
Dramaturgy by Kyla Searle
Project Assistants: Keenan Hurley and korde arrington tuttle
Set by Arnulfo Maldonado
Costumes by Oana Botez
Lights by Solomon Weisbard
Sound by Elisheba Itoop
Songs by Jomama Jones with Bobby Halvorson and Samora Pin-
    derhughes
Music arranged by Samora Pinderhughes and Truth Bachman

FEATURING:
Jacques Gerard Colimon as JACQUES/ALEX
Tenzin Gund-Morrow as TENZIN/THE BA/SWEET T
Toussaint Jeanlouis as ANUBIS/SAINT
Daniel Alexander Jones as DANIEL
Jomama Jones as JOMAMA JONES
Stacey Karen Robinson as MA'AT/MRS. ROBINSON
Kaneza Schaal as THE SCRIBE/LALIBELA

THE BAND:
Truth Bachman on KEYS
Josh Quat on GUITAR
Ethan O'Reilly on BASS
Mareike Wiening on DRUMS

To the night flowers, made of stardust. Your hour is nigh.

This lobby is like an entrance to a tomb. Cordoned-off areas contain empty wooden bookshelves, crates, and flower beds. Empty picture frames, wire curling out of their backs. A sense of having been cleared and hastily arranged to accommodate the audience. A layer of dust. Faint smell of incense, of resin. Bare incandescent bulbs on wrapped cords pepper the space and the hallway to the theatre.

A stained and faded craft paper banner with construction paper letters hangs on one wall, its lower left corner curling up; it used to read:

[BLACK] AMERICA READS!
Ask your librarian for suggestions.

...but now the "BLACK" has fallen off. Opposite hangs, barely, a faded craft- and construction-paper American flag with several of the fifty stars fallen down to the floor, slightly brighter blue on the background on the flag where they used to be, like now-missing teeth, and at least one of the white stripes just gone.

Faded photographs of librarians, readers, learners. Covered in a thin layer of dust.

A cracked display case contains the contents of a grade school report on DUAT – THE ANCIENT EGYPTIAN AFTERLIFE.

TENZIN sits at a small table and hands audience members small folded Xerox reproductions of the report. He stamps each one with a stamp of a feather and an arrow before handing it off. He does not speak to anyone. He just hands the report.

With confirmation of their upcoming attendance, audience members should be invited to bring a book to give away, should they wish to contribute to "the archive." If audience members have brough books, they will place them in a dark, canvas bin. TENZIN will hand the audience member a small slip of paper that reads:

"Thank you for your timely donation to our archive."

HEART

(TENZIN *clears the library table. He turns off a record spinning on a turntable. He spies a book on the table. He picks it up and reads the page to which it is opened.*)

TENZIN. " ...and in the afterlife, the soul uttered the list of negative confessions, as a spell of purification and preparation, before the heart was weighed against the feather of Ma'at, the Goddess of Truth and Justice."

(*He closes the book and reads the title.*)

TENZIN. *Duat.*

(*He takes the book with him into the darkness. Light up on* DANIEL.)

DANIEL. How is your heart? How is your heart? I act like mine is fine, but it is not. If I'm quiet, I can hear it beating. As long as it's beating I can't complain, right? I *shouldn't* complain. Beating, standing, moving, breathing. Like I am. Like we are. Like they were.

Do stars have hearts? How is your heart? Is your heart in your body? My body is fine. Not like "fine" but fine. Aches and pains and scars and all that comes with getting old. Er. Older. It's breathing, moving, standing ...Like it is. Like theirs were. Before they were torn apart. Why do I feel my heart coming to pieces?

It wasn't supposed to be this way.

(*The library is revealed as* TENZIN *turns on the lamps.*)

TENZIN. Confess.

DANIEL. I love libraries.

(*To* TENZIN) I was a library page! At our neighborhood library, i.e., The Black Library. In the mid-1980s.

(TENZIN *walks away.*)

Our librarians? Mrs. Sylvia Humphrey, immaculate in her starched and pressed cotton dresses, and Mrs. Bettye Webb who strode in each morning looking like Lena Horne with frosted hair.

MRS. HUMPHREY. "Mrs. Webb, have you ever wondered how stars are made? Kindly point young Miss Jackson to the section on Astrophysics."

MRS. WEBB. "Have you ever wondered, Mrs. Humphrey, how so many languages are spoken on the planet Earth? Take a gander at these new Swahili instructional cassettes!"

MRS. HUMPHREY. "Have you ever thought about how brave you would have to be to seek your own freedom? This young lady must read *Incidents in the Life of a Slave Girl* by Harriet Jacobs!"

(TENZIN *places a box on the table. He removes an old, worn book and places it on the table directly at* DANIEL's *seat.*)

They taught me the basics of Dewey Decimal. To properly shelve books—yes, that's a thing. To add cards to the card catalogue. To create new library cards! To collect late fees, or, learn when you should waive them with a smile.

(DANIEL *moves to the table and handles
the book.*)

Jean Toomer's novel, *Cane*, lay wounded on the counter—torn
pages, coffee stains.

> MRS. HUMPHREY. "Karintha ...Karintha at twenty, car-
> rying beauty, perfect as dusk when the Sun goes down."

> Some things, Mrs. Webb, are beautiful beyond measure
> or capture; so beautiful that some folks seek to ruin
> them because their light pierces the darkest heart.

> MRS. WEBB. A generous stance, Mrs. Humphrey, but
> that book was nearly ruined through sheer neglect.

Mrs. Humphrey took me back, back, in the way-back of *our*
Library, with its steady stream of poor and working-class
readers; homespun philosophers and curious learners ...It was
the heart of the heart of our neighborhood. Inside that space,
they tended the books like rare black flowers; portraits of great
writers, artists, politicians on the walls: Dr. George Washington
Carver, Mary McLeod Bethune, Florence Mills, Odetta ...the
sounds of jazz turn-tabling in the way back-back, I felt whole.

JACQUES. This is a mixtape
of songs and confessions
made—after hours—at the
Winchester Square Public Library
May 1, 1986
from the heart of Danny Jones
directly
to you.

DANIEL. Paper tape.

JACQUES. I love the night.

No, wait.

DANIEL. Pink Pearl eraser.
Art Gum eraser.

JACQUES. I'm not afraid to love *in* the night.
No, wait.

DANIEL. Needle and thread.
Binding tape.

JACQUES. I love hardest in the night.
...
These confessions are
deliberately unedited.
I will not hide anything.
I will be totally naked.

DANIEL. Horse glue.

JACQUES. Quote:
"Her skin is like dusk.
Oh, can't you see it?
Her skin is like dusk,
When the Sun goes down."
That's from this book I like.
Cane, by Jean Toomer.
Jean was a boy.
Jeannie is Mom's name.
So I'm used to it being a girl's name?
But what is a girl's name or a boy's name.
What is a boy or a girl?
These are some things I wonder in the night.

DANIEL. "These are the tools to mend, Danny," she said.
Back-back in the way back, we tended the broken book.

Fingering its pages.
Binding its snapped spine.
I swear, my fingers could almost feel a pulse within it.

JACQUES. I can see auras. For real.

DANIEL. "Her skin is like dusk."

JACQUES. His is purple, mostly.

DANIEL. "Oh, can't you see it?"

JACQUES. It's like a light shimmering around his skin.

DANIEL. "Her skin is like dusk,"

JACQUES. Hmm. Does your aura taste purple, too?

DANIEL. "When the Sun goes down."

JACQUES. Just wondering.

> (JACQUES *and* DANIEL, *three gestures, in staggered unison.*)

DANIEL. When a library closes on Earth, what closes in the universe?

TENZIN. Confess.

DANIEL. I don't know how we mend this.

TENZIN. Confess.

> (TENZIN *brings* DANIEL *a card catalogue drawer.*)

JACQUES. Nobody said anything today in school today about your eyeliner. But I couldn't stop looking because it makes your eyes even deeper. I like how your curl hangs over one eye. And how you cut your tee-shirt short, and I can see the hair under your belly button. Your skin is like honey. You are the prettiest boy.

"I Feel For You" by Prince.

(TENZIN *turns on an overhead projector.*)

DANIEL. October 26, 1968. Jeannie Jones's veil is whipping in the wind. Art Jones got that side-part, pomade slick-back. "It was one of the nicest weddings I've ever been to, a cross section of people from any way you want to look at it," my Grandmother Bunny said. Mom and Dad met working at the Springfield Girl's Club. Bunny had hired my Dad. They all worked in the community. Summers, she ran an overnight camp for girls. She said Dad had made an unannounced visit, and at the end of the day, when they lowered the flag after dinner, Dad asked Bunny for her permission to marry Mom. "Well, there'll be problems," she said. "Not only are you Black, but you're Catholic. Some of your family won't like it. Some of my family won't like it. But as far as I'm concerned you're a fine young man. Jeannie has a lot of love to give, and I'd be happy if she gave it to you. Simple as that." She always thought it was so symbolic that she had the American flag in her arms when he asked her.

Growing up we were like our own maroon society. They moved onto a street in our predominantly Black and immigrant neighborhood. We had two preachers on our street. Reverend Morgan, Trinity Baptist, right there, and Reverend Watts, A.M.E., down there. Two halfway houses, the one with one-toothed Ramona over there, and the one with Crazy Willie, behind that house there—Crazy Willie looked like a Black Frankenstein, with yellow eyes, and would chase us like "uuurrururrurhhhgggh!" But we didn't pay him no mind because he had one short leg and couldn't catch us for nothing.

My favorite day was always Christmas Eve. My parents bundled us up and we paid visits to all the neighborhood elders. Mr. Burr who was like a Native American and Black Santa Claus. Mrs. Bertoldo, the widow from Italy, who was in mourning for my entire childhood, but who smiled on that night, sipping red wine from a short glass, recounting braiding flowers into garlands as a little girl in Italy, her fingers tracing the air. At the end we'd come to a small wooden house. Mrs. Pitter sat, like a frail bird with bright glassy eyes, wrapped in a blanket in front of the fireplace. Mr. Pitter would say, "You wanna taste something sweet, I got something sweet for you," and give my brother and me a ceramic cup filled with fresh spring water. We sipped that cold water, in that house, with the Pitters, who had been born in the 1800s.

> (TENZIN *hands* DANIEL *a large manila envelope.*)

DANIEL. A visual archive of extinct things.

> (DANIEL *and* JACQUES *sing* "*Extinction Song.*" *Operating the overhead projector,* TENZIN *names/speaks the following as he places their images under the light.*)

DANIEL & JACQUES.	TENZIN.
Christmas Island Shrew	Christmas Island Shrew
Dusky Flying Fox	Dusky Flying Fox
Carpathian Wisent	Carpathian Wisent
Eastern Elk	Eastern Elk
Bubal Hartebeest	Bubal Hartebeest
Javan Tiger	Javan Tiger
Caspian Tiger	Caspian Tiger
Bali Tiger	Bali Tiger

Eastern Cougar   Eastern Cougar
Japanese River Otter   Japanese River Otter
Miriam's Elk   Miriam's Elk
Red Gazelle   Red Gazelle
Nelson's Rice Rat   Nelson's Rice Rat
Eastern Hare Wallaby   Eastern Hare Wallaby
Libythea Cinyras   Libythea Cinyras
Unsilvered Fritillary   Unsilvered Fritillary
Silver-studded Blue   Silver-studded Blue
Giant Fossa   Giant Fossa
Polydamas Swallowtail   Polydamas Swallowtail
Danish Clouded Apollo   Danish Clouded Apollo
Once were flying   Osiris
Once were snaking
Once were trodding
Once were devouring

Once were moulting   Isis
Once were fucking
Once were multiplying
Once were generating

Once were here   Ma'at
One by one
Rent from being
Not all violence is swift.
Just as sharp.
Just as vengeful.
Just as lethal.

Moving slow as epochs.   Thoth
*Some violence hides in
time.*
Hungry for the future.

274

> *Its mouth stretched wide*   Anubis
> *at the opening womb.*

TENZIN. Confess.

DANIEL. The thing that really strikes me about this photo? The shadow behind them. It was barely a year after *Loving v. Virginia*. And by October of 1968, MLK and Robert Kennedy had both been killed, and just a week or so after this, Richard Nixon would be elected on a campaign of restoring law and order. Mom and Dad? They stood at the edge of the void, and they leapt.

JACQUES.
> *Have fun again*
> *I want you to*
> *Have fun*
> *Have fun again*
> *I want you to*
> *Have fun*
> *Just like little children*
> *Like the little children*
> *Know how they have fun?*[1]

I'm just going to say this. I need to kiss you. If we kiss my heart will just break out of my chest. I will not be the same. And you won't be the same. I think you know that. That's why you're so distant. Like the Moon.

> (JACQUES *holds up Diana Ross's* Diana *album.*)

JACQUES. Diana Ross is distant like a goddess of the Moon.

DANIEL. Ancient gods peered out from record covers.

---

1   Ross, Diana. "Have Fun (Again)." *Diana.*

Stevie Wonder the Sun god shone Hotter than July.
Marvin Gaye sailed into the afterlife shattered into pieces.
Nina Simone the mourning witness.
Tina Turner had magic to bind the atoms of a broken life back together.

JACQUES & DANIEL. And transform them.

JACQUES. I make homemade altars of records, candles, and love notes. Sometimes I put honey.
And wildflowers from the yard.

DANIEL. Ra, Osiris, Nephthys, Isis. I was obsessed with Ancient Egypt since little-little. I read every book in the library. "There are many histories hidden inside his story," said Mrs. Webb. Saw family in the faces. Aunt Evelyn even looked like Queen Tiye.

JACQUES. Are we really here or are we ghosts? Have you ever wondered? Like, what is life? And what is *after* life? And what if after life is *now*. And, if now is after life, then what is next? I like Ancient Egypt. They had afterlife all mapped out; and told you to be prepared. My favorite Egyptian god?

DANIEL & JACQUES. Anubis.

JACQUES. I got a statue of Anubis from that witchy store at the mall, where the white kids who listen to Depeche Mode hang out. It was in the *back* of the store. Just saying.

DANIEL. The sad god, with a jackal head.

TENZIN. "Anubis, the guardian of the balance, tended the dead, then walked their souls through the trials of Duat. He managed the main ritual. He weighed the heart against the feather of Ma'at— the Goddess of Justice. The petitioner made their confessions and prayed their heart would not be carried off."

DANIEL.
> *So many*
> *so many*
> *hearts*
> *in the dark.*

JACQUES. Light hearts go to paradise.
I'll take you to paradise.
Adventures in Paradise, that is, by Minnie Riperton.

TENZIN. Confess.

> (TENZIN *puts a card catalogue drawer*
> *down, and hands a card to* JACQUES.)

JACQUES. Jones, Arthur L. 1935 –

> (JACQUES *hands the card to* DANIEL. *He*
> *reads:*)

DANIEL. Jones, Arthur L. b. 1935 –
Winter mornings
I ask for more heat.
Art Jones says
"my feet stuck to the floor
in our cold water flat
on Essex Street.
I'm living proof—"

DANIEL & JACQUES. "You don't need no damn heat."

> (JACQUES *hands* DANIEL *a card. He reads:*)

Jones, Joseph. Birth date unknown, d. 1972.
There's no photo of Joseph Jones.
I scan my aunt and uncle's faces
to try to piece a glimpse.

Dad says
"the last time I saw him
was outside a bar."

DANIEL. "Called me over, said
'This right here, this is my boy.'"

(JACQUES *hands* DANIEL *a card. He reads:*)

Jones, Daisy Mae Twiggs, b. 1911 – d. 1996
Grandma Daisy Mae
holds her stories in closed fists.
One hot summer night,
light spits from the baseball game on TV
she recalls her cousin
back home in South Carolina
who played for the Negro Leagues
"I loved him like Jesus," she says.
Then falls quiet.

Later, Uncle Gus tells the whole of it;
cousin had a Model T Ford with white-walled tires.
That pissed off the white folks, they slashed his tires.
Being a Twiggs, he went straight to 'em and handled his business, dig?
When he went missing they all went searching.
Daisy Mae, the littlest one, found him,
when his blood dripped on her face from the tree above.
They sent her climbing up to get something down to bury,
her fists full of his burned flesh.

(JACQUES *hands* DANIEL *a card. He reads:*)

Jones, Gussie, b. 1930 – d. 2003
Uncle Gus laughs with his whole body.
His whole body is muscle.

He muscled all over Asia in the Merchant Marines—
was a Boxer, a Player, and a Buddhist.
Uncle Gus says beware the righteous, and that Malcolm X
was the smartest one because he learned to change his mind.
Uncle Gus was in the room when they killed Malcolm.
Nobody fucks with Uncle Gus.

(JACQUES *hands* DANIEL *a card. He reads:*)

Jones, Louis, b. 1929 – d. 2005
My Uncle Lou has a painting of himself styled like Johnny
Mathis. He wears a wig and is in and out of contact depending
on various family feuds. We don't talk about him being gay.
He has thousands of records from when he was a deejay on the
radio. His greatest fantasy, which he often describes, is to enter
large public spaces crowded with white people and scare them
to death. "I'll tell you what I'm gonna do. Gonna go to the
mall, incognito. They'll be there with their carts and carriages.
I'll reach in my pocket and take out a rope; I'll throw it up over
the railing; then drop my coat and climb on up. They'll start
screaming, oh, no, oh, god, who is that, run, run, get out! And
I won't give a good goddamn, cuz I'll be swinging, over their
heads, buck naked with a bone in my nose!"

(JACQUES *hands* DANIEL *a card. He reads:*)

Jones née Leslie, Georgina b. 1937 –
Mom reads us to sleep
fertilizes our dreams
with a gardener's devotion.
When she is sad, which is often,
She retreats to her books.
I imagine their pages filled with flowers.

TENZIN. Confess.

DANIEL. The white people I have loved have eschewed the kind of whiteness that...

TENZIN. Eschewed?...Confess!

DANIEL & JACQUES. I never wanted to be white.

JACQUES. Jean Toomer passed for white. Sad, right. Everybody at school assumes because Mom is white that I'm all, "I'm mixed, I'm better than you". But I don't bother with them because they are too literal. I hate boxes. I'm Black. Black isn't a box. It's a universe outside their boxes. Jean Toomer was a mystic. That's the way we connect. Through his words. Across time.

> At this point, DANIEL improvises stories of school and the madness of integration around the following points:

DANIEL. (*Improvising.*)
1. I was an integrator from way back.
2. First grade teacher driven insane by integration.
3. Ms. Heaps replacing Ms. Grey as the new first grade teacher.
4. Second grade dime shakedown/non-violence
5. Mrs. Davis—the first in a line of Black Women teachers: resilience, self-reliance, fairness.
6. The schools I attended taught us all apart, but Black women taught me how to live through killing contradictions.

JACQUES. I don't do sports. Except tennis. I like tennis. Everyone's all like, that's such a gay sport. I'm like, yeah, and? Martina Navratilova is my favorite. She is unstoppable. They can call me a faggot all they want. I'm unstoppable, too.

DANIEL. (*Improvising.*)
Story about 7th grade and Tanya Williams.

JACQUES. I saw you in the shower after gym class. That's basically all gym class is good for. The showers. I appreciate *the whole* of you. Does that intimidate you, me staring at you? Naked? I appreciate others, too. José, and José, and Jacob. Does that make you jealous?

Skin is our first garment. That's what Miss Camp says in art class. I should be able to take double art class and not gym. I could easily do fashion design. We went to the Ebony Fashion Fair last night. Bunny takes me every year. Do you think she knows? Like knows, knows?

Shayla Simpson is the host, she's all "I'm Shayla Simpson, welcome to the Ebony Fashion Fair...

> (TENZIN *strides in dramatically, carrying an album.*)

Pamela Fernandez is feeling bold and playful, wearing a one of a kind ensemble by Gi-ven-chy."

(*A sigh of exultation*) Uhhhhh. My response to our beauty is automatic.

> (TENZIN *places one record from Prince's* 1999 *on turntable. They dance to the entirety of* "Automatic."[2])

JACQUES & DANIEL.
A-U-T-O-matic, just tell me what to do, ooh
A-U-T-O-matic, I'm so in love with you

> (TENZIN, *the first of the three to stop dancing and gesturing, rings the bell.*)

DANIEL. Oh, my God. The bell!

2   Prince. "Automatic." 1999, Warner Bros, 1982.

(DANIEL *improvises the story of the summer of 1991.*)

1. Graduated with Africana Studies Degree. No job. Living with parents.
2. Father left house.
3. Mother crisis.
4. Grandmother moves in, growing blind. Little Dutch Girl Bell.
5. Sudden collapse of time and space, discomfort of closeness and scrutiny.
6. Reports of serial killer Jeffrey Dahmer's crimes.
7. Mother's abhorrence and confrontation.
8. Grandmother's reporting—the bell.

(TENZIN *collects the bell. He brings another drawer.*)

DANIEL. As I got older, I would come to the library to read all the things I did not learn in school. About radicals and rebels. About intraracial tensions of class and color.

(*He sends* TENZIN *away.*)

And to learn about my body. About being Queer. About being Black *and* Queer.

JACQUES. Sometimes I feel like I recognize you. Like from before-before.

DANIEL. Let me tell the truth of it. We had started writing each other letters, out of the blue, a year before. He was coming out. "How does it feel to kiss a man?" he wrote me.

JACQUES. I believe in past lives. Do you?

DANIEL. That same Jeffrey Dahmer summer, we both ended up back in Springfield. We had grown up together, but hadn't seen each other in forever. On the first night we met up, I was shocked by his appearance. He had been running track and field. Some of y'all know what I'm talking about!

JACQUES. Can I tell you a secret?

DANIEL. "Are we going to do this?" he asked. "Yes, I said." We walked softly into my room and took off all our clothes.

JACQUES. I had a really bad fever when I was seven. It wouldn't break no matter the medicine, and I got really, really skinny. During that time, something happened. It was late at night. I felt myself leave my body.

DANIEL. I felt my body against his body. His perfect arms, his thrumming heart, his full lips, his silvery eyes...

JACQUES. I could suddenly see
all the lives connected like a web.
I know it's weird but I saw across time.
So many paths. Some so beautiful. Some so horrible.
I couldn't look away.

DANIEL. My mouth opened and his mouth opened and my fingers traced the six shades of brown that shimmered atop each other and called themselves his skin. And some ocean salt smell pulled me away from his lips and down his neck and down his chest and down and down and gave me a firsthand understanding of why Patti LaBelle had to sing "*So good, so good, so good,*" at the end of her song.

JACQUES. Then it zoomed out and I saw galaxies bind into a great midnight blue body
I felt a pulse like rolling thunder
I took a breath and in an instant I snapped back into the room, covered in sweat. The fever broke.

DANIEL. Sticky, glistening, panting, I sat up and looked at him in the dark.

JACQUES. We are all a part of a giant body. And she is beautiful, beautiful, beautiful.

DANIEL. You are the prettiest boy. I said. That summer, every night we could we fucked until dawn.

JACQUES. I'm not afraid to die because of what I saw. But I do get scared about what could happen while I'm alive.

DANIEL. Last year, he wrote me on my 45th birthday. "Every part of my body," he said, "has a rich memory of you." I couldn't write him back.

> (DANIEL *removes a photograph from one of the catalogue boxes.*)

DANIEL. These are my friends, my little brother, and me. Around 1981. Before the trickle-down impact of Reaganomics gutted the city and choked our neighborhood. We are all dressed as Wonder Woman—our favorite superhero. I liked that she pulled truth and justice out from within you. And she dressed fierce.

> (DANIEL *removes a pair of doll-sized panties from his jacket pocket.*)

Wonder Woman's panties. All I have left. I could tell you the story about my Wonder Woman doll. Tell you about her disappearance and my father's direct involvement in it; draw some conclusions about Black masculinity, repression of queerness, and the disintegration of justice. But what I really want to tell you is about the way my father sought to protect me, with no words, from the violence that he knew awaited. Our personal version of a conversation that happens countless times. But there is no protection. There has been no end to the breaking. Black bodies shattered. Queer bodies under constant assault. Race war, class war. Public schools fucked, safety net nonexistent, libraries closing, bees vanishing, oceans dying. Can we love the broken with all our hearts?

TENZIN. Confess.

DANIEL. In our house, we rode hard for the dead. Tended their stories like saints on the wall.
History.

> (*During the following song,* DANIEL *puts the chairs on the table and prepares the stage for Part Three.*)

DANIEL.
Medgar can't talk because the words spill out onto the driveway.
Four little girls can't talk because their words have been crushed under brick.
Martin can't talk because the words spill out of the hole where his jaw used to be.
Bobby can't talk because the words spill out of the hole in the side of his head.
Malcolm can't talk because the light spills out of the holes and the holes and the holes in the body of him.

We keep our grief close like prayer
Dead hope is feather soft
We tend our little garden
Secret behind walls
Secrets within
What will become when I am undone?
What will my atoms become?
A balm or a bullet?
A screen or a cradle?

A fox or a hawk?
A stream or a tree?

Not history. Right here, right now, new stars are shattered into atoms faster than they're being born. An endless list of new names. Growing as we speak—if I started, I couldn't stop. Right here. Right now.

We thought we were doing something. I thought I was doing something. Thought I was representing.

My heart. My heart.

JACQUES. This mixtape is way more talking than music.
You should come over. I'll play you my records. In person.
Plus we could study for Ms. Hoffman's final.

DANIEL.
So many.

JACQUES. I have decided to offer you all of me.
My mess, my drama, my fierceness.

DANIEL.
So many
hearts
in the dark.

JACQUES. I wonder, in the future. Will I tell bad jokes?

DANIEL. Oh, I tell bad jokes.

JACQUES. Will I feed my friends?

DANIEL. Milk and honey.

JACQUES. Will I wonder about new words, new worlds?

DANIEL. As long as I can, I wonder.

JACQUES. Will I stay awake?

DANIEL. ...

JACQUES. Will I let go of what I can name?

DANIEL. I wash my hands, I wash my eyes, I wash my face in water.

JACQUES. Will I remember the names?

DANIEL. I call the names, make offerings to the forgotten.

JACQUES. Will I offer my body like a feast?

DANIEL.
　　Oh, my heart.

JACQUES. Will I kiss?
　　Will I savor?

DANIEL.
　　Oh, my heart.

JACQUES. Will I hold space for others to dream?

DANIEL.
　　Pray, weigh my heart.

　　　　　　　　　(TENZIN *returns in a new costume. It sug-*
　　　　　　　　　gests a different world/dimension than that
　　　　　　　　　which he's been in. He carries a card cata-
　　　　　　　　　logue drawer that glows softly from within.
　　　　　　　　　He stands, still, clear, knowing.)

JACQUES. Will I shimmer like dawn, will I conjure like night?

DANIEL. Will I bring joy to the table?

JACQUES. In the face of fear, will I delight?

DANIEL. It wasn't supposed to be this way. But we failed.

(DANIEL *exits.*)

JACQUES. I'm running out of tape.
In closing—this is the sound of my heart.

> (JACQUES *exits.* TENZIN *remains alone onstage. His catalogue drawer glows brighter. It contains a feather. He reaches inside and lifts the feather in a clean, angular gesture. A crack, like lightning and thunder compressed into an instant. The library wall dissolves to reveal a massive bank of five-pointed stars. Three Ancient Egyptian deities step forward through undulating waves of light. One,* MA'AT, *extends her hand, and* TENZIN *gives her the feather.*)

BLACK

(STACEY (MA'AT), *with* KANEZA (THE SCRIBE), TENZIN (THE BA) *and* TOUSSAINT (ANUBIS) *perform a weighing of the collective heart.*)

MA'AT. At the beginning, I set the order.

Not rigid lines. But fractal patterns.

My archive, my library.
Continuous unfolding space for infinite possibility.
Everything that ever happened.
Every imprint.
Every word.
Every lie and every truth, each and every utterance.
Every kiss, or sweet caress.
Every death or reckoning.
Each undoing and remaking.

And that?
That was justice.

Back at the beginning it was
willed that will,
your will,
would reckon with responsibility.
You could choose to glow—or to consume.

So are you not responsible—for this?
Living brokenhearted like the living dead.
And all because you were too afraid to feel?
To feel the fear of your ultimate undoing.

The smallest resistance blocks the flow.

You know? You know?! You know.

One by one. The stars blink out and what will replace them if not your dust? One by one. The stars blink out and what will ignite new lights if not the spell of a flowering song? You were meant to be the notes. Melodies, moving, changing, shifting, expanding the skins they are in.

But, y'all were afraid of the dark.

I wish I could have saved you from your fear.
But you've tried to press the all
into a singularity
all us gods and feathers,
all your pith and failures,
all that radical continuance.
All our reinvention.
All our syncretism.
All our bronze endurance.

You. Are you going to wash the bodies?
You. Are you going to draw out the blood?
You. Are you going to spread the resin?
You. Will you anoint?
You. Will you gather the flowers?
Who among you will bind the limbs?
Who knows the spells?
Who among you?

Hmmmmph.

I didn't dress for a funeral. But here we are.

What you think is your heart
is merely a husk.

I pray for you the coming dark

is a womb
not a tomb.

Lights out!

(*All is plunged into pitch darkness. Break.*)

FLOWER

JOMAMA. Why hello there! It's so lovely of you to come out to our final school pageant rehearsal. You know, everyone said to me, Miss Jones, this is no time for a pageant, given the state of the things out there. *I say*, there's never been a more important time!

Together, for a moment, let us be historians—this is my classroom, after all. The history of pageants is rich! Why, did you know, 100 years ago, W.E.B. DuBois's Star of Ethiopia Pageant gathered together hundreds of performers to celebrate over 10,000 years of Black History at the height of the Plague of Lynchings in our country? And if we reach way back thousands of years, we might consider the Abydos Pageant Play in Ancient Egypt: everyone dressed up in their fiercest fashions to tell the story of that African god Osiris, who was shattered into pieces, then remembered and resurrected by Isis. The original ISIS. See how they do?

Osiris moved through the long nighttime hours of the Afterlife—the Duat—to have his heart weighed against the feather of Ma'at. That was one serious pageant.

With everything going on, in these serious times, one might be forgiven for wondering if this is some kind of afterlife, with its bizarre twists and turns, distortions, and fat, obscene demons spouting bile and groping at things.

The part of the story that gets left out is what happens next! Osiris became a green god—his heart, revealed to be a husk, trembling like a seed planted in the Earth. And that, *that*, gave me the theme for our pageant! The students have been working so hard. And there's one in particular I'm a little concerned for. I hope you'll help me keep an eye on them. Here we go!

I'm on the lookout for our music teacher...why, Mx. Bachman, hello!

> (JOMAMA *improvises a saucy statement about* MX. BACHMAN, *which embarrasses them, then transitions to her classroom. She stands at the board, singing the names of the flowers she writes. As she does so,* TENZIN *sneaks in and sits, glumly, at a table.*)

Bleeding Heart
Heliotrope
Cynoglossom
Delphinium
Freesia
Narcissus
Lily
Rose
Lotus

You're here early, Sweet T. How long have you been there, quiet as a mouse?

> (*Discreetly,* MISS JONES *indicates to us that this is the student about whom she is concerned.*)

SWEET T. You mean, quiet as a *seed*.

JOMAMA. A *salty* seed, evidently.

SWEET T. I still can't make up my mind
　　What kind of seed I am.
　　And it's our final rehearsal!
　　I tossed and turned all night.

JOMAMA. Sometimes it's useful to close your eyes and pick—just try one on for size.

SWEET T. But I've tried so many on for size!
Forsythia was too like this (*Makes a pinched-face, rustling gesture*)
And Iris was all (*droops head*)
And Saxifrage was so tiny I was all "look at me, look at me" and nobody would.
Tell me, Miss Jones.
What should I be becoming?

JOMAMA. Now that's a question for the ages. You know what I'm going to say in response.

SWEET T. I'll have to find out for myself.

JOMAMA. Precisely.

SWEET T. Why'd you make me play a seed?!

JOMAMA. Tut-tut. Nobody *made* you do anything. It was the logical assignment. You have so much potential. Who knows what's locked inside that shell of yours.

SWEET T. But, I'm shy.

JOMAMA. I was too.

SWEET T. You?!

JOMAMA. I was a wallflower. Albeit a tall and irresistibly magnetic one.

SWEET T. How did you break out of it?

JOMAMA. I was, shall we say, *compelled*.

SWEET T. I want to be compelled! I want to make everything glow and be unforgettable. You do that.

JOMAMA. Yes. But in my way. You'll have your way.

SWEET T. Why am I shy?

JOMAMA. Shyness can be useful. You can see things that others may not from your perspective. The loud and the bold get a lot of attention. But they often miss the rest of the story.

SWEET T. Ugh! You don't understand!

JOMAMA. Oh, you think I've never been in your shoes. There was a certain Black History Month pageant competition at a certain elementary school that a certain little girl, I wonder if you can guess who, took part in. Everyone else's pieces were ordinary. We had five little Martin Luther King Jrs. with drawn on mustaches reciting the same passage from the "I Have A Dream" speech; three Harriet Tubmans running runaway slaves up and down the aisle of the auditorium, yelling "Keep it low, don't look back, I've never lost a passenger." Perhaps the most edgy was one angry little boy with a box of matches calling himself Nat Turner but he froze onstage in front of the audience and nearly caught the curtain on fire. Thankfully, my little friend and rival, Tamika, who was one of the seven Sojourner Truths, whipped off her shawl and smothered the flames. I, on the other hand, had gone weeks prior to the library and begun deep research. "Have you ever wondered how brave you would have to be to seek your own freedom?" asked the librarian. "You must read *Incidents in the Life of A Slave Girl* by Harriet Jacobs!" She was a house slave who was beset upon by her enslaver. She managed to flee and hid in the tiny attic of her grandmother, Molly, where she hid, for *seven years*, in order to be near her children, before finally escaping North. I set to work. I made a shift of rough muslin. I constructed a scale model of the attic from popsicle sticks and glue. I put it at the side of the proscenium and, factoring ten minutes for each year, created a seventy-minute endurance performance that straddled the pageant's performance time. Periodically I would peer out from the slats to gaze longingly at the basket of doll babies I had sewn to represent my abandoned children and set at the opposite side of the stage. A small tape player looped them crying "Mother, mother, lawd why'd you leave us?" My tears were real. And, as a final touch of verisimilitude, I peed, furiously, into a mason jar, at hour six. When the principal, Mrs. Jackson-Johnson announced me as the winner, the audience rose to its feet in unanimous acclaim; even dear sweet Tamika with her singed shawl was moved to clap. You might say I bloomed under the lights that day.

SWEET T. I want to bloom!

JOMAMA. You will. You will. When the time is right. Now, Lalibela and Alex and Saint should be here any second. I'll go get ready. You can practice for when your classmates arrive.

> (JOMAMA *exits. Softly, almost under his breath,* SWEET T *practices a song and movement sequence.*)

SWEET T.
We are seeds
Hearts called by the Sun
Yearning to come undone
Knowing our time has come

> (LALIBELA *roars in with take-charge energy, disrupting* SWEET T*'s song.* ALEX *and* SAINT *follow, looking at their pages.*)

LALIBELA. Come on, come on! I want to see it on its feet before I add this part in for sure. (*To* SWEET T) I have new pages. Can you be thunder?

SWEET T. (*Makes thunder sound.*)

LALIBELA. "Scene: A rare black flower grows in the middle of an otherwise barren field. Dark storm clouds roll in. Time is of the essence! What's that flying close? Go."

> (ALEX *circles around* SAINT *and then kisses him.*)

Keep going. But more ardent!

> (ALEX *pulls back, immediately.*)

ALEX. Ardent?!

SAINT. It says "ardent" in the stage directions.

LALIBELA. Yes, you've got to *get in there* and get all the nectar.

ALEX. I'm following my instincts, not being "ardent."

SAINT. You're *definitely* not ardent.

ALEX. What's *that* supposed to mean?

LALIBELA. Look. Trust what I put on the page, okay? Just do it. Use your hands.

ALEX. But I don't have hands. I'm a bee.

LALIBELA. Move! Like this!

> (LALIBELA *kisses* SAINT *passionately and uses her hands. He 'swoons.'* ALEX *flutters around them, making his case.*)

ALEX. If I'm a bee I have *legs*, not hands. I'd be using my wings. And my proboscis. Do you even know what that is? A worker bee extends her proboscis to tap the nectar.

(LALIBELA *releases* SAINT.)

LALIBELA. Well looky there. I tapped the nectar. Just like that. And I used my *hands*.

SAINT. Ardent.

ALEX. I value scientific accuracy. Anthropomorphizing bees contributes to a lack of regard for complex systems and sentimentalizes something that should be viewed with objectivity and rigor.

SWEET T. This is a pageant. It's supposed to be exciting, not dry.

ALEX. Accuracy is not dry.

SWEET T. Kinda.

(SAINT *addresses* ALEX.)

SAINT. Science looks at the bee and says "Apis mellifera," placing it in a rigid box. But bees are at once object and metaphor; external fact and interior calling; particle and wave.

LALIBELA. Poetry ain't dry.

(SAINT *walks away from* ALEX, *who is a little ...flustered.*)

ALEX. Whatever.

SWEET T. You're blushing.

ALEX. No I'm not.

ALL. From Seed to Flower and Beyond.
A Pageant.
In preparation.
Go!

JOMAMA.

>*All that lives is of a piece.*
>*Though spirit moves beyond all boundary,*
>*the wonder of your body*
>*happens only one time.*
>*What a wonder I behold.*
>*I love to watch you dance.*
>*It's a miracle.*
>*Magic is unfolding*
>*all around you.*

ALL.

>*You show me,*
>*you show me your*
>*flowers.*
>
>*I show you,*
>*I show you my*
>*flowers.*

JOMAMA.

>*Tell the world the truth of you,*
>*your anger and your passion*
>*and your beauty.*
>*Never hide your sweetness*
>*or your vulnerability.*
>*From your truth is born a flower—*
>*fragrant promise meant*
>*for sharing.*
>*There will never be another*
>*being like you.*
>
>*Temporal, ephemeral,*
>*fall upon the ground.*
>*Loss is in the bargain*

yet the living call.
Better spread love all around
don't give in to fear.
There's no need to fear
for nothing has the power of our flowers.

So many splendid flowers.
So many splendid names.
Countless incarnations.
No two are the same.

> (*With the following song, everyone picks a*
> *name from the board and does that "flower*
> *dance.")*

Pretty flower
What's your name?
Pretty flower
What's your name?
Pretty flower
What's your name?

> (MRS. ROBINSON *enters pushing her cart of*
> *books and objects. She sneaks closer to the*
> *circle—then takes it over!*)

MRS. ROBINSON. Miss Robinson is my name
Books are my game
Just got in a big donation
Making records and citations
I stay organized, to leave room for surprises!

Oh, oh, oh! You know I'm running late, but I'm running!

JOMAMA. You right on time! *Right* on time! Miss Robinson, your responsibilities as our school librarian are many. It is a gift to us all that you are able to attend our rehearsal.

MRS. ROBINSON. Now you know I wouldn't miss this pageant for anything in the world.

JOMAMA. Why, what do I spy on your cart, Miss Robinson? Could it be a box of seeds?

ALL. Oh!

MRS. ROBINSON. And not just any seeds!

JOMAMA. Really. Are they especially significant?

MRS. ROBINSON. Why not ask them?

JOMAMA. Why hello there!

ALL AS SEEDS. Hello, Miss Jones!

JOMAMA. Aren't you quaint in your little box.

ALL AS SEEDS. Yes! Yes!

JOMAMA. Miss Robinson says you're pretty special. Are you sunflower seeds?

ALL AS SEEDS. No!

JOMAMA. Are you mustard seeds?

ALL AS SEEDS. No!

JOMAMA. Are you "Punkin" seeds?

ALL AS SEEDS. No!
We are seeds from Alabama
Born of flowers wild
Gathered by a scientist

Who was at heart a flower child

JOMAMA. What a riddle!
Alabama
Scientist
Flowers...
Could we be at Tuskeegee?

> (JOMAMA *has written "Tuskeegee" on the*
> *board.*)

SAINT. Greetings! I am Dr. George Washington Carver!

LALIBELA. Fine, fine, fine! I'm Booker T. Washington. Welcome to
my Tuskeegee Institute!

SAINT AS CARVER. Education is the key to unlock the golden doors
of freedom for our people! It is my pleasure to be here.

LALIBELA AS WASHINGTON. Well, get to work.

SAINT AS CARVER. But, Mr. Washington, where is the science laboratory
you promised in your letters? And about my private residence,
surely you didn't mean for me to stay in that musty shack!?

LALIBELA AS WASHINGTON. Yeah, yeah, yeah. You'll figure something
out, if you're as inventive as you claimed. Listen, I've got a
long day of fundraising, political accommodation and masking
ahead. I'll leave you to it.

SAINT AS CARVER. My, my, my. Ninety-nine percent of failures come
from people who have the habit of making excuses. I shall make
no excuse and make of this situation a success! Why look at
these old cups and jars. I can use them as beakers!

ALL. Time passes! (*Gesture.*)

SWEET T. Dr. Carver! Dr. Carver! What great success! So many inventions from the sweet potato and the peanut! Balms and lineaments, powders and cures, feeding the hungry, healing the sick! How did you do it, with no resources, no equipment, no manuals? How did you discover such marvelous things?

SAINT AS CARVER. Would you really like to know my secret?

Nothing is more beautiful than the loveliness of the woods before sunrise. I rose each day at 4am and walked; there I took my counsel with those most delicate of God's creations. They told me how to do!

If you love a thing enough
it will reveal its secrets to you.
Unlock all its codes and keys
and send its message through you.
So says the man
who talks to flowers.

Science yes, but so divine.
In nature you will find your guide
to mystic senses
that escape definition.
So says the man
who talks to flowers.

In wee hours of the morning
I walk to the woods to greet first light.
All my worry, all my wanting
grew pale beneath the verdant might.

In the flower is a portal
to the universe so wide.
Its trumpet ear placed to my eye,
nameless wonders I do spy.

So says the man
who talks to flowers.

My life in service to the science.
My life in service to the race.
An elegant tale to tell.
A flower in my lapel.

If you love with all your heart
and love without an ounce of fear,
you will surrender all you know
and open up your sacred ear.

For if you love me as I do you,
I will visit in your dreams.
Whisper secrets bold unto you
leading you to mystic streams.

So says the man
who talks to flowers.

So says the man
who talks to flowers.

So says the man
who talks to flowers.

(MRS. ROBINSON *and* JOMAMA *excitedly surround* SAINT.)

MRS. ROBINSON. Yes! Yes! Oh, you captured the essence of Dr. Carver—wouldn't you say, Sister?

JOMAMA. Absolutely. His sweetness and his vulnerability.

SAINT. I tried to show his optimism in the face of adversity. That's important to me.

MRS. ROBINSON. That was crystal clear. And the way you used your hands! Just so special.

SAINT. (*To* JOMAMA) Do you have any notes?

JOMAMA. Well, as we prepare for what's next. I want you to carry that spirit forward. Like a glistening thread from Dr. Carver to you and beyond. There is one other thing. Dr. Carver was a vessel for so much good. I want you to be able to receive as well as to give.

Ah?
Ah.
Ahhh.

> (ALEX, *who has been watching, casts his "spell"; all else slows as though caughtin honey. He intones the words, which tremble on the edge of being sung.*)

ALEX. Semipermeable plant cell wall separates the interior from its environment
I want to permeate your plant cell wall suffuse what's within with particles of light
If I ask humbly will you allow quantum entanglement within and without your plant cell wall.

> (*Back to normal.* SWEET T *watches* LALIBELA *who has been staring at her hand mirror.*)

SWEET T. Lalibela. Why's your face all twisted?

LALIBELA. She won't look me in my eye.

SWEET T. Your eyes are amazing.

LALIBELA. (*Small gesture*) Changing.

SWEET T. (*Repeats gesture*) Changing?

LALIBELA. Changing demeanor. Changing face. Not looking back.

SWEET T. Maybe it's just a phase?

> (LALIBELA *speaks the bracketed text to herself—an internal confession.*)

LALIBELA. No. She won't meet my eyes.
[Mine but not mine eyes are changing.]
Far off.
[And with the change my questions rise.]
Hard where she was soft.
Soft where she wasn't.
[Pit of my belly some stirring quaking.
Something we aren't being told
About what lies ahead for us.]
I can't grab a hold to her.

> (*She looks over at* JOMAMA, *suspicious.*)

SWEET T. (*Owning the gesture. "Aha."*) Ah. She's *changing*.

LALIBELA. See? I told you.

SWEET T. Tell her what you feel.

LALIBELA. How? She won't see me back.

SWEET T. I know! I know! Write it down. *Nobody* writes stuff down anymore.

LALIBELA. Nobody writes stuff down anymore? How would *you* know what they doing?

SWEET T. That's what Ms. Jones says all the time.
Write a note.

You can draw your amazing eyes on it. Like (*gestures*).
But no hearts like that (*gestures*).
That's tacky.
...

LALIBELA. Sho'nuff, Sweet T.

SWEET T. I'm gonna write lots of love notes. That's gonna be my
"thing."

LALIBELA. I think I'm too melancholy to write a love note. Too tuned
in to the shadows.

SWEET T. That's okay. Some people like to, you know, come to the
rescue of sad people.

LALIBELA. I'm not trying to rescue nobody or get rescued, you hear?!

SWEET T. No, not you, not you.

LALIBELA. Independent, me.
Resilient.
Autonomous.
Self-contained.
Bad ass / bitch.

SWEET T. Bumble bee.

LALIBELA. Don't act quaint.

SWEET T. Don't act like you hard or you'll stay that way.

LALIBELA. You so old.

SWEET T. The oldest.
I'm telling you.
Write a note.

Lalibela means the bees obey you.
Lalibela means the bees obey you.

ALEX. Hey, little seed!

SWEET T. Hey!

ALEX. Whassup?

SWEET T. Just chilling.

ALEX. Pretty wildflowers in that field over there, huh?

SWEET T. They're resplendent!

ALEX. You know what's amazing? Those flowers are like one measure of music in a larger song. One variable in a larger equation. One rung on a ladder.

SWEET T. I got the first metaphor.

ALEX. Smart seed.

SWEET T. So, what's the bigger picture?

ALEX. Touché, little seed! Cycles of flora and fauna in a constantly unfolding interdependent environmental dance. Close your eyes and feel that sensation. Could it be—pollination?! Who got the buzz?

ALL. You got the buzz.

ALEX. I said, who got the buzz?

ALL. You got the buzz.

ALEX. Whaaaaaaaaaaaaaaat???

Which came first—the chicken or the egg?

Flower or the fruit?
Beetle or the juice?

What goes further—talons or the hands?
Missions or the plans?
Branches or the roots?

Do you know the story?
Held up by the science,
Yea that's living proof.

I'll tell you the truth.
First I might delight.
Then I bring the news.

It's about the pollination.
You know I'm integral to all of creation.
Angiosperm, a flowering plant.
Taking messages to whole populations.

I am a male and a female.
I draw a lot of attention.
I change the behavior
With the help of all my buzzing friends
I ensure you see the fruits of my labor.

Open myself to the sun and sky.
Colored patterns seen by many eyes.
Colored petals span the spectrum of your dreams
I made colors that were heretofore unseen.
Vibrate, agitate, liberate, free state, that's what I do.
And I keep it fresh, all in fractal forms, if you don't like it—
fuck you!

Organs ooze with nectar.
Bees swarm, flies gather, beetles buzz, hummingbirds hum.

Make a heady spiral.
Crash and climb, burrow to the middle, put your fingers in the mud.

Don't you want to smell?
Don't you want to land?
Don't you want to drink?
Don't you want to fly away?
Carry me to another day?
Don't you want to pray?
Don't you want to love!

I smelled the signal scent upon the air, and spent the time spreading grains.
I am the mover, the stick, and the root, put my finger down to make the seed in the plains.
I am the one who attracted the mothers.
They dust and they cover, from one to another.
My beauty's a marvel—that's what they tell me at least, I don't know the game.

Look for me in the fields of California.
Look for me in the schools in Arizona.
Look for me in the hills of Tennessee.
Look for me in the depths of memory.

I'm around, yea, I'm around.
Send it up, then we carry down.
And for anybody that claims they don't know—
Now you can tell 'em how the story go.

> (MRS. ROBINSON *grabs* ALEX's *arm, and, a little like an Auntie trying to be cool, shares her memory.*)

MRS. ROBINSON. Thrilling, just thrilling! I once did a pageant! I sat with my mother and we cut the pattern from gingham and made satin flowers for my hat. I was Sunbonnet Sue and I did a little dance. A flower dance. Sweet and pretty. Just thought you kids would like to know!

SAINT. That was really nice poetry.

ALEX. It's really hard science.

SWEET T. Can't you take a compliment?

ALEX. It's fact, not poetry.

LALIBELA. He can't take a compliment.

SAINT. I'm being sincere, here.

ALEX. Compliments remind me of the decorous patterns some flowers produce on their petals. They are invisible to humans but visible to (*gestures*) bees. They have a purpose. To get the bees to pay attention and land on the ultraviolet landing strip. So what is the purpose of your compliment?

(SAINT *walks away.*)

JOMAMA. Miss Robinson. There seem to be so very many feelings welling up around us like shoots from garden soil.

MRS. ROBINSON. Indeed, Miss Jones, indeed.

JOMAMA. What do we do with all that feeling?

MRS. ROBINSON. Oh, I don't know...tamp it down, lash out, triangulate, dissipate, harden up, walk away?

JOMAMA. Mmmm-mmmm-mmmm. Well, that certainly seems to be what's happening in this rehearsal. And it is blocking our flow! Everything living expresses without what it feels within

and thereby promotes the pulse of life. Fragile and temporary,
every flower must open wide.

If you need a hand to hold,
first offer your hand to someone else.
If you need a shoulder to lean on,
lift a weight from someone's back.
If you need a word of wisdom,
look inside the questions of your life.

Give yourself to save yourself.

If you've been betrayed,
place your trust in another's arms.
If you've grown too serious,
make somebody laugh out loud.
If you've fallen so far down,
look to new mountains you can climb.

Give yourself to save yourself.

ALL.
Open your heart wider.
Open your eyes wider.
Open your hands wider.
Open your eyes wider.

SAINT.
If your soul feels so damned empty,
welcome all the space inside.

SWEET T.
If your world falls apart,
rearrange the broken pieces.

ALEX.
> There is no work harder,
> than expanding what can be.

ALL.
> Give yourself to save yourself.

MRS. ROBINSON.
> If hatred rules the day,
> spread your love like rain.

LALIBELA.
> When the darkness falls,
> set up a light and shine it bright.

JOMAMA.
> Stand up straight and tall,
> in all your possibility.

ALL.
> Give yourself to save yourself.
> Open your heart wider.
> Open your eyes wider.
> Open your hands wider.
> Open your eyes wider.

> (*The boys go to arrange flowers.* JOMAMA
> *and* MRS. ROBINSON *peruse the things she
> has brought.* LALIBELA *pulls out a folded
> paper and approaches them.*)

LALIBELA. Miss Jones, Miss Robinson?

JOMAMA. Yes, Lalibela?

LALIBELA. May I read you something?

MRS. ROBINSON. Come over here with us. (*Under her breath about the others*) They ain't talking about nothing.

LALIBELA. "In the periphery
  Little girl glimpses
  Brown limbs moving in concert
  Laughter and blushing voices
  Whispers to wide open arms
  A thrum of possibility

  Yet, in the shadow of my glance
  I spy stark fragmentation
  Splitting bones tearing flesh
  Stilling limbs
  Flashing lights and sirens
  Some crushing cycle
  Motors on"

MRS. ROBINSON. I'm not familiar with that poem. Who's the author?

JOMAMA. Why she is.

MRS. ROBINSON. And the title?

LALIBELA. *Untitled (What's Next?)*

MRS. ROBINSON. Oh, my.

> (*She and* JOMAMA *share a look.* JOMAMA *gestures to the books/objects.*)

JOMAMA. What's all this?

MRS. ROBINSON. Oh, just a few odds and ends I've put together for a kind of care package to send along. For the pageant. Get a gander:

LALIBELA. Langston Hughes   JOMAMA. Seeds
       Zora Neale Hurston   Flowers, Nectar
       Carter G. Woodson   Fruit
       Eleanor Roosevelt   In every book
       Toni Morrison   Light
       Alice Walker   and Shadow
       Toni Cade Bambara   Rhyme
       Essex Hemphill   and Reason
                                                        Evidence

JOMAMA. All flowers are temporary, whether they fade on the vine
or are crushed underfoot. But their sweetness is eternal. Keep
writing.

(LALIBELA *goes and writes furiously.* MRS.
ROBINSON *hands* JOMAMA *a booklet.*)

JOMAMA. *The Picture-Poetry Book* by Gertrude Parthenia McBrown.

MRS. ROBINSON. Illustrations by Lois Mailou Jones. One of our
great painters.

JOMAMA. How I remember.

MRS. ROBINSON. I earmarked one.

JOMAMA. "Elizabeth Eliza," would you look at that.

MRS. ROBINSON. (*Gesture: go on.*)

JOMAMA.
    "Elizabeth Eliza
    was cracked in a fall,
    but she's a nice doll.

    Elizabeth Eliza

hasn't any hair,
but I don't care.

Elizabeth Eliza
is a little bit lame,
but I love her just the same."

JOMAMA & MRS. ROBINSON.
"Elizabeth Eliza ...
I'll kiss you twice.
Now! Isn't she nice?"

JOMAMA. We can't stop, can we?

MRS. ROBINSON. No, ma'am.
No protection from life.

JOMAMA & MRS. ROBINSON.
But we have to do it
anyway
But we have to choose it
anyway
Have to take the leap,
have to move our feet,
have to make love what we do anyway.

MRS. ROBINSON. Well, I don't know about you but I'm still stepping!

JOMAMA. Don't you start with all that.

MRS. ROBINSON. I don't know about you!

JOMAMA. I can still shake a leg. Now, I may not be able to see where I'm shaking it, but it's gonna be shaking.

MRS. ROBINSON. That's right!

JOMAMA. "Elizabeth Eliza" ain't got nothing on me.

LALIBELA. Miss Jones? I'm ready.

> (LALIBELA *sings, the group accompanies her, chorally.*)

LALIBELA.	ALL.
My heart	*Making my*
My heart's	*Making my honey*
now	*Making my*
honeycomb	*Making my honey*
chambered chambers	*So sweet my*
expanded geometry	*So sweet my honey*
pieced from broken,	*So sweet my*
refracted lines,	*So sweet my honey*
filled with regurgitated	*Come get my*
longing	*Come get my honey*
thickened by the beating	*Come get my*
of wings.	*Come get my honey*
Amber light	
a distillation	
of a wild, untamed field	
of persistent blooms,	
beautiful and brave.	

SWEET T. Damn, *that's* whassup!!!

JOMAMA. You'd better tell it.

LALIBELA.
> *All of this to save the world*
> *All of this to feed the world*
> *All of this to soothe the world*
> *Oh, my honey*
>
> *All of this to save the world*

All of this to feed the world
All of this to soothe the world
Oh, my honey

Nectar gathered
Battles won
Scars unraveled
Notes undone

Cook the sugar
Sweet transform
Brighten eyes
Come on, come on

I can craft it
Sweet delight
I'm gon' share it
Through the night

LALIBELA.   ALL.

   Ooh my honey gonna save   *All of this to save the world*
   the world   *All of this to feed the world*
   Ooh my honey gonna save   *All of this to soothe the*
   the world   *world*
   Ooh my honey gonna save   *Oh, my honey*
   the world
   Oh, my honey

                 (SAINT *turns to* ALEX. *He casts his spell in*
                 real time.)

SAINT.

   I abide with the bee
   just it and me
   sense sensually
   its

boxless
buoyant
brilliant
bodacious
buzzzzzzzzzz

> (*He and* ALEX *kiss passionately.*)

LALIBELA. Oh my god.

JOMAMA. If you couldn't see that coming ...

SWEET T. He's got that nectar now.

MRS. ROBINSON. Hush your mouth. You need a tissue Miss Jones?

JOMAMA. Just beautiful.
Just beautiful.

> (SWEET T *taps* ALEX *and* SAINT *on the shoulder and they stop.*)

SWEET T. You made Miss Jones cry.

> (*A sound like a slow bell, beautiful and a little ominous.*)

ALL.
We are flowers
Born of stardust
We are flowers
Humming, humming
We are flowers
Resonating
We are flowers
Born of love.

JOMAMA. It's time for your number, Sweet T. Inside each seed, a purpose lies coiled. What's your purpose?

ALEX. Continuance through connection.

SAINT. Ecstasy through vulnerability.

LALIBELA. Profusion of wisdom across time.

JOMAMA. Sweet T, you have to choose.

SWEET T. I wish I was bold, not shy.

JOMAMA. You know, not all flowers bloom by day in a gaudy show of things. Some dance under the moon, and their celestial kin—the stars. Quiet—like at the cusp of dawn.

Drinking the indigo deeply
you call yourself into being
as to the slumbering lovers
all of the night birds are singing.

SWEET T. I think …I think I'm not just shy. I'm scared.

JOMAMA. There you are!

SWEET T. What?

JOMAMA. You had to find it for yourself. You should be scared.

SWEET T. Don't say that!

JOMAMA. It's true. You should be because what you will find is wholly unknown.

SWEET T. Are you scared?

JOMAMA. Just between you and me?

SWEET T. (*Nods.*)

JOMAMA. If I wasn't, even just a little bit, I'd know I wasn't putting my heart into it.

SWEET T. I'll just have to be brave. For myself. And for everybody else.

JOMAMA. Well, I think you've found what sort of flower you need to be.

SWEET T.
> *Night flower*
> *only under stars will I bloom*
> *tender flower*
> *rescuing us all from the gloom*
>
> *Night flower*
> *have we been the same all along?*
> *Tender flower*
> *witnessing the new being born*
>
> *Petals*
> *like butterfly wings*
> *unfolding into the blue*
>
> *I ply my transformation*
> *caressed by the glow of the moon*
> *I'll summon us back*
> *past edges of heartbreak*
> *moving from midnight toward dawn*
>
> *Out from our rooms*
> *filled with longing*
> *and memory*
> *moving the circles along*
>
> *Night flower*
> *only under stars shall I bloom*

tender flower
rescuing us all from the gloom

Night flower
have we been the same all along?
tender flower
witnessing the new being born

JOMAMA. Go along, my loves. Make of your lives something luminous.

> (*They begin to exit. Catching* ALEX *and*
> SAINT.)

Now, no hand holding!

ALEX. But…

JOMAMA. Trust me. You'll find each other on the other side.

> (LALIBELA *runs up to* JOMAMA *and hands*
> *her the hand mirror she's been holding.*)

LALIBELA. Imagine me from time to time.

MRS. ROBINSON. Well, we'd better be about it. See you, Sister!

SWEET T. Have we been we before?

JOMAMA. I wonder. Us.

SWEET T. What is that glow?

JOMAMA. Go find out.

Oh, day!
Yonder come day
Oh, day!
Yonder come day
Oh, day!

Yonder come day
Day done broke
Into my soul
Yonder come day
I heard 'em say
Yonder come day
Oh come on day
Yonder come day!

(As the song concludes, flowers burst from the schoolroom windows as if they were in a three dimensional time lapse photo. The light turns honey-colored, then deepens and darkens. JOMAMA *is rendered in profile silhouette; for a brief moment before blackout, she is a hieroglyph.)*

EXIT INSTRUCTIONS

There are shafts of light: green, pink, golden.

As the audience leaves, they encounter a garden where there was none.

In wooden beds are paper flowers. Those closest contain small photographs of the dead. Some sepia-toned, some bright and colored. They stare at us like eyes.

Those nearest the exit contain mirrored centers. We can see glimpses and glimmers of light and our own faces within.

On the wooden shelves (or desk) are books. There are signs on the shelves that read:

SEEDS—TAKE ONE.

Nearest the door, a small homemade altar with devotional candles, feathers, mirrors, honey. A vessel of water sits under an illuminated sign that points toward the outside:

JUSTICE

←—

THIS WAY.

SONG CREDITS

"EXTINCTION SONG"—Music and lyrics by Daniel Alexander Jones

"MEDGAR CAN'T TALK…"—Music and lyrics by Daniel Alexander Jones

"FLOWER SONG"—Lyrics by Jomama Jones; music by Bobby Halvorson and Jomama Jones

"THE MAN WHO TALKS TO FLOWERS"—Music and lyrics by Samora Pinderhughes and Daniel Alexander Jones

"POLLINATOR RAP"—Music and lyrics by Samora Pinderhuges; story by Daniel Alexander Jones

"OPEN"—Lyrics by Jomama Jones; music by Bobby Halvorson and Jomama Jones

"HONEY"—Lyrics by Daniel Alexander Jones; music by Samora Pinderhughes and Daniel Alexander Jones

"STARDUST"—Lyrics by Jomama Jones; music by Bobby Halvorson

"NIGHT FLOWER"—Lyrics by Jomama Jones; music by Bobby Halvorson and Jomama Jones

"YONDER COME DAY"—Traditional, arr. Bessie Jones and the Georgia Sea Island Singers

clayangels

a biomythographic prayer at sunrise

FOREWORD

In the '90s, Austin, Texas is sleepy and casual. We do everything off-line and analog. We stay in touch by landline and send plays in the mail. In the mid-'90s, if you want to be part of any scene you have to get in the room where it's happening, and people do. There is a lively theater scene going on in Austin and people travel in and out all the time to share work.

My friends Annie and Jason and I are running a theater called Frontera. Frontera is about adventure and openness. We operate with no money and a lot of permission. Frontera has an incredible audience who loves to see adventurous, well-written theater that transports them to epic personal places. Our building, the Hyde Park Theatre, is small. The stage is a weird triangle and the audience sits in cramped, hard chairs. There is no backstage. Actors frequently run around the outside of the building during shows to make their next entrance. There is a large homeless camp between our building and the gas station next door.

A lot of barter and gifting lifts our theater and keeps it going.

Lots of cool artists come through Austin, and Frontera, during this time. Many give birth to themselves in this weird little theater. Sharon Bridgforth and root wy'mn are working here. Graham Reynolds plays concerts on Mondays. Luke Savisky projects video installations in the alley. Katie Pearl and Lisa D'Amour make early site-specific art together. Morgan Jenness says Austin is like Paris in the '20s.

In 1994, Daniel Alexander Jones comes to Austin for the first time. Our theater loves a play called *Talking Bones* by Shay Youngblood, and we are looking for the ideal director. I reach out to Lou Bellamy at Penumbra because they have recently produced Shay's play.

Lou leaps on this—"I have the perfect person"—and sends Daniel directly to us.

I am elated when I meet Daniel at the gate. I have no idea who will get off the plane—but there he is! Twenty-four years old, tall, long curly hair, shiny eyes, huge smile, headphones and a walkman. We are enthusiastic and trust each other. Daniel and I are both young souls that people mistake for old souls.

Talking Bones is a big success and Daniel becomes a member of our Frontera family. In 1995, Daniel is on board to direct again. We send each other lots of plays to consider, and Daniel mails me his own script *Earthbirths, Jazz and Raven's Wings*. I don't know Daniel is a writer and his work blows my mind! I have already been working in new plays for ten years, but I have never read a play that combines this kind of orchestral storytelling with a painter's attention to light and shadow, detail and texture. I want to hang it on my wall and live inside it every day, or sit on my porch and listen to it on repeat. I'm not sure how to engage and I love it.

Between 1995-1997, Daniel writes, directs, and performs in a trilogy of plays at Frontera. The plays—*Earthbirths, Jazz and Raven's Wings*, *Blood:Shock:Boogie*, and *clayangels*—are about family, place, internal mapping, and the transformation of one's self amidst pieces of family history. Stories re-mapped and collaged into an epic journey of souls. Daniel is all confidence. It is incredible to see him opening this space around him with his voice and vision! In this window of time and repetition of place, Daniel pretty much delivers himself as an artist and his art changes us. Watching, it looks like Daniel knows exactly how to do this work from the get-go. How to be present in a collaged universe, to choreograph ideas in gestures and music, to juxtapose layers of sight and sound, to compose incredible symphonies of theatrical jazz. In retrospect, I see that he must be learning on his feet, experimenting loudly, letting these vivid portraits fly, remembered into the weird little triangle we all share. This is an event. A revolution. We inhale this moment together, and it is breathtaking.

clayangels, commissioned by Frontera, is the third play in Daniel's trilogy, and a duet with his younger brother Todd. The piece is directed by the doctor herself, Laurie Carlos, with musical direction by Grisha Coleman and dramaturgy by Omi Osun Joni L. Jones. It is breathtaking to witness this group work. Rehearsals are organic—lots of food, storytelling, writing on one's feet. Music is made in the moment. Gesture and rhythm are idiosyncratic to the actor. Set in Springfield, Massachusetts, primarily in the '70s, and composed of sibling rivalry, Egyptian mythology, neighborhood gossip, PBS science shows, and intimate communal truths, *clayangels* routes and re-routes the evolution of two sibling gods, born from the same womb, and riffs on their divergent paths of evolution and transformation. Throughout the piece, Daniel shares the personal biographical history of his parents' individual arrivals in Springfield, their interracial courtship in the '60s, and their family's journey to "the Hill" and beyond. These intimate portraits, built with old bones, ancestral voices, moonlight through glass, and survivor's humor, are among the greatest treasures in Daniel's work.

How do we get to the room we wanted to be in? How do we find each other? Sometimes it takes an epic passage, mapped and re-mapped through time. Other times we throw out old maps, sit a bit, listen to night, and chart a new path together. Daniel traveled to Austin and transformed our community with his voice and vision, and we are lucky to have shared the journey with him.

– Vicky Boone

ALTAR NOTES | the quiet side

Around the time that we were working on *clayangels*, Laurie Carlos said, *listen to this*, then, as she often did, pressed play on a recording that blew my mind. The sure, low hum of upright bass, a swirl of strings and the delicate waterfall of a flute gave way to Morgana King's tremulous, pinpoint-focused voice hovering just in the space between song and sensuous whisper. "When it all comes true, just the way you planned, it's funny but the bells don't ring. It's a quiet thing…" In his elegant book, *The Sovereignty of Quiet: Beyond Resistance in Black Culture*, scholar Kevin Quashie writes:

> "In humanity, quiet is inevitable, essential. It is a simple, beautiful part of what it means to be alive. It is already there, if one is looking to understand it. An aesthetic of quiet is not incompatible with black culture, but to notice and understand it requires a shift in how we read, what we look for, and what we expect, even what we remain open to. It requires paying attention in a different way."[1]

Written in 2012, Quashie's words affirmed the core truth of *clayangels*. I created the piece with my brother Todd and we were joined by director Laurie Carlos and musical artist Grisha Coleman for both the New World Theater developmental process in Amherst and its premiere at Frontera@Hyde Park Theatre in Austin. Todd and I were interested in the truths held by the inward-facing experience of growing up in our family. The parts of growing up in a so-called "interracial" family that were tucked inside the rhythms of the making of the beds, the mopping of the floor, the touch of hand to forehead to check for fever; the refraction of the larger political Dream within lived everyday reality. The things that were hidden from public view.

---

[1] Quashie, Kevin. *The Sovereignty of Quiet: Beyond Resistance in Black Culture*. Rutgers University Press, 2012.

The quiet things. We settled on PBS as a source in part because it was such a fixture of our childhood, from *Sesame Street* and *The Electric Company* to *The French Chef* and my grandmother's allegiance to the *MacNeil/Lehrer Report*. But also because in some way, we realized we were making a frame for folks to gaze into the inner workings of an ecosystem of sorts, our "natural habitat," not unlike one of PBS's nature documentaries, or museum tours.

The dearth of narratives and images of interracial families during my upbringing had little direct impact on us. But, Todd and I and Grisha (who is the product of a Black and Jewish marriage) reflected on the television shows, movies and books we *had* seen. Tom and Helen Willis and their daughter Jenny on *The Jeffersons* were probably the most consistently visible, but their Manhattan high-rise sophistication bore little resemblance to the world I knew directly in Todd's and my working-class New England city, or the real-life, workaday Manhattan where Grisha grew up. When stories of interracial relationships appeared, they were two-dimensional and melodramatic. The white partners in interracial relationships were most often presented as culture vampires fetishizing their Black partners while appropriating fashion, slang, and movement. The Black partners, when women, were most often portrayed as bitter and scarred by alienation from Black folks, and when men, portrayed in a frenzy of desire for white women and disgust for Black women, as in *Jungle Fever*. Any "mixed" progeny almost always were portrayed as thrashing violently through full-blown, self-hating identity crises. And you'd best believe that somebody was dying at the end of any of these cautionary tales: parent, child, white, Black—somebody. None of the stories had positive outcomes; rather, most had a funeral scene where one of the living is overcome by regrets and throws themself on the coffin. None contained an iota of truth from the lived-side of our family's experiences, nor from the experiences of any of the other interracial families I met over the years. They reinscribed the sentiment my parents often heard when they were engaged. *It's fine for you to play at this, but what about the children?* The idea being that interracial love will never *really-really, for-real-for-real* be acceptable, and that the children, for lack of a defineable identity, "caught between two opposing worlds," will be doomed to a life of continuous non-belonging.

What was true in real life were the specific ways others' stories about who we were would press against our skins when we left the confines of our house. Without realizing it most times, I would loudly exhale when we walked back into the house. However subconscious and however subtle, meeting the overly curious or downright hostile gazes, feeling the sticky film of projections, and resisting the narrativizing took a toll. Though our neighborhood and surrounding community was by and large accepting, there were some who absolutely were not. And let's not get it twisted, it wasn't just white folks who were disapproving, some of us were, too. (Miss Lillian and Miss Vivian in *clayangels* embody those folk). Growing up in a Black cultural context, it seemed for most folks, especially our peers, that our "mixedness" was simply biographical information, as in: *That's your Mom and that's your Dad?* Yeah. *Cool, get your skates.* It felt to us of no more significance than our height or whether or not we could run fast. And, yes, it could be weaponized in a fight but was no more likely to be hurled in a verbal battle than your height or whether you could run fast. It was a descriptor not a determinant. Whereas within white spaces, it took on great significance and had reflexive repercussions as we learned the value placed on proximity to whiteness in all things. Because I knew better and felt no pull toward whiteness, I became more confusing to the system—I wasn't thrashing around *tragic mulatto*-style. I abided on the inside, the seam side, the quiet side. Quashie notes:

> "Quiet...is a metaphor for the full range of one's inner life—one's desires, ambitions, hungers, vulnerabilities, fears. The inner life is not apolitical or without social value, but neither

is it determined entirely by publicness. In fact, the interior—dynamic and ravishing—is a stay against the dominance of the social world; it has its own sovereignty. It is hard to see, even harder to describe, but no less potent in its ineffability. Quiet."

To work from and toward that quiet as a vital, pulsing, and consequential site is to risk illegibility in a cultural context that recognizes Blackness only in the aforementioned ways. The luminous films of Charles Burnett, Julie Dash, and Haile Gerima were oases for me in part because of their trust in interiority. When someone questions the Blackness of my work, I often smile because I've grown familiar with the fact that in the United States we rarely see the inside, the seam side, the quiet side of Black life, let alone Black Queer life, or a Blackness that can hold an interracial family in its self-conception. This despite the fact of interracial love in many folks' actual families, extended if not immediate. Consequently, the private, quotidian truths of interracial families shaped by the electric hopes of the Civil Rights Era and and dashed dreams of the Reagan Revolution were not only illegible but unimaginable. Our stories were inscrutable *ancientfuture* relics.

My parents were readers and contemplative souls. Both my brother and I inherited their propensity to get lost in books. I studied Ancient Egypt and Black American arts since I could read; Todd immersed himself in Native American history and Ancient Chinese culture. When we started creating the piece, he'd talked to me about the terracotta army of Qin Shi Huang. I did a deep research dive into the meticulous artistry in funerary preparations in the ancient world. I asked Kimberlee Koym to make us a tomb. We talked about the objects in tombs as ciphers: simultaneously sources of and repositories for story. Todd and his homeboy, Porn Siphanoum, who designed the artwork for *clayangels*, talked to me about the centrality of the cypher in hip hop and how that cypher exists, always, in time and space, and it is activated by the gathering of deejay, dancers, rhymers, and audience/community members who come together in a circle—the circle and those in the circle are also called the cypher. My family felt like a cypher, conjuring our own reality, which somehow always existed; so too our community. Todd and I and Laurie and Grisha and Kimberlee and all the folks involved in making and witnessing the piece were yet another cypher. All of us touching histories, epic and intimate, revealing and changing meanings with each touch. Poet Robert Hayden, in his poem "american journal," wrote:

> america   as much a problem in metaphysics as
> it is a nation earthly entity an iota in our
> galaxy   an organism that changes even as i
> examine it   fact and fantasy never twice the
> same   so many variables

I often smile recalling my trip to Cairo with Kaneza Schaal in 2017, where we visited the Egyptian Museum. Many of the funerary objects I had researched for *clayangels* were there before me in three dimensions. We saw thousands of sculptures, most carved in one of a handful of formal stances. Ancient Greek sculpture is heralded as the innovative leap for its lifelike depictions of the body in motion. In art history classes, Greek statues are often juxtaposed with Ancient Egyptian sculpture, the latter minimized for its rigidity and the purported lack of distinction between figures. Such master narratives flatten and distort vision. And they sever our collective connection to the complexities, multiplicities, and nuances of history.

I recall a PBS docuseries released a couple years after *clayangels*. *An American Love Story* chronicled the lives of an interracial family, Black dad, white mom, and there were moments where I could see echoes of the way it felt in our house. Those moments were all tiny, quotidian things. The rise of an eyebrow. Hands resting in laps. Moments when the family members' eyes lingered upon one another's faces, or out the window. Moments when they were caught in thought. These moments affirmed the innate power of interiority to manifest a broad and vital "now" through an imposed narrative, like insistent roots pressing through concrete. In Cairo, I stood in front of the massive legs, huge hands, long torso, and cryptic gaze of the one statue I'd longed my whole life to see. I locked eyes with the Pharaoh Akhenaten and thought as I always do, oh, they don't remember the inside, the seam side. The quiet side.

– DAJ

clayangels
Premiered at Frontera@Hyde Park Theatre
Austin, TX
July 1997

Songs by Daniel Alexander Jones, Todd Christopher Jones, and
    Grisha Coleman
Directed by Laurie Carlos
Additional original music and musical direction by Grisha Coleman
Dramaturgy by Dr. Joni Jones
Installation by Kimberlee Koym
Costumes by Andrea Lauer
Sound by Kevin Freedman

FEATURING:
Daniel Alexander Jones
Todd Christopher Jones

Players be:

DANIEL, the fractured dog-child, and
TODD, the son of clay and will—

> brothers who touch fragments and become the
> others.

Settings be:

The *doorway* to an underground chamber which is a cracked wall
lined with pictures and shapes, yawning;

The *tomb* which is a burrowed space in their minds' eye. Dry light
fingers through the space, angled darkness in negative, memory cracks
and shifts under bare feet—blinding hot;

The *river* which is the passage to abyssal water, begging transformation through soft light. Cerulean breath licks the edge.

OSIRIS CHANT

(Sung from offstage.)

Come, come, come.
Your flesh your thought your spirit.
Come, come, come.
Your every breath in freedom.
Come, come, come.
Come under to the place where I am that you may know your
brother.

(While initiating ritual gestural language, DANIEL *and* TODD *enter. They sing "Imagine," a prayer.)*

IMAGINE

DANIEL.
Imagine. Imagine.

TODD.
What if?
What if?
What if?
What if?

DANIEL.
Imagine. Imagine.

TODD.
What would happen?

What would happen
if I commanded this clapping of thunder?
It's a question I ask to make you wonder,
as I wonder
can a man be more than a man?
Can a woman be more than a woman?

DANIEL.

Imagine. Imagine.

TODD.

The demons? They've stalked, leading you to walk
into traps called identity.
Me? I pray to be
superhuman.
I'm assuming you remember days
when we would masquerade.
Life is but a play in five acts.
Smell, taste, sight, touch, and sound contact.
But beyond that
we must stop our reactions
to become figures of action.
That's why I'm asking
what if?
What if?
What if?

DANIEL. My name is Daniel Jones.

TODD. My name is Todd Jones.

DANIEL. We were born and raised in Springfield, Massachusetts.

TODD. Our mother's name is Georgina Leslie Jones.

DANIEL. Our father's name is Arthur Leroy Jones.

DANIEL & TODD. We breathed the same air.
　　　We played the same games.
　　　We looked in the same mirrors.
　　　Together we watched the sun...
　　　set.

TODD. Set. Genesis.

DANIEL. Before all that is was the abyss.

TODD. The abyssal water thought of itself and came to know itself as rock, fire, air, and sea.

DANIEL. Geb, earth father, and Nut, sky mother, were born from these elements.

TODD. Geb and Nut had four children. Isis, Osiris, Set, and Nephthys.

DANIEL. Osiris ruled the kingdom and Set grew jealous.

TODD. He killed Osiris and hacked him into fourteen pieces, feeding his phallus to the crocodile. Crocodile snacks.

DANIEL. Isis searched, and gathered all the pieces, remembering him, and making a phallus from clay.

TODD. She called upon Anubis, guardian of the dead, and together they resurrected him.

DANIEL. Osiris rose from the dead and he and Isis were reunited and it felt so good.

TODD. They created a son, Horus, who vowed to avenge his father's murder.

DANIEL. Osiris descended into the underworld, Anubis at his side, and became the judge of the dead.

TODD. Horus battled Set—striving to defeat him, from sunrise to sunset, sunset to sunrise. The battle continues without end.

DANIEL. The mouth of the underworld opens.

> (*Over the course of the following voice-over,* DANIEL *and* TODD *initiate circles and pushes, culminating in a stare-down.*)

TRANSISTOR RADIO/DR. INGO SCHLAPP. What we see
on a worldwide scale
is a general trend for amphibians to decline.
We're losing species...
like whole species
are uh—lost.
Totally, unfortunately.
And we're also losing populations in...in most species that...
that have been looked at
intensively.
So why's that?
There is a number of reasons for that.
Annnd none of these reasons is probably universal.
None of those probably applies to all species at any time.
But just to name a few...
one thing that has known negative effects is acid rain,
for example.
That's responsible...
That's probably responsible for, um, a lot of damage in individuals.
It's damaging the tadpoles or the eggs.
Or, eggs are more...more prone to fungus infections.
Things like that.
So relatively not...not really easy to find effects
but they are often related to some environmental cue.
Then there is...

um...
and that's so...
most of these things have
a component of human behavior,
and we can work on that.
So...
there are more factors of course
more than I can name here—
increased UV light
intensity of ozone depletion—
one other thing is
that...that has a very direct component of human behavior
is habitat destruction.
And I think that...that accounts for most of the species losses.
Just to give you a very simple example if you look again
at rainforest species like in...in the new tropics...
American tropics...
Africa...
wherever...
go to Madagascar...
anywhere,
the more trees you cut down,
the more habitat you destroy,
the more species you lose.
And among those species of course you lose amphibians.
We may be losing species that we didn't even know about.
So we're losing something that we hadn't yet recognized
which to me is really painful.
Personally I don't expect this to shift back.
Um...I think we're, we're working on...
conservation biologists are trying to work on containing some
of these effects.
Basically you have to be very clear about this:

whenever a species is lost
it's gone
forever.
No way to get it back.
Absolutely no way.
This is the product of a very long evolutionary process
and once it's perished
it's gone
forever.

> (TODD *and* DANIEL *begin speaking the PBS*
> *text along with the radio.*)

That's also true for populations.
Once you lose a population
even if some specific individuals of the same species
recolonize an area where you have lost a population
still that particular population with all of the traits
it had
is lost.
Forever.
It's gone.

PBS

TODD. Shut that off.

DANIEL. No.

TODD. I'm tired of hearing that shit.

DANIEL. I don't care.

TODD. I'm serious, man, shut if off.

DANIEL. No.

TODD. I'll do it myself.

DANIEL. Don't you do that.

TODD. I'll do what I want to do.

> (TODD *begins poking* DANIEL *in the chest.* DANIEL *curls in to protect himself, kind of poorly.*)

DANIEL. Stop that.

TODD. Uh-uh.

DANIEL. Don't mock me. I hate it when you do that. "Uh-uh…"

TODD. Oh, I hate it when you do that…

DANIEL. Turn it back on.

> (TODD *turns it on, reluctantly. They begin a series of dynamic, argumentative crosses.*)

DANIEL. You just hate anything having to do with educational programming. PBS?

TODD. That's not true. I grew up on PBS just like you and I love documentaries. You just have no taste in programming. You're always watching bad nature shows or crafts shows or shows on the Holocaust.

DANIEL. I like history, okay?

TODD. But you watch the same thing over and over and over and over. It gets really played. You've listened to this how many times before?

DANIEL. Three.

TODD. There, that proves my point. What could you possibly gain from hearing this three times?

DANIEL. Phylogeny!

PHYLOGENY

> (*During the following voiceover text,* DANIEL *and* TODD *curl into a pietà position.* DANIEL *examines* TODD's *body, curious, familiar.*)

TRANSISTOR RADIO/DR. INGO SCHLAPP. If you divide the animal kingdom into some major parts
like invertebrates and vertebrates,
which is animals having a spine like we do,
then you'll place frogs somewhere between ...
well, they are the first vertebrates that left the sea.
In terms of phylogeny
this is the first group that probably made the transition from water to land
which was a major step in evolution.
And this is neatly repeated in their individual life cycle.
Most frogs have aquatic tadpoles
that then metamorph
into adults.
It's often so that you have aquatic tadpoles.
It doesn't have to be that way,
but the typical frog that you and I would know
really makes this transition
within his or her individual life.
The metamorphosis

is a major reorganization of certain organs.
If you think of an aquatic tadpole it has to have certain
organs certain adaptations to live in the water
for example
gills
to breathe in water
and those have to be changed into lungs to breathe on land.
The skin's changed.
They lose their tail…
well, they don't lose it they kind of um reabsorb it and then somehow
legs appear.
And it's really neat to see that in an individual.
So basically what tadpoles do is they transform a lot of their tissue.
It's totally rearranged
and basically transformed into something totally new.

160

DANIEL. Miss Vivian

TODD. Miss Lillian

> (TODD *and* DANIEL *transform into* MISS
> LILLIAN *and* MISS VIVIAN. *Game.*)

MISS LILLIAN & MISS VIVIAN. We like simple things.

TODD AS MISS LILLIAN. Preserved peaches.

DANIEL AS MISS VIVIAN. Vanilla ice cream.

MISS LILLIAN & MISS VIVIAN. Shortbread cookies.

MISS LILLIAN. Fine entertainers. Lena Horne.

MISS VIVIAN. Lillian always has borne a strong resemblance to Lena Horne, minus the flaws in Lena's figure.

MISS LILLIAN. You're too kind.

MISS VIVIAN. We're quiet people.

MISS LILLIAN. Good people.

MISS VIVIAN. We do have high expectations.

MISS LILLIAN. High standards.

MISS VIVIAN. We've been on this street since nineteen forty-five. At one fifty-eight.

MISS LILLIAN. And one sixty-two. Vivian's husband worked in the die-cutting factory.

MISS VIVIAN. And Lillian's husband maintained his own building.

MISS LILLIAN. We're both maiden Freedmen from North Carolina.

MISS VIVIAN. We've been on either side of one sixty long enough to see the changes. It can be difficult, having standards.

MISS LILLIAN. Neither of them came from much.

MISS VIVIAN. Sister.

MISS LILLIAN. It has to be said. To put it all in context.

MISS VIVIAN. The wife had opportunity, her father was a musician. And Scottish.

MISS LILLIAN. Her mother, the dear, embodied the social graces.

MISS VIVIAN. Old Massachusetts family. I wouldn't bear to think of what crossed her mind when that Jones boy began to come around.

MISS LILLIAN. It's not that those…arrangements can't work.

MISS VIVIAN. Why, when we first came to the Hill there was another family *like that* on the next block up.

MISS LILLIAN. Not our block.

MISS VIVIAN. And they were no bother. Kept to themselves.

MISS LILLIAN. Didn't make a show of it. And their little girls were just as mannered.

MISS LILLIAN & MISS VIVIAN. But one sixty.

MISS VIVIAN. It was like a revolving door.

MISS LILLIAN. All those *different* folks. All "peace and free."

MISS VIVIAN. Right next door.

MISS LILLIAN. When it comes down to it, in an arrangement like that it is always the children who suffer.

MISS VIVIAN. Children.

MISS LILLIAN. You can take the "N"-word out of the ghetto, but you can't take the ghetto out of the "N"-word.

MISS VIVIAN. It's going to show up somewhere. In the children.

MISS LILLIAN. The wife was nice enough. Although we had a word for young white ladies who fancied colored men.

MISS VIVIAN. Lillian.

MISS LILLIAN. She didn't know about that Jones family.

MISS LILLIAN & MISS VIVIAN. We knew.

> (DANIEL *and* TODD *return to pietà position.*)

DANIEL. Well in the first place I had asked for a brother and then around my birthday Mom and Dad said that I was going to get one and they had found out for sure it was coming. So they told me and I got ready for it and everything, cuz you have to get ready. And then it was supposed to come but they said the um, stork was um, it was late but I knew he just didn't want to come out yet cuz I had talked to him and so the doctor said we're gonna go in there and make him come out so Mom and I we took a picture in the backyard right near the flowers. And she went in to the hospital and we still had school because we had had all the snow days but all we had to do practically was color and start times tables and then it was Flag Day and Mrs. Finn had us coloring some flags and I had already told Shannon and Porfirio that I was going to get a brother and Porfirio said something but he was Puerto Rican and me and Shannon were teaching him English but he still didn't make sense sometimes and Shannon asked was the baby gonna look like me cuz I was half and half and she didn't know which half, and you know the eyes, and I said I didn't know, and I wasn't gonna tell them anyway and then the principal came in and started talking to Mrs. Finn so I knew it was time and he came over and told me my father was in the hall and I gave Mrs. Finn my flag and said I had to go! And my father said I had a baby brother and the principal shook my hand. And we went to the hospital and went in but when we got there the lady said I couldn't go in there all the way cuz visiting hours were over and I didn't get to see my mom or my brother. But they made—my mom called and she asked what should they name him from two choices Todd or Christopher? And I said easy—Christopher—cuz Todd sounded stupid and Christopher was his true name and anyway they named him Todd.

TODD. My first name is Todd. Publicly spelled with two *d's*. Truly with one. Its meaning is death, in German. I am sure to live up to my name. Death. *(Rhymes) I wake up every morning to the name of death. I fear nothing but myself and the life I left, may I resurrect.* My last name is Jones. Jones is what some call a slave name. From my understanding the former slaves took their names in freedom. As far as I am concerned, Jones means freedom. Freedom. My name, my name is Death Freedom. It is my pleasure to meet you.

DANIEL. *(Aside)* Your name isn't Todd.

> (DANIEL *begins a series of gestures that become phrases that loop and repeat as* TODD *tells this story. New gestures are born from details of the story. They are not illustrative, but rather essential responses to the story. At its conclusion he repeats the whole composition in the voice of* ISIS.*)*

TODD. My father asked my grandmother for my mother's hand in marriage out on that beach. I was on the other side.
I had this dream, I was on the other side,
the other side of the lake, looking across to that beach.
We went fishing there, me and my father. Sometimes with my brother.
Most of the time it was just me and him.
So I had this dream, it was me and this girl,
you know how girls are always sneaking up in dreams,
we were on the other side of this lake, looking to the beach,
I said
damn I got to get over there.

I didn't know why, but I had to go.
So I took a step out on the water.
Underneath my footsteps the water froze.
It can happen, walking on water.
Step by step, frozen water
so I got to the other side, and the girl she floated over in a blue bubble,
looked like her aura just scooped her up, and I moved across the beach
to the beginning of the woods, which are next to the beach.
Tall grass, plants, weeds, bushes decorated the gate of the forest—I was about to push my way through when I saw him—
I saw the wolf.
This beautiful grey wolf, his coat reflecting the moon,
slipping in and out of darkness, weaving in and out of trees.
Damn! Wait till I tell my mother I saw a wolf, she'll love it.
So I'm all excited, but then—
then the wolf looks behind himself—sort of nods, gives some signal,
and then I see
this huge figure, another wolf, but not quite, moving along, moving along.
I look closer—it had this
long black mane, these huge shoulders, its body more catlike than canine, but I knew it was a wolf,
and once a man. Then it turned, and looked at me…everything stopped. Its eyes looked right through me, and they glowed blue electric light. It was me. I turned to the girl and told her I had to follow. Then I walked into the woods following its lead.

DANIEL AS ISIS. (*Intoned*)
I and I am I.
Be river
be ocean

be sea.
I and I am I.
Light cast by the moon
to pull you from yourself
into yourself,
pull through myself
through water to land from land to water again.
May fortune gaze upon your
new penny skin
freshly died, freshly born.
You bear the mark
under my light.
Change
through the night,
change
through the night,
change
to
radiating sun,
radiating son.
I will meet you by the riverside
where the sun
falls down.

(DANIEL *howls like a wolf.*)

VITAMIN T

TODD. Set and Anubis.

TODD AS SET. The Earth is a child in God's womb. Such a quaint and
dramatic statement. Full of idealism, based upon the realism

seen by genius. But death is coming. Even if it was not meant to be feared. I have fallen. Fallen astray. Away from the path which does not exist. I can remember little of what brought me to this hell. I know that it surrounds me. Suffocates me. Why? I remember little.

DANIEL AS ANUBIS. Huh? Huh? Huh?

SET. Hello.

ANUBIS. What?

SET. Hello. It's well past rising time.

ANUBIS. It is? Yes, of course it is. Of course. I'm sorry.

SET. No need.

ANUBIS. No. No. This has been happening a lot.

SET. It has.

ANUBIS. I know. It has been upsetting.

SET. Truly.

ANUBIS. I think maybe malnourishment.

SET. You haven't enough to eat?

ANUBIS. No, no, not at all, not at all. I am not in any way saying that. I am simply saying that I haven't been eating as well as I should have of the food you provide, which is, I must say, an ample amount—I could have sworn I heard the thunder, didn't you feel everything shaking?

SET. The alarm clock.

ANUBIS. Certainly. But, it felt like something more, something just way-out big!

SET. No.

ANUBIS. I think I'm hallucinating. Got to be the food thing. I look at myself and see: sluggish, slow to rise, borderline lethargic. I really ought to look into vitamins. Vitamin B. Vitamin D.

SET. Tea.

ANUBIS. Vitamin T? Is that for the liver? I just know my liver is caving in. I can just feel it caving.

SET. I'd like to have tea.

ANUBIS. WHOA! *You* want to ...look at me! Selfish? Self-centered, self-self ...goddamn! When will I get it right?

SET. Just bring the tea.

ANUBIS. At once. Pick yourself up. Pull yourself together. Cream?

SET. Light and sweet. Always light and sweet.
What's that in your pocket?
A book?
A book of plants and flowers?
Reptiles, maybe?

ANUBIS. Frogs.
A frog.
Such a thing could certainly move in the water
and make sounds and eat things and it would have to have the
sun ...it changes, you know?

SET. Sing for me.

ANUBIS. The frog has ...cells that ...protoplasm—energetic, gelatinous, pulsing, contained by a membrane ...eggs ...

SET. What else did you learn today?

ANUBIS. The beautiful sorrow song of the Negro.

SET. Show me. Entertain me. Inform me, move my spirit.

ANUBIS.

> *One of these mornings*
> *It won't be long*
> *You'll look for me and*
> *I'll be gone*
> *Yes, one of these mornings*
> *'Bout twelve o'clock*
> *This old world*
> *Goin' to reel and rock*
> *Death is goin' to lay*
> *His cold, icy hands on me, Lord*
> *On me*
> *Death is goin' to lay*
> *His cold, icy hands on me!*

> (*Transformation into* MISS LILLIAN *and* MISS VIVIAN.)

MISS LILLIAN & MISS VIVIAN. We value education.

DANIEL AS MISS VIVIAN. Learning a trade.

TODD AS MISS LILLIAN. All our great leaders valued education.

MISS LILLIAN & MISS VIVIAN. Booker T. Washington. Our daddy shook his hand.

MISS VIVIAN. Five fingers on the same hand …and a toothbrush in every mouth.

MISS LILLIAN. Our great leaders understood the nature of things.

MISS VIVIAN. Shouting, violence, agitation really don't lead anywhere.

MISS LILLIAN. If you don't like it you can always move and drop
your bucket somewhere else.

MISS VIVIAN. You see what that other falderal brings.

MISS LILLIAN. Confusion.

MISS VIVIAN. Confusion.

MISS LILLIAN. Confusion.

TRANSISTOR RADIO/MALCOLM X. It isn't something that made me lose
confidence in what I'm doing because my wife understands.
And I have children from this size on down and even in their
young age they understand. I think they would rather have a
father or a brother or whatever the situation may be who will
stand in the face of any kind of reaction from narrow-minded
people rather than compromise and have to grow up in shame
and disgrace...[2]

TODD. Uncle Gus.

(TODD *and* DANIEL *embody* GUSSIE JONES.)

GUSSIE JONES. I was there the day he died.
He was giving these weekly talks at uh...the Audubon Ballroom
which is right across from Presbyterian Hospital.
He had been there a week before and two weeks prior
and I'd seen those two
and I wanted to make damn sure I went down to this one, you
know?
So, I got there and we sit down
and they walk up on top of the rostrum on top of the stage
and we're just sitting there,
everybody's sitting in their seats,

---

2   Malcolm X, "Speech at Ford Auditorium," 1965.

and all of a sudden
the commotion
just jumps up quick
and they shot up the place,
you know?
People started jumping and moving fast, you know?
Like we—and running like crazy!
I didn't know what the hell was going on.
I...and I was trying to get up, get up to the front of the crowd.
Found out, found out he had gotten shot.
And that was it.
The crowd got a hold of one guy.
Then they talked about...
they're still saying...two people got away.
To this day they're saying two people got away.

TRANSISTOR RADIO/DR. CONSTANCE BERKLEY. Let me start off by
        saying that the serial assassination of all of those figures
        had the psychic trauma of an atomic bomb explosion in our midst.
        As you were asking the question I got a vision of the explosion
        and the
        scattering of energy,
        the dispersion,
        the instantaneous dispersion
        of the top energy,
        but then the slow destruction
        and dispersion and
        reshaping, reforming—
        mal-forming by the way—
        malformation of the energies that were left there.
        If I were writing something I would use that as the center in
        this piece, as the center somewhere.
        And then you have things building up to that and after that
        it's like the tornado.

The devastation you see there.
The floods.
Where do people begin to clean up?
That's what happened.
That's what happened.

> (TODD *rhymes.* DANIEL *hums a folk song as a countermelody underneath the following piece.*)

TODD.

> *I am the radiating sun*
> *I am the radiating sun, gladiating one*
> *I am the radiating sun*
> *I am the radiating sun, gladiating one*
> *I am the radiating sun, gladiating one against many*
> *I am the radiating sun, gladiating one against many*
> *Devilish men, embellished in sin*
> *I am the radiating sun, gladiating one against many*
> *The twin angel fallen, stalking myself*
> *For the self is the devil, the devil is the self*

DANIEL. The last day of school was four days after you were born. I went in that morning and threw up all over my second grade class. They sent me to the nurse.

TODD. So you threw up on the last day of school. Boo-hoo. What's your point?

DANIEL. Dad took me to Dr. Shuman, there were blood tests, they didn't know what was wrong, and since you were about to come home, well, they couldn't have you come home to a house full of germs so they sent me off with Bunny to her house. I was there for several weeks. I had a fever practically all the time. No medicine seemed to work. I was placated with a book on

King Kong and a plastic model of the Empire State Building. Eventually, they let me come home, but they kept me away from you for almost two months. I was still sick.

(*Long-ass pause.*)

They were giving me erythromycin, that's a substitute for penicillin, because Mom is allergic to penicillin, so they couldn't give it to me, right, cuz you know, stuff passes down. But Dad said he slipped me penicillin anyway. I could have died.

TODD. Did you get better?

DANIEL. I got better straight away. Two weeks before the end of summer vacation. They said I had scarlet fever.

TODD. Scarlet fever. Do you remember in high school when you had chicken pox?

DANIEL. How could I forget. Belisa gave them to me, she was playing Eliza, remember, when I was in *My Fair Lady*. They were too cheap to buy another makeup sponge and they just ground the contagions into my face. This scar ...

TODD. Man, memory is ill. Because I had my fever on the last day of school. You gave me the chicken pox. I knew I was going to get them from you when you got them. And I was mad for a long time, but then I resigned myself to the fact that I was going to have them and if you had suffered through it, I could. We were brothers. Such things are bound to happen in a family.

(*Pause.* DANIEL *walks away.*)

MOONWALK

TODD AS SET. You were asleep, dreaming. What were you dreaming?

DANIEL AS ANUBIS. About these two guys. Talking. I think they were brothers.

SET. Your brother?

ANUBIS. I don't know.

SET. When did you see him last?

ANUBIS. Some time ago. Through the window.

SET. How would I know him?

ANUBIS. Oh, you'd know. His teeth are sharp and pointy and he moves smooth as the moonlight. Moonwalk. He would moonwalk all around the house in full circles. I gave him a *Thriller* jacket when he was seven. Moved just like Michael Jackson. He outgrew it but he can still move just so. So you'd know him that way.

SET. Where is your brother?

ANUBIS. In the shadows of buildings. In the shadows of stray thoughts. He walks nameless among the nameless.

SET. How will you know him, nameless?

ANUBIS. (*Sniffs*) I'll know him by his smell.

SET. Nameless, nameless, book of names…could it be Williams?

ANUBIS. By his smell.

SET. Surely Johnson?

ANUBIS. By his smell.

SET. Well…I'll be…Jackson? Brown?

ANUBIS. By his smell.

SET. Jones?

(ANUBIS is still.)

SET. Yes, of course, Jones. Genesis Jones…start.

GENESIS JONES

DANIEL & TODD. Black slaves named Jones lived in South Carolina. They were emancipated by Abraham the Great and moved onto rich and challenging lives gainfully employed as sharecroppers, railroad men, and some, mostly those with Injun blood, opened their own businesses. Well, among every score of colored there's got to be one uppity nigger and one of those in our line started some ruckus or other with the whitefolk and they strung him up sure enough and came after the other "mens."

DANIEL. Well, those colored folk ran out of town on the spot, loads of them, heading north to cities where they dropped their carpet bags and raised some Canaan! Cities like Chicago, Philadelphia, Springfield, and Newark, where they became negroes and worked in factories, or some of the ladies, in homes. They continued on in their part of town, mingling with poor Poles, Italians, and other negroes with other names who, in Springfield, lived in the North End.

TODD. They lived in apartments and rickety houses with cold water and vermin and the little boys' feet stuck to the floor in wintertime it was so cold. They also came into chance contact with refined negro people who were descended from free Blacks, were from North Carolina, or were just generally light-skinned. These refined negroes attempted—through charitable actions like yard work, opportunities, and chaperoned socials where etiquette might be instructed—to make some difference for the rough country negroes who were filling up the streetcars. Serious business.

DANIEL. One of these young, countrified Joneses was invited to monthly teas with the Little Men's Club, up on the hill, where the whites and society colored lived, organized by a North Carolinian Jones, no relation, where he learned social graces and proper dance steps. As he grew into an upstanding young negro, his exposure to such higher culture and cultivated interest in reading and thinking gave him a sense of responsibility to his community.

TODD. He embarked upon a career of service to the people in his neighborhood, just as the American government bolstered its cities' infrastructure with a new set of highways, up...where we gonna put 'em?...well how about through the Black neighbor-hoods? Need to clean up those parts anyway and so, the poor Springfield North End negroes scattered in many directions, some climbing right up that old hill.

DANIEL. So the Jones boy and his brothers went up the hill and that one boy began to associate with a certain lady a certain white lady that worked in an adjoining service agency and so they took a liking and it was the sixties and all and sure enough the negro asked the lady for her hand in marriage, etiquette, and they got married with all kinds of neg-Blacks and whites talking to each other and sitting eating at the reception and all that and they moved into a house on the hill right next to the lady named Jones who had taught that same little boy how to hold a napkin,

TODD. ...and she near 'bout died.

DANIEL. But they were friendly nonetheless and there were other Blacks, preachers even, and Italians and old nondenominational white people, and Puerto Ricans and Jamaicans and Cape Verdians and all that all up and down the street and bang they made a baby and put it out there in the street anyway and it played with all those other people's babies and got all kinds of ideas and was rebellious from kindergarten and well the story goes on from there just a keepin' up with the Joneses by day and by night...

(*Howl of wolf, beginning of wolf-chant.*)

DANIEL. Did you hear that?

SET. Absolutely not.

TODD & DANIEL. Var-ulf. Wargus. Waw-kalak. Lupo mannaro. Loup-garou. Apollo Lycaeus. Anubis. Werewolf. Where? Where? Where?

(*Transformation into* MISS LILLIAN *and* MISS VIVIAN.)

MISS LILLIAN & MISS VIVIAN. We did Hallowe'en together.

DANIEL AS MISS VIVIAN. We love children.

TODD AS MISS LILLIAN. Little children.

MISS VIVIAN. Mischievous (*miss-chee-vee-ous*).

MISS LILLIAN. Clever.

MISS VIVIAN. Cute as buttons.

MISS LILLIAN. Vivian's favorite holiday was always Hallowe'en.

MISS VIVIAN. Spooky little ghosts and goblins all up and down the street.

MISS LILLIAN. We'd play trick or treat.

MISS VIVIAN. Mostly treats.

MISS LILLIAN. Cookies.

MISS LILLIAN & MISS VIVIAN. Butterscotch candies.

MISS VIVIAN. Hershey's chocolate kisses.

MISS LILLIAN. We'd open our doors and those little gremlins would say, "Trick or treat?"

MISS VIVIAN. "Trick or treat? Trick or treat?"

MISS LILLIAN. And I'd say, "Oh, look it's a passel of ghouls, Vivian, I'm so scared!"

MISS VIVIAN. Some of the little children couldn't afford costumes but we played right along as though they could. No sense in embarrassing.

MISS LILLIAN. Of course that's how you began to see something wasn't quite all together with the boys next door.

MISS VIVIAN. We'll never forget opening the door expecting a dandy mouse or a sunflower Sue and seeing a poor crippled child wrapped head to toe in bandages limping with the last of its energy to the door and sniffling at the stoop.

MISS LILLIAN. We couldn't believe it—didn't know whether to cry or holler. It reached out its pitiful hand and I didn't know what to do.

MISS VIVIAN. It didn't have a mouth. How could it be capable of chewing candies?
I looked out to see if there was someone accompanying this crippled child.

MISS LILLIAN. I just shouted out, "Whose child is this?! Who let this poor broken child climb up these steps to get candy?!"

MISS VIVIAN. We were outraged.
And up the walk came those Joneses.

MISS LILLIAN. They said that was their boy and that he really believed he was a ...*muddy.*
What did they call that Vivian?

MISS VIVIAN. Mummy.

MISS LILLIAN. Mummy.
They said that's how those things were done up and all with real bandages.

MISS VIVIAN. We said there were certain things one didn't joke about and crippled children was one.

MISS LILLIAN. No candy for that child.

MISS VIVIAN. They should have asked for money to buy that child a proper costume.

MISS LILLIAN. And there are limits to pretend.
Of course he turned out to be an actor.
A performer.

MISS VIVIAN. We love performers.

MISS LILLIAN & MISS VIVIAN. (*A shared knowing look*) Harry Belafonte.

MISS VIVIAN. Well, little Danny was fair of face.

MISS LILLIAN. And light of step.

MISS VIVIAN. *Lillian.*

MISS LILLIAN. *Well*, the father wasn't at home as much as he should have been. I did the best I could to make some impact on the father since his own youth, to teach manners and decorum, but all those Jones boys cared about was stealing glances at my DeeDee's ankles during tea.

MISS VIVIAN. The other little one next door.

MISS LILLIAN. Todd.

MISS VIVIAN. He spent a lot of time on the porch with my husband, Allyn. That's probably what kept him from going off too far.

MISS LILLIAN. Well I don't know about that. I do recall catching him in my bushes dressed up like a wolf-man and it wasn't even near Hallowe'en.

MISS VIVIAN. The "N"-word will rear its ugly head.

MISS LILLIAN. Better an "N"-word than an "F"-word.

TODD. Set. *Set.*

DANIEL. Set.

TODD. I was thinking about taking that name. I was right. Remember when I talked to you about Set?

DANIEL. Definitely.

TODD. The Egyptians actually had temples for Set. He wasn't seen altogether as a devilish god, he was the deliverer of death to life, and worshipped as such. Man I have never been so scared.

I found this old copy of *The Book of the Dead* and pronounced his name out loud. His real name, not the anglicized version. It's true, you call a name and the spirit will follow. Man I went through that book reciting everybody else's name hoping that if he was coming maybe someone else could protect me. But whatever, the name Set, I thought about taking it.

DANIEL. I don't know why you are always talking about changing your name.

TODD. Because I just don't feel comfortable with my name sometimes. Like I'm outgrowing it or like it isn't me. Besides, you're one to talk.

DANIEL. Daniel means, "God is my judge." I like Daniel.

TODD. What name is on your birth certificate?

DANIEL. Don't go there.

TODD. Well? Proves my point.

DANIEL. I chose Alexander because it was our grandfather's name. I wanted to incorporate his energy into mine.

TODD. Wasn't it already incorporated? And besides, you really hurt Dad by taking his name out.

DANIEL. I really hurt Dad?

TODD. Yes.

DANIEL. Daniel Alexander Jones. That's me. Joni said in numerology, when you take a new name it totally shifts the energy around your life. That's my name, that's my energy.

TODD. Daniel Arthur Jones. Your real name, not the anglicized version. Say the name and the energy will follow. Word. Word.

(Tomb language.)

TRANSISTOR RADIO/DR. INGO SCHLAPP. My particular favorite?
It's the European common toad.
Its Latin name is more specific.
Bufo bufo.

> (DANIEL *and* TODD *echo the words* "Bufo
> bufo.")

They have...
they just have beautiful eyes.
You wouldn't believe it.
You wouldn't believe how beautiful their eyes are—they have,
so overall they're pretty ugly,
but they have this copper...
copper colored iris with dark little spots in them...
they're just...beautiful.
Mmm. It's a nice species.

QUINTESSENTIAL

TRANSISTOR RADIO/RACHEL M. HARPER. I think I'm very aware of
that...
of feeling like a guinea pig.
To be...to be from mixed worlds
in terms of race in terms of class and education.
I think that I am at the same time the experiment gone right
and gone wrong.
Do you know what I mean by that?
I feel it's much easier for me to have a sense
of community and family than of nationhood.
And that upsets me.

I mean I…I don't…
Like I came from this completely liberal and
optimistic stance on my parents' part,
not to say that there's not love and other things going on there,
but, but in the sense of bringing this biracial child into the world.
But then my my existence and my own life
and my sense of life force from that is almost null
So it's…it's sort of like I am everything and I am nothing.
I am the quintessential American and I have no country.

DANIEL. Anubis.

DANIEL AS ANUBIS. Horsemen, wolfmen with stars which are seeds. Smell them coming. Smell you coming in the breeze. Brother mine. Seven and seven and seven again. I am the witness of the falling, of the breaking. You are the avenger. Waited for you to come. I am the child of my mother and father's darkness. I have waited. Dog. Jackal. Mineomineomineomine. Knew you by your smell I did, knew you by your smell.

TODD AS VOICE. What are you doing?

ANUBIS. I'm sorry, I thought you were asleep.

VOICE. You were looking out the window, I told you not to do that. It's dangerous. There are things on the other side of the window which do not mean you well. Bad things.

ANUBIS. What sort of things?

VOICE. Mishaps. Maladaptations, malformations. Zombie-like things. VERY VERY SCARY.

ANUBIS. Where did they come from?

VOICE. The water.

ANUBIS. Isn't that where I came from, the water?

And my brother, too.

VOICE. Lights out.

TODD. Where's Dad?

DANIEL. What's this?

TODD. It's a show. Where's Dad at?

DANIEL. I think he went to play his numbers. What's this about?

TODD. A show on Vietnam. I find it rather interesting.

DANIEL. That's not Vietnam.

TODD. That's the flag-raising in WWII, Iwo Jima. I think that's right. One of those guys is an Indian. I guess that they're reviewing America's modern war history in order to place it in a larger context.

DANIEL. In a larger context.

TODD. That's how I have to deal with you.

DANIEL. Do you know his name, the Indian?

TODD. Hayes? Where's Mom?

DANIEL. Upstairs. Ira Hayes. What do you know about him?

TODD. I know about the pain of his death. He drank himself to death.

DANIEL. He did movies, too. With John Wayne and what's the brother's name? ...

TODD. The *brother*?

DANIEL. Woody Strode.

TODD. The brother.

DANIEL. Woody Strode, on the Hollywood set, had a separate entrance, as did Ira Hayes. But Ira Hayes said he didn't mind about the entrance cuz at least he wasn't a black nigger. He beat his wife, several women...

TODD. What about standing on a beach shrapnel flying? Bombs bursting in air. Raising our flag.

DANIEL. "America must defend the world..."

TODD. Why isn't Ira Hayes your brother? Why isn't Ira Hayes your brother while Woody Strode is your brother?

DANIEL. Brother is a figure of speech.

TODD. Did you learn that being an Africana Studies major?

DANIEL. Man.

TODD. Am I a figure of speech, *man*? Isn't that a "sexist" piece of language?

DANIEL. Look. If you want to be lazy and just lay up inside of an oppressive discourse, that's your choice. If you want me to do that, that's another question.

TODD. No, not at all, not at all. I just want you to shut up. Please. Be quiet. That's how I have to deal with you.

DANIEL. What do you mean deal with me?
Did you bring the chair in from the porch?
Fix the flag like Dad said?

TODD. Please, Daniel, be quiet.

DANIEL. You see? You see how you are?

TODD. Do I see how I am? Introspection. Looking inwards towards the self. A smaller context. A bigger context; that's how I have to deal with you, put you in a bigger context. Native raises the flag, bombs bursting in air, Daniel can't stop being Daniel. The scheme of things, the bigger context.

DANIEL. Oh, the bigger context. Just put me away and throw away the key.

TODD. I've given you all you need, Mr. Transformation. You can pick and choose. You do so already, Dan the Man.

DANIEL. Daniel.

TODD. Okay, Dan, now be quiet so I can get back to my program.

TODD.
The moon transforms.
On nights of the full moon
I would perform this ritual.
On the nights of the full moon
when I was just a child
I would wait to transform.
I would walk to the window,
the small iron window
which was too small and out of the way
to serve any normal purpose.
Underneath that window I would gaze at
the moonlight on my hands
waiting for the transformation,
waiting for the fur and the claws.
It's what happened in the movie,
in the stories,
in the dream.
The Wolfman.
I was just a child.

Not yet a man.
But still I believe.

MISS LILLIAN & MISS VIVIAN. He was a drunkard.

TODD AS MISS LILLIAN. He knew he wasn't good enough. A white wife, a house on the hill, won't erase where you come from. "Peace and free" or not.

DANIEL AS MISS VIVIAN. She didn't leave him. If it had been I.

MISS LILLIAN. It wouldn't have. Again. It's the children.

MISS LILLIAN. You remember his hospitalization. When he fell in the house and broke all his ribs, too drunk to see the stairs. Little Danny discovered him. The sins of the father.

MISS VIVIAN. The pressure of those …*arrangements* …is great. We brought little Danny some custard that time, do you remember, Lil?

MISS LILLIAN. He lapped it right up, poor pup.

MISS VIVIAN. They tried to start again with little Todd.

MISS LILLIAN. To see him with little Todd, driving that dilapidated used car while intoxicated.

MISS LILLIAN & MISS VIVIAN. It's hard not to wonder why she stayed.

TODD. Mom? Is that you?

DANIEL AS JEANNIE AS ISIS. Here, boy.

TODD. Mom?

JEANNIE AS ISIS. Son of mine.
    No son of mine.
    Some son of mine?

Is that you, honey?
Is that what I'm supposed to say?
Some son?
Somebody's supposed to be mine son?

TODD. Mom?

JEANNIE AS ISIS. Yes?

TODD. I can't see you. Where are your hands? Your eyes?

JEANNIE AS ISIS. Sweet little brown baby, don't you know me?
I know you by the shape of your head that I wrenched,
I wrenched the meat of my bones to thrust out.
Your sweet head born from inside me splitting, poking, tearing me.
Hospital tests hurt less with your sweet face at the end.
Your sweet head that I turned in the crib to keep a nice shape.
A shape so familiar, like your brother's, yet your own.
I know you.
Don't you know me?

TODD. You've been calling me in from outside.
Calling me in for bedtime.
For a warm bath and powder.
Soft, fanned air with music playing.

JEANNIE AS ISIS. Your hair is like your father's and the downward
turn of your mouth. Marks.

TODD. That's not fair to Dad.

JEANNIE AS ISIS. Sweet little brown baby.
The father you recall through your breathing is a thin shard
who cuts my palm. He is the smell of lemon, the taste of pot
likker.
Your memory stings me.

TODD. That's not true. You love him. Don't talk that way.

JEANNIE AS ISIS. Strong wedding light on clean skin.
  Ivory soap and still dreaming through wounded vision.
  Bullet gleams are birds in the air flying, flying and landing.
  Catch each other and bury fire in earth.
  Sowing. Sowing. Bullets flying. Gods falling. Feathers flying.
  Your brother and I would play inside, safe inside as they fell
  and flew.
  Your father walked through the madness, crooked, bearing
  witness.
  Dead gods. Dead boys in body bags draped with flags
  in the corners of the television and the newspapers.
  Scarecrows in alleys and shadows where no angels would tread.
  Your father walked through the madness, your brother and I
  saw him fall one day.
  Fall down the stairs and land at our feet, broken ribs, broken
  bones, feathers flying.
  Pieces scattered through the house down the street to the river.
  I put him back together.

                    (*Sniffs.*)

  Stale liquor smell.
  Sweet rot of softening teeth and spine.
  Clouding gaze and all.
  Your shaking brother's dog hand on his heart in the hospital room,
  yelping quiet in his mouth.
  I put your father together.
  Not for a movement,
  not for his fallow friends,
  not for your brother,
  but for me.
  I wanted him back.

I needed to feel that what I had held, had been drawn to,
had welcomed inside me was real.
I formed his fullness from clay.
Made him strong where he was not, inside me.
My pleasure marked your coming.
You are a child of the dirt, of the clay and my will.

TODD. I just want us all to stick together. We're a family ...Mom...
Mom?

JEANNIE AS ISIS. Son of mine, some son of mine.
You can't see me.
I am the sound under the dirt which is your flesh.
Look for your brother.
He is a shaking dog startled by feathers and light.
Give your prayer to him.
Somebody's supposed to be mine son.

TODD. Mom.
(*Chanting*) *The four horsemen you can hear them coming.*
Listen carefully to their hoofsteps drumming.
For centuries they waited in underwater dungeons.
Listen carefully hear their hoofsteps drumming.

In a moment they will turn our everything to nothing.
This moment listen to their hoofsteps drumming.
The four horsemen you can hear them coming.
Gabriel's melody they will be humming
Over their hoofsteps drumming.

What a beautiful music they make.
Their drum beats break into earthquakes.
They devastate with the pen and create with the sword.
The truth you would ignore but you can't ignore the war of the
Four horsemen.

For centuries they waited
In underwater dungeons
And anticipated the call.
Let civilization fall.
From fall to spring to winter to summer
You'll find no reason in the season to come.
The four horsemen they come.
You can hear them coming drumming crushing
All you non-believers straight to the gates of hell.

> *(To the rhythm of Grisha Coleman's "Feel That Way."[3])*

DANIEL.

Nowhere to go.
Nothing to show.
No rings around.
No vow.
No oath.
No small degree.
No short delay.
It's not at all.
Or all the way.
It seems you've slipped.
I felt you slide.
You cracked your shin.
Pulled back the skin.
I'll tell you how.
You tell me when.
We're gonna feel that way again.

I face the wall.
You hit the dirt.

---

3   Coleman, Grisha. "Feel That Way."

Now we can't see.
Is this the end?
The end again?

How can I know
what matters most
if I don't make it matter?
It seems you've slipped.
I felt you slid.
Right off the fence.
On to one side.
I'll tell you now
they'll be no fight
if you can't feel that way.

Hoo ah hey ah
Hoo ah hey ah
Hoo ah hey ah
Hoo

The love you weaned then left behind.
It's not just me that acts unkind.
When you begin to feel this way.
When you begin to feel.

Hoo ah hey ah
Hoo ah hey ah
Hoo ah hey ah
Hoo

DANIEL. Could you lift your feet?

TODD. I could.

DANIEL. Would you lift your feet?

TODD. Grammar?

DANIEL. I always get those two mixed up. Like can or may? Ability and willingness are two different things.

TODD. Too bad.

DANIEL. Feet?

TODD. Psssh. What are you doing?

DANIEL. I'm trying to clean up in here.

TODD. Oh, you're trying to clean. That's a novel idea.

DANIEL. Seriously, man. It's nasty in here. All dusty.

TODD. Suddenly it's become important for you to clean. And you interrupt me to do it?

DANIEL. Nigga just move your feet.

TODD. I'm not moving anything.

DANIEL. Why you got to be difficult?

TODD. You need to stop pretending. You wouldn't even be cleaning this up if you weren't all of a sudden thinking about keeping up appearances. You're shifty.

DANIEL. That's not even true. I'm always cleaning. Practically.

TODD. That's why that pot of spaghetti was in the refrigerator for two weeks?

DANIEL. Look, that's different.

TODD. Oh, that's different?

DANIEL. It is, I was going to eat that.

TODD. Were you going to eat the contents of the laundry basket, too?

DANIEL. Man, just move your feet! I have to clean up so I can work.

TODD. Happy feet, I've got those happy feet…

DANIEL. Names.

(The following is spoken simultaneously.)

TODD. Your name is Daniel Jones.	DANIEL. Your name is Todd Jones.
You are my brother.	You are candle-lit nappy patches
What does it all mean, beyond the word brother?	where thoughts propel magic.
It means that I will carry you if you have fallen, but you won't fall.	You grow feathers out of sleepy mornings.
I love my brother, we shared the womb.	You animate a postcard of Malcolm,
We share life.	a Mayan painting torn from a library book,
What could be a better blessing, than to have someone to share life with?	as you conjure Marley through your bass laugh.
Life is your stage Daniel, claim it, as you do your language, so that life may manifest your every divine thought.	You cultivate yourself and I become your father, your grandfather, your mother, your sister, and yes, your brother.
Water is the burden you bear.	Watching you stand through to your fullness you are my spirit mirrored.
Water is the burden you bear.	Together we dance devil music
Water is the burden you bear.	with God's cadence.

DANIEL. That was very *Afterschool Special* of us.

TODD. Word. ABC. Word.

PRAYER AT SUNRISE

DANIEL & TODD. We were born and raised in Springfield, Massachusetts.
    Our mother's name is Georgina Leslie Jones.
    Our father's name is Arthur Leroy Jones.
    We breathed the same air.
    We played the same games.
    We looked in the same mirrors.
    We pray the same prayer
    at sunrise.

> (*Sunrise.* DANIEL *and* TODD *fill the air with sound as new light floods the space.*)

THE BOOK OF Daniel

Chapter 10: Wonder (Us)

FOREWORD

Can we inhabit the body that made these words by saying the words ourselves? Only one way to find out. *The Book of Daniel* as recorded here may be freeing for you to read aloud. Hold this book in your hand. Move about the room. Do not be shy. Say it. Sing. Try making up the notes.

Does there need to be someone else there with you when you do? Not always, but at some point, you may need to turn over the words to another body. Can you get a witness?

Or, can you use *The Book of Daniel* as a directive? Improvise the story of your becoming based on the landmarks here: a photograph of a significant event before you were born; a song you carry in you. In this practice of becoming there are no accidents. There may be improvisations, but these can be honed.

o

On some level—and maybe this is too much of a reach, but I need to try, in the spirit of practiced courage that pervades Jones's theatricality—I think *The Book of Daniel* revels in an America that is simultaneously improvisation and myth, both of which Jones reframes by turns. Grandmother happens to be holding the flag. She recognizes the significance. It gives our story a new sense of itself. Here we go.

And if there is some mythical American Boy who is supposed to play with a certain type of action figure, Daniel's American Boy plays with Wonder Woman. Same red white and blue, different emphasis on how to kick ass. By playing in the room with us, our American Boy, gazed upon by the man, becomes part of a new myth. Right now. And if our American fathers are supposed to be knowing and strong, the father of this chapter's Daniel achieves something like grace through a fumbling attempt at protection.

By elevating this story, with its altered and sanctified symbols, we might find we have more room in the stories of this country, of our cultures here, for what really happened, and happens. I think about my own parents' marriage—a Jew and a WASP—and how that created first hysteria and then a slow settling in. I think about my father's quiet desire to keep me safe or feeling okay about myself, when I was a misfit boy in Minneapolis around the same years *The Book of Daniel* describes. I think about playing with a Baby Alive doll with Tessa Scherkenbach next door, how it must have been a relief for my dad when I stopped, even though I stopped because of other boys' cruelty.

o

I see that in Jones's larger project, liberation remains central: collective, individual, textual, physical. We are meant to free up—ourselves, something, someone—through these enactments, these enchantments, through our presence together. Pieces come and go over many years, they collect insights and disseminate music, collect personae, rediscover themselves, and grow in practice.

In *The Book of Daniel*, people find themselves making choices before we know what they mean. Isn't that the job of the mythical figure and the improviser both?

This play, this series, this approach to embodied language made in a moment of shared presence, is a tool for you. Please wield it with the appropriately adventurous spirit.

– Aaron Landsman

ALTAR NOTES

Aishah Rahman gave me many gifts. One of the greatest was her proclamation that if something you have written for performance doesn't move the bones, it has to go. Whenever, for example, I directed performers who were starting with a new text, I'd refuse "table work" in favor of sending them off to "say the words aloud, over and over. Begin right there. And let the words move your body. Always." Words repeatedly sounded through the body guide performers toward revelation. The spell unlocks. I drew upon this idea, along with Anna Deavere Smith's oft-repeated statement, given her by her grandfather, "If you say a word often enough it becomes you." I knew the words I wrote first had to move my own body, pulsing from faint impulse through marrow toward utterance. When I wrote, much to the amusement of anyone I was around at the time, I'd shake and shimmy, mumble or shout, sounding out the statements and moving myself through space to figure it all out in my body before it ever went onto a page.

As I entered my thirties, I looked in the mirror and proclaimed that I was just talking smack if I wasn't ultimately willing and able to compose long-form, on the spot, *in performance*. I always left room in written scripts for improvisation, and I knew how to riff off of a set moment in a live show. And for sure I could be extemporaneously cute for five or ten minutes. But what would it mean to make a big shape, with multiple moving parts, in real time? I knew I had to jump into that fire of my own accord if I was going to fulfill the promise of my beloved mentors' investment in me. In my mind's eye I could feel the bemused observation of Aishah, along with Laurie Carlos and Robbie McCauley (two masters of improvised performance practice). I thought about the spectacular compositions that I'd encountered through recordings (film or vinyl) made by folks like Betty Carter, the Nicholas Brothers, or any number of the Astral Jazz All-Stars of the '60s and '70s. And, of course, as I got deeper into the practice, I became familiar with Lawrence D. "Butch" Morris's capacity to weave multiple players' improvised parts into a shimmering whole in real time.

The Book of Daniel resulted. From 2001 through 2011, I created a series of improvised performances. All but two were lengthy compositions between 60-90 minutes. Most were repeated (with inherent variation). Some were one-time-only deals. I cannot consider my body of work, thus far, without naming this series of performances. They annealed me as an artist. And they were all—absolutely—living altars.

This chapter was improvised at the Pillsbury House Theatre's Late Night Series in Minneapolis in November 2011. I selected the following elements beforehand: the traditional "Let Your Little Light Shine"; a memorized snippet of verbatim text transcribed from an interview conducted in 1992 with my grandmother, Bernice G. Leslie; a photograph of my parents' wedding day and an accompanying story about the photo; and a Wonder Woman doll. Other than memorizing the interview, I intentionally prepared no text beforehand. This is a transcript of the resulting performance.

○

I gave a lot of attention to the visual composition of the *Book of Daniel* chapters. Because several of them were presented in "budget" circumstances, I often had few objects and elements to work with. So precision was key, as was the sequence of how information coded in objects, in space, and through the light spectrum was revealed. Given the intimate nature of the work, I had the luxury of, for example, investing a lot of energy in a postcard of Malcolm X. In the fifth chapter, the simple card and the story attached to it—about being in a spirit-dialogue with the dead Civil Rights leader through a postcard I kept on my wall—became a point of entry for "Brother

Malcolm on the Postcard," a guide, a provocateur, and a kind of high priest inhabited by my collaborator Walter Kitundu. For Chapter 5, presented at allgo, in Austin, TX, I also commissioned short texts from Robbie McCauley, Erik Ehn, Rachel M. Harper, and Grisha Coleman, which became the equivalent of a spoken setlist for me and Walter. We responded to these texts by designing and hand-making the installation inside of which the performance happened, by discovering the "story" that bound the text through a series of movement and musical improvisational sessions, and, finally, through our spontaneous nightly explorations of everything we knew, anew.

The lighting design for this, Chapter 10, was improvised by Mike Wangen, in real time. Mike and I discussed a "palette" of emotions, locations, and intentions; these corresponded to the palette of colors and textures he used. Mike "played" light live like a musician. While he had expertly designed hundreds of traditional plays over the course of his career, his love for the dynamic and immediate creative meeting place of composition and performance was palpable. He talked to me once of the psychedelic light shows that fascinated him as a young person. Mike understood the ritual use of light. In the moment, I was elated to weave together my own emerging impulses, the shifting connections with audience members, and Mike's vibrational conversation—it was *always* a conversation—into a whole through the movements of my body and various soundings. I listened to Mike's light. It told me when and where to enter. And, Oooo-whee when we hit a "chord" together? Magic.

Imagine the light as you read. And see, do the words move your bones?

– DAJ

Book of Daniel Chapter 10 "Wonder (Us)"
Improvised at Pillsbury House Theatre's "Late Night Series"
Minneapolis, MN
November 2011

Created and performed by Daniel Alexander Jones
Lighting Design by Mike Wangen

(DANIEL *enters singing.*)

DANIEL.

> *Let your little light shine,*
> *shine, shine*
> *Let your little light shine,*
> *shine, shine*
> *Let your little light shine,*
> *shine, shine*
> *There may be someone down in the valley*
> *Trying to get home...*[1]

How y'all doing tonight? So to tell this story—which is a story of forgiveness—I have to go back...

2011
2010
2009
2008
2007 (meh)
2006
2005 (yeah, yeah)
2004
2003 (not a very good year)
2002
2001
2000 (mmm)
1999
1998
1997
1996
1995
1994 (first time I came to Minneapolis)

---

[1]   Traditional

1993
1992
1991
1990
1989
1988
1987
1986
1985
1984
1981
1980
19-and-79
1978
1977
1976
1975
1974
1973
1972
1971
1970
1969
1968 …

1968.

The year my parents were married. It's a pretty wedding picture, isn't it? My mother's veil is blowing in the wind (*gesture*). All kinds of drama. My father is leaning in for the kiss, coming in on the side. They were married in October of 1968. I once asked my grandmother, Bernice Leslie, who used to run the Springfield Girls' Club Family Center overnight camp for girls …

only girls—no boys...about the day that my father asked her for my mother's hand in marriage...

(*Gesture/shift to become* GRANDMOTHER BERNICE LESLIE.)

Well. They came out to the camp for dinner. And I didn't think anything about anything. And they sat at the head table, and after we went down for flag lowering. Your father...uh... came down with me, your mother stayed up at Head Cabin. Your father said... "Mrs. Leslie, may I speak with you..." and I thought it was quite symbolic, I had the flag—American flag—in my arms—United States flag—and I said suuure...let's walk down to the lake...and he told me that your mother and father had grown quite, uhm, fond of each other and he wanted my permission to marry her. Well! I said, there'll be problems, I said not only are you Black—you're Catholic. Some of your family won't like it, and some of my family won't like it...but as far as I'm concerned, you're a fine young man. My daughter has a lot of love to give someone and I'll be happy if she gives it to you. As simple as that. And we walked back up the hill. And your mother had been pacing back and forth and they left immediately because they had to tell each other everything. But I always thought it was so symbolic that I had the flag in my arms when he asked me.

(*Quick shift back to* DANIEL.)

And these are the people that I came from. So...1969, 1970, 1971, '72, '73 I start as a little teeny tiny tot to go out in the summers to be with my grandmother at the all-girls camp! I was the only boy at the all-girls camp and I felt just fine. You know why? Because women do it better!

Sorry. They run things and they get things done. If they got

a problem, they sit down, work it out and they get the thing
done. Going out, 1974, 1975, remembering

(*Movement phrase begins.*)

Watching the women
in a line going down the hill
down to the lake over to the right
into the grove of trees
gathering in a circle
moving in a circle
lighting a fire flames flying high licking the sky sparks
sparks flying
in all directions
the light
the burnished light
the amber light
glowing on the face of my grandmother as she stood before the
encampment and said
to all of the campers
"You must act with love
you must act with respect
you must take care of the land
you must take care of one another" and they would sing
those beautiful Kumbaya camp songs let your little light shine
let your little light shine
here may be someone
down in the valley
trying to get home.
white girls
Black girls
Asian girls
exchange students from India exchange students from Africa
I got to sit on everybody's lap.

The only boy in a land of girls ...

(Shift.)

1976 1977 ...

Holding it down in Springfield, Massachusetts. My brother is born. I am proud. I am seven years old and I have a baby brother named Todd.

But 1977 was marked by something else, it was love. Have y'all ever been that kind of crushed out, nasty, crushed out love of second grade? I loved—and I'm not ashamed to admit it—a little white girl named Shannon. I loved her with all my heart. She used to wear pants that had daisies on them. Bell bottoms. She had that Farrah flip – Farrah Fawcett hair? I loved her so much that I asked my father for a nickel and I went to the machine where they had the thing and you would put it in and turn it and it would go click-click-click boom and it would pop out a fake ring. Anybody know those machines at the grocery store? Yeah? Now I don't want what they would give you. But I took the ring and I wanted to give it to her, I was so nervous that I brought it to school and I had a lump in my throat the whole day. I couldn't give it to her. I brought it home—sweating—and I said ... "I've got to mail it to her." So, for some unknown reason I went into my mother's room, I went into her sewing basket and I found some yellow yarn. Go figure, y'all. I took the yarn and I wrapped it around the edge of the ring ... and I started to think about her ... as I thought about her I started to wrap the ring until it started to snowball and grow into a large knot and I kept wrapping it, thinking I hope she likes the ring, I hope she likes the ring ... I love her so much ... I want to marry her ... I want to run through a field with her ... I'd heard some weird thing about hot dogs and buns and I thought you ran toward the girl and you carried a hot dog and she had a

bun and you met in the middle of a field and exchanged them...
and I made a big fat ball of gold yarn and I said "Mom, I have
to mail this" and she said, "Are you crazy?" And I mashed it
into a little box and I wrote the address with my pen—because
I could print like a motherfucker—I gave it to my mom and
asked her to send it off and I waited and this was right before
my brother was born. I went to school and I saw her, she...

(Gesture to show ring on her finger.)

she said..."Thanks." And it was OVER. I was in love. I got
so nervous. At least I thought it was nerves. I proceeded to
throw up all over the desk. Not just like a little bit. It was one
of those—uuuuuuuuuggggggggggghhhhhhh—covering the desk.
Just stank, just nasty, just wrong. So, back in the day—and
already the poor white teachers...we got bussed there, it was
the beginning of bussing in Massachusetts...you think only the
segregated South? nah—worse than you'd imagine up North...
and so they were already spun out cuz they had to deal with
the little Negro children and the Puerto Rican children and
they were already nervous and now one of them throwing up
on the desk. It was too much. They call the parents and one
of them comes...my father came and got me...and...oh...My
Dad came and got me...

My Dad My Dad My Dad

He said "you got a fever, Danny, you got a fever..." And that
fever was a problem because my brother had just been born.
He hadn't come home yet—but they couldn't have me in the
house with him. So, they sent me to my grandmother, which
was fine by me. I loved my grandmother. She'd retired from
the camp, so I went over to her house. But the fever set in my
bones. And all I was looking forward to at the end of school—
you know you go play—and we were playing superheroes! Me

and my friends Ako, Joia, Kieyan, J.P., we were ready for our superhero games, you know. Spiderman, Batman, Superman... and the pièce de résistance—Wonder Woman! Ain't nobody better. That's why they can't make the movie, because they did it right the first time.

I'm yearning to play my superhero games, and I'm laying in the bed with the fever, and they brought me several times to the pediatrician. They could never really find out what was wrong. And I tell you that I lay for almost six weeks with this low-grade fever. And during that time something happened to me...

The fabric of time and space started to come apart.

I lay in a fever dream state and I started to see things. Like the little bits of dust that you see in the air? Moving in patterns. I started to hear voices.

(*Movement begins.*)

Back back back back back
back back from the way back
back back from the way back
back from the way back
mixing with the voices and the sounds of the footsteps from the street outside mixing with the voices and the sounds of the footsteps from the other room ring ring of the call of the telephone of the talk talk talk
back back
in out
in out
night day
night day
and I started to feel myself leave my body
look down on my body

and look outside of time

my body grew smaller and lighter
and limp
I couldn't breathe deeply and it felt so ...good

the water coming off my back soaking into the pillow soaking
into the sheets
and on and on it went

and finally
my father came
and quietly in the night
in my Grandmother's house
he fed me pills
(which I later found out he was not supposed to give me)
he stripped off the bed sheets
and he began to
rub my legs with alcohol
rub my belly with alcohol
rub my arms with alcohol until the fever broke

I'll never forget when they brought me home and
I had my first chance to walk outside
I heard my brother
my new brother
crying—
he wasn't going to be good for a little while
he still had to grow before you could play with him—

but I could feel ...
y'all ...
I could feel everything humming.
The light was like honey on my skin and I could see a single
bee flying through the air

landing on a little stalk of clover
I could feel it like the clover was my skin
as the clover bent and dipped
and I felt that
I am connected to something so magical
before I even had the words
I felt like I had seen outside my life
to the light
to the light
to the light
that connects us all
and when I came back into my body
the door didn't close.

And so a little bit even just a little bit even just a little bit
and I'm telling it like a confession even just a little bit
I felt from that time forward slightly apart from
everyone and everything that I would meet because I had one
foot
on the other side
when I would meet people
and I would see people
I could see the shimmer in them
or I could see the shadow in them
I could see what they didn't want me to see.

(*Shift.*)

The other good thing about being sick is that you can pimp
your parents for anything you want. So, my father said, "Well,
are you doin' good Danny, you doin' good? What do you want
for a present?" And I said, and I don't know what he was
expecting, "I want to go to Child World," which was before

Toys R Us—you know that's a seventies name, "Child World," right?—"And I want the Wonder Woman doll."

And there was a beat.
A long beat.
And he said … "Alright, okay."

And I got the doll. And I'm trying to tell you this. Another reason that Wonder Woman is the best? You got Peter Parker—a little hipster, now, for his secret identity. Peter Parker becomes Spider Man. Clark Kent, very fifties … Wonder Woman in the 1970s was serving you some beautiful, polyester, big print dresses—Diana Prince was the hotness. So the Wonder Woman doll was not only Wonder Woman, she was also Diana Prince. You could change her back. And she was giving you model looks. You pulled the hair back in a bun. And then you could whip out the little bracelets and you could whip out the tiara—it was fabulous—and all my friends, J.P. the preacher's son, my friend Kieyan (who came from a family where all the boys had names that started with a "K"—Kieyan, Kyle, Kensin, Kevin and Keith—I loved Black People in the seventies—I do, it's never been the same since—and my friends Ako and Joia—now here's the deal. All of us boys on the street—not Joia, the little girl who we made do routines—dressed up and played as Wonder Woman. So there was a culture on Thompson Street. It was very special. I'm going to tell you I took Wonder Woman everywhere.

A story of forgiveness … 1978.

My father is called for jury duty. One year later. Summer. High profile trial. Now back in the day jury duty, you get sequestered. He's not going to be able to come home—he can't call, we can't call him. So, he says to me before he leaves, he says, "Danny, I want you to take care of your mother and your little brother."

Now that's some big responsibility at eight years old. But I take everything seriously. Too seriously ...

(*Gesture.*)

One foot in the other side

...and I say I will do it. You know why I know I can do it? Because I've got Wonder Woman on my side. We've got bullet-proof bracelets. We've got an invisible plane. We've got a lasso of truth. We can leap over a tall building. Because we're just that bad. Because why?

Women do it better.

No problem. He goes off. And I go to find her. I'm like, where's she at, where's she at? Looking in my room. Looking under the bed. Looking on the shelf. Looking ... looking ... she's not in my room, where I always put her ... back ... she has a place like Paradise Island where she always goes back to ... go outside and look for her ... run around and look for her ... I spend a long time looking and finally I run back into the house and scream, "Mom, Wonder Woman's missing!"

(*Look around as* MOM. *Five long beats.*)

MOM: You'll have to ask your father.

ME: Um. He's sequestered.

MOM: You'll have to ask your father.

(*Shift.*)

I'm familiar with the mail. I get my piece of paper and write:

Dear Dad.
How are you?
How is court?

WHERE. IS. WONDER. WOMAN?

Fold it. Stamp? Mail it, please.

Two days. Three days. Get a letter back:

> "Dear Danny. Court is good. You would be fascinated by the judicial system of America. It is fascinating to be in a court where there are so many diverse voices. I cannot discuss the trial ... "

No answer to my question. He ends with "Take care of your Mother and your Brother."

> Dear Dad.
> Maybe you didn't read this part ... WHERE. IS. WONDER. WOMAN?

And so forth, and so on. For six weeks. When my father comes home, he says to me, "There's something I want to tell you." My heart quickens a little bit. "I'm gonna take you to Child World and we're gonna buy the Hulk." Now, let's look at this. When evil villains got to work and Diana Prince got wind of it, she would quickly and discreetly slip away, do her fabulous turn and BAM, become Wonder Woman, leap back on the scene and handle business. But with Bruce Banner and the Hulk? It didn't go well! There's a problem. The man breaks his clothes off, then comes all "Rrrroooaaaaarrrrrrrhhhhh" like this, leaves behind a trail of destruction, good or bad, get out the way!

My father never mentioned Wonder Woman again.

And so, for years, for years, I carried the story, right, that he was ashamed that he had a son that loved Wonder Woman. And the obvious connection that we can make—that your little boy is going to "turn out gay"—which I did. (And I wasn't the only one on the street.) It became one of the things that became a wedge between me and my Dad. And part of my frustration was he never had the courage to come out and tell me. Tell me where she was, tell me why he did it, none of it, none of it, none of it…

None of it.

So I was just evil…And let alone that I already told you I was one foot out…In a small way, even from eight years old. It made me feel less trust in men. In general.

You know one of the greatest blessings and one of the greatest curses of my life is that I actually grew up, until I went to junior high school, with very few men in authority and without ever coming into contact with a white male in authority. That just happened to be my life. So when I did, and they started acting funky, I was like, "What y'all doing?" But it wasn't only white men. My own father, a Black man, a brotherrrrrrr…had done this…

So, I was cleaning my house. And I found that old photo album. And I found this picture, which I'd seen a hundred times. I want to point out this one thing…behind them is a shadow. You see the shadow? They were married in October of 1968. Not the Summer of Love, 1967, though they knew each other then. Not in March, but after April, April 1968 when Martin Luther King was killed. Not in May, but after June, June when Robert Kennedy was killed. They got married at a time when a shadow was falling on the country. And did that shadow fall.

As I looked at the shadow it became for me the most interesting part of the picture and I started to think for myself, the man and the woman in this picture, who got married, transgressed at a time when people didn't do this as a popular thing. The man and the woman in this picture knew that they were doing something out of love. The man and the woman in this picture, who were my parents, came from people, my grandmother, a white woman who approved of it even though everyone in her family told her how sorry they were, and she said, "I'm so proud and you needn't call me again." Something clicked in me. As I remembered the end of that summer. Before my father came home from jury duty. And it was one of those memories that you just push back in the way back of your head?

Down at the end of the street there was a halfway house. There were a lot of halfway houses back then because they let all the people out of the state institutions because they were cutting budgets. And one night, there was a fight. Bricks were thrown. There was a gunshot or two. And all of a sudden the house at the end of our street—only three houses down—was lit on fire. I remember my mother, in a frenzied state, calling the firemen, calling 911, and grabbing my brother, my baby brother, my baby brother, my baby brother who was still so little.

And I remember walking, unbeknownst to her, to the front door. And I remember opening the front door.
And I remember stepping out onto that front porch and feeling... has anyone ever been by a big fire where you feel the heat—the wall of heat coming at you.

I walked down the sidewalk.
And I stood there, and I faced the fire. And I said, I will protect them.

I called on the spirit of WONDER WOMAN! I did.

I waited until the flames died down. My mother, when she found out where I was, gave me a rare, but memorable, spanking.

Looking at this picture recently, I remembered that moment and I said, oh.

My father wasn't ashamed of me. The story that I'd been telling myself was wrong. My father wanted to protect me. Because he knew how deep and how dark this shadow was.

And now I can say to him, and I can say to all of us. There is no protection from the shadow. That shadow fell, and continued to spread and it has been so thick and so dark and so deep … that it has shaped the America we live in right now, and its incredible volatility. But guess what? Inside of you is a light. Inside of us is a light. Inside of me was a light. It was the light that got so delighted by Wonder Woman. It was the light that got so delighted standing in the circle with the flames leaping high and the sparks leaping in the air and the amber light on the side of my grandmother's face when she said, "You must love one another, you must respect one another, you must respect the Earth, you must take care of one another." Which, in retrospect, I saw that my father, in the way that he knew how, had done with me.

(*Singing.*)

Let your little light shine, shine, shine
Let your little light shine, shine, shine
Let your little light shine, shine, shine
There may be someone down in the valley
Trying to get home …

CHRONOLOGY | the book of daniel

2001 – Chapter 1: Testimony of a Flock of Ravens
Text-based extended riff. Published in *Spirited*, RedBone Press, 2005.

2002 – Chapter 2: Jazz Rite in Lecture Format
A meditation on rice and race, using my parents' interracial wedding in 1968 as the central ritual. Performed as a solo for the Austin Project.

2004 – Chapter 3: Dis/Integration
Integrating schools through bussing in Massachusetts in the mid-1970s. How has education reinscribed divisions? Also included: a meditation on the death of Ronald Reagan. Performed as a solo at allgo in Austin, TX with installation by Dr. Joni L. Jones.

2004 – Chapter 4: 33:66
The tenuousness of health/body. Mother's breast cancer and the shift from child to caretaker. Performed as a solo with community testimony at Goddard College in Vermont.

2006 – Chapter 5: My Favorite Things
Commissioned texts from Erik Ehn, Robbie McCauley, Rachel M. Harper and Grisha Coleman performed in duet with Walter Kitundu, including community response. Installation by Jones and Kitundu. Performed at allgo in Austin, TX.

2006 – Chapter 6: Sunshine/Son-shine
Performed as octet at UCSB Summer Theatre Lab (Jones, Kitundu, and students). An interpretation of the myth of Horus. Malcolm X as Osiris, Josephine Baker as Isis. No sense.

2007 – Chapter 7: Immortality
Performed as quintet (Jones, Kitundu, Tea Alagíc, Azure

Osborne-Lee, and Patrick McKelvey) with installation by Leilah Stewart. At the UT Austin/CAAAS Performing Blackness Series.

2008 – Chapter 8: Wheel
Performed as duet (Jones, Sonja Perryman) at FlipFest at Angel Orensantz Center, NYC.

2009 – Chapter 9
Performed at Black Lavender, Rites & Reason Theatre, 2009 with a cast of student and community performers.

2011 – Chapter 10: "Wonder (Us)"
Performed at Pillsbury House Theatre's "Late Night Series" in Minneapolis, MN.

BLACK LIGHT

A musical revival for turbulent times

FOREWORD

By the time *Black Light* premiered at Joe's Pub in January 2018, Jomama Jones was already nearly a decade into her diva comeback, inaugurated by the soaring hopes and harmonies of her show, *Radiate*, back in 2010. But whereas *Radiate* opened with the parting of a milky white curtain and the celestial shimmer of the disco ball's refracted light, *Black Light* began in the dark with the sound of Jomama's solitary voice and the floor shuddering under our seats as the subway surged away from its station beneath us.

Lucky for us, Jomama kept coming back. We needed her now more than ever, as we braced ourselves for the inauguration of a new and nefarious political regime. Perhaps she stuck around precisely because she had seen it coming all along, or because she knew it had been there from the beginning. She was from the future and the past, after all.

Black Light calls us to meditate in the darkness. *Be a witness. Join the revival*, the publicity posters beckoned. To be a witness is to sit, as Aunt Cleotha does, armed and alert in the dark to ensure that the new year brings with it hard-earned freedom. To be a witness is to see deeply into a dark girl's latent desires and to say to her, as Miss Stutts urges, *Feel all of your feelings*. To be a witness is to partake in the Black freedom tradition of standing up and standing guard and sometimes breaking into a run or a song or any action that will bear the load of our witnessing for and among our people.

Black Light is a revival in all senses of the word. Revival as resurgence, as the diva's return. Revival as a theatrical re-staging, as the repetition-with-a-difference of all the Black divas who've shaped and sometimes saved Black life. Revival as resurrection, as the spirit of Prince come alive again when Jomama sings, *I brought you purple fire / It shimmers on my skin*...And, above all, revival as a holy gathering where folks can give and get a witness and lift their voices and their hands and their spirits. *Black Light* creates a sacred space that redeems us from the ship's hold, that holds us close. And we are rendered nearly whole again, brought back from our dead, redeemed in our desires, revived.

– Deborah Paredez

ALTAR NOTES | on altar-egos & matters of light

I call Jomama Jones my altar-ego. She is both an altar and the energy that courses through it. I'm her vessel. There are long-standing traditions of drag performance and theatrical persona-building that I and Jomama are frequently linked to. Things have different meanings in different contexts, and people bring their contexts with them when they encounter work. I was keenly attentive to this as a teenager when a number of the recording artists I loved, who were beloved on Black radio, began to have huge "crossover" success on mainstream—a.k.a. white—radio. My friends and I felt a deep disorientation seeing the differences between how they were contextualized on *Soul Train*, for example, versus *American Bandstand*. The artists whose records I collected were anchors for whole constellations of folks we came to know through comparative study of liner notes, and through their personal stories shared in print in *Jet, Ebony, Black Beat, Rock & Soul* and *Right On!* magazines. In our context, for example, Whitney Houston's crossover superstardom was inextricable from her youthful appearances on television, radio, and recordings prior to her first album. The sound of her music was linked to the legacies of producers like Kashif—who in addition to B.T. Express and his own recordings had created the electro-soul sound that brought Evelyn "Champagne" King, Melba Moore, and Howard Johnson massive hits—and Narada Michael Walden, who had been an anchor of Mahavishnu Orchestra and had produced so many records I loved for Stacy Lattisaw, Sister Sledge, Angela Bofill, and Patti Austin prior to working with Houston and Aretha Franklin. In "our" world these artists were part of a mighty congregation and held distinct meanings for us. Crossed-over, they were often stripped of those unassimilable meanings and were coated in slick projections of universality. It seemed clear to us that Black culture was the font, and the mainstream was the great extractor. I am particular about linking Jomama to the lineage from which she was directly born; and I am unambiguous about her purpose. Jomama-as-altar contains my record collection, contains the double-helix of Black music culture as soul food and emancipatory practice, contains the rapturous aesthetics of artists whose identities held the crossroads of individual expression and collective illumination. Her grandeur flows from Josephine Baker, Lena Horne, Diahann Carroll, Lola Falana, Josephine Premice, yes, but also from the grand ladies I knew in my community growing up: Mrs. Sylvia Cope, Ms. Helen Thompson, Mrs. Peggy Carroll, and our librarians, Mrs. Sylvia Humphrey and Ms. Bettye Webb. Her style, changeability, and electricity exist in great measure because of the examples of many of the aforementioned artists who were my lifeblood, but also because of the way I learned aesthetics in my everyday cultural context: the styles of the people, their angles and lines, their sway and their pop, their determined self-expression. The Queer magic of Jomama can be traced to the lodestar presence of artists like Joan Armatrading, whose quiet certitude and directness offered trustworthy witness, as well as to the brave and bold yes in Sylvester's megawatt presence and Jermaine Stewart's unabashed hair flips. I well remember Sylvester's appearance on Joan Rivers's nighttime talk show in the mid-1980s. She referred to him as a drag queen and he stopped her in her taxonomical tracks: "I'm not a drag queen. I'm Sylvester." Was Sylvester dissing drag? No. Was Sylvester making clear that he abided in infinite possibility and foll better recognize that in context? *Well …* And, of course, Jo reflects the long line of storytellers from next door neighbors to Ossie and Ruby, exemplars of the long tradition of Black oratory-as-congregation-stirring practice. These things and more make up the living context of Jomama's origin. If you pinch a piece of her to examine under a microscope, all these things would always be revealed within—they are inseparable. Too, in the over twenty-five years of my association with her, she has continuously revealed new layers of being and meaning that invite new connections to this historical

After her scorched-earth appearance in *Blood:Shock:Boogie*, Jomama did not perform again through me for years. When in the late 2000s she appeared to me again, gone was the arch-diva aspect of her personality. In its stead was an urgency of civic purpose and a wholly unfettered radiance. If in *B:S:B* she had talked about being an "Afro-American astronaut", upon her return to me it was clear she had gone to the furthest reaches of inner and outer space and come back on a mission and with a message. By 2008, when Jo showed up in my body to record *Jomama's Hope Warriors*, an unreleased series of filmed interviews with a range of folks that she found inspiring, I understood somatically the shift in her perspective. She quickly urged me to contact Bobby Halvorson, then an aspiring musician based in Los Angeles whom I'd met briefly while working on one of the Book of Daniel chapters at UCSB through Naomi Iizuka's Summer Theatre Lab in 2006. We wrote and recorded our first album *Lone Star* in just about ten days, working DIY style in the tiny Santa Monica apartment he shared with three other guys. I'd never felt the kind of whole-body alignment that snapped into place when he played the first chords and I sang the first phrase of our song "Endless Summertime" into the microphone. I knew I was eternally home in this music and that Jomama had been wise to challenge me to do what I'd longed to do since I was a child—make a record. On my 40th birthday, February 9, 2010, at the gracious invitation of Shanta Thake, we played the album's songs live at Joe's Pub among an audience filled with strangers and loved ones. There that night was Sarah Benson, who'd been a supporter of my work and practice; she "got" Jo entirely and brought Jomama into Soho Rep's next season with the support of New Dramatists' Full Stage initiative. Shanta and Sarah opened performance homes where there had been none for me in NYC theatre. As I write these notes, there is a flourishing of a dazzling range of Black Queer art across all media; it is a powerful shift, especially for those of us who, as we traveled for decades beyond the boundaries of our "home" communities and spaces, found hard, cold ground and often had to make a way out of no way, to, as Zora Neale Hurston said, "throw up a track through the wilderness."

We recorded our second album, *Radiate*, which became the anchor for the show of the same name that premiered at the Walker Street space that December. In a glorious full-circle, the legendary Nona Hendryx even participated in a panel discussion about the work—the singular recordings by her pioneering group, Labelle (Hendryx, Patti LaBelle and Sarah Dash) comprise a holy solar barque. We toured *Radiate* for several years and I created two more albums with Bobby, *Six Ways Home* and *Flowering*. When I met Josh Quat during the preparations for *Duat*, I found another incredible songwriting collaborator and we began composing new material. People responded to Jomama directly and passionately. They "knew" her somehow and many said they felt a sense of homecoming when in her presence.

Mystery blooms in the zone between the known and the unknown which performance traverses. By the time I began work on *Black Light* in 2015, Jomama had assumed her rightful oracular place in my own soul's solar system. I had long ago learned the delicate, changing balance between utterance and silence. Indeed, one of the things that folks remarked upon the most who'd come to hear Jomama in concert or see her performance pieces was her comfort with silence, with waiting, with deep listening. As the nation turned a corner towards a particularly rancorous passage, I, too, was listening.

Enter (again) Shanta Thake. Then director of Joe's Pub, Shanta and her stalwart right-hand man, Alex Knowlton, and I would meet in her office at the Public. They gave me plenty of space to build the work which came into being through mixing up setlists, improvisation, call and response with audiences, and thoughtful dialogue with Shanta and others who were watching the events of 2016 unfold like a slow-motion trainwreck. When in November of 2016, *Duat* closed at Soho Rep and the presidential election took its sobering turn, preparation for the work took on new urgency. That urgency had little to do with the notion that *Black Light* or any show would somehow change our circumstances and everything to do with our bone-deep sense of the necessity of holding out a light during what was sure to be a dark night of the soul for the nation. I had experienced time and again the power that live performance had to orient us toward possibility and to continue its dialogue with us long after the performance itself concluded. I wanted to make an altar that would invite an engagement with courageous imagination.

I was blessed to collaborate with lighting designer Ania Parks, who worked meticulously with me to create distinctive, saturated looks for each of the songs. We drew heavily on research into the design concepts for the concerts I'd loved which were all their own kinds of rituals. Ania went above and beyond the call to perfect the angles, get the exact tones, and deal with Jomama's propensity to wander out of her light to go talk to folks who were beyond the reach of Ania's instruments!

Because Jomama is the altar, adorning her body was key. Oana Botez, the genius designer, has worked with me since Jomama's comeback. What you see (when Jomama finds her light) is the product of the meeting of Oana's and my souls. Oana's designs reflect her meticulous attention to historical research, dramaturgical context, and spiritual impulse. Among my favorite New York City memories are my trips with Oana to the Garment District to the tiny back rooms and basements in the fabric stores she frequented. She knew all the owners, knew how to cut deals, and knew each and every fabric so well that she could gauge its quality and durability by gazing at a bolt across the shop. She could spot a tuft of fabric tucked behind four or five heavy bolts, defy physics to extract it, and end up with the perfect material for an otherworldly gown. Most importantly, Oana knew that she had to create garments to conjure, not illustrate, pieces that would move and breathe and shimmer just so, to allow my body to shapeshift energetically and refract timespace in the subtlest and most effective fashion for Jomama to manifest in full. Oana is a master of her craft. And her riotous laughter, anchored in her loving heart, would always keep the flow going as we all navigated charged waters under great pressure.

Finally, I will call the entire community of Joe's Pub and the Public, who went out of their ways to shepherd *Black Light* from its first wild experiments in 2015, its foundational run in Under the Radar in 2017, to its premiere and six-week run in 2018. We made it a point that all rehearsals and sound checks would be open and inviting places for anyone to stop by, drop in, take a rest. On performance nights, audiences would linger long afterward to commune. Every security guard, desk worker, waitstaff, busboy, and custodian we met became a guardian of the show and the performers. When I feel shaky, I go back to the notes and cards and messages I received during that run. What people said, again and again, was that our show was a light in the darkness.

Black Light
Premiered at Joe's Pub at the Public Theater
New York, NY
February 2018

Created and performed by Daniel Alexander Jones
Music direction by Samora Pinderhughes
Costumes by Oana Botez
Lights by Ania Parks
Sound by Jon Shriver
Songs by Jomama Jones with Bobby Halvorson, Dylan Meek, Josh
      Quat, Samora Pinderhughes, and Tariq al-Sabir

FEATURING:
Jomama Jones as JOMAMA JONES

THE VIBRATIONS:
Truth Bachman
Vuyo Sotashe

THE BAND:
Josh Quat on GUITAR
Michelle Marie Osbourne on BASS
Sean Dixon on DRUMS
Tariq al-Sabir on KEYS

Black Light was commissioned by Shanta Thake, Joe's Pub, and the
Public Theater as part of its New York Voices initiative.

Black Light was subsequently produced Off-Broadway by Diana
DiMenna in October 2018 at the Greenwich House Theatre under
the direction of Tea Alagić.

(The room is crepuscular, shadows deep-
ening swiftly, then dark. Dark. Dark. Bells
sound with steps and gestures of approach.
Into this breath, JOMAMA *enters. She speaks*
to us.)

JOMAMA. What if I told you it's going to be alright?
But what if I told you not yet?
What if I told you there are trials ahead beyond your deepest fears?
What if I told you you will fall down, down, down?
What if I told you you will surprise yourself?
What if I told you you will be brave ...enough?
What if I told you you are not alone?
What if I told you our hearts are on the line?
What if I told you we won't all make it through?
What if I told you that is as it must be?
What if I told you it has been foreseen?
What if I told you that I have seen the future?
What if I told you I'm from the future?
What if I told you it began tonight?
Here, at the Crossroads.

BLACK LIGHT

JOMAMA.
Come together in the twilight.
Open up your hands,
open up your eyes.
See the veils all lifting,
showing us the darkest night.

Crossroads calling.

Move your feet upon the ground.
What will be lost?
What will be found?

You can run, but you can't hide.
Time is tight on every side.
Here together
There's more than meets the eye.

Starlight,
Starbright,
wish I may,
wish I might
have the wish I wish tonight.

Starlight,
Starbright,
wish I may,
wish I might
have the wish I wish tonight.

Under the Black Light.
Under the Black Light.
Under the Black Light.

Particle or wave?
Cowardly or brave?
Which road leads to mystery?
Which road is your destiny?

North or South or East or West.
Above, Below, Within.
Where you gonna go?
Will you trust the unknown?

Starlight,

Starbright,
wish I may,
wish I might
have the wish I wish tonight.

Starlight,
Starbright,
wish I may,
wish I might
have the wish I wish tonight.

Under the Black Light
Under the Black Light
Under the Black Light

Open the way so we may see.
So we may see how we be
Together.
Under the Black Light.

> (*Lights warm so all the faces can be seen as* JOMAMA *steps forward and speaks directly with us. Her eyes linger on ours; we are here in this pulse of time together.*)

JOMAMA. Good evening!
Ladies, gentlemen, and otherwise described,
I am Jomama Jones.
And these...are my *friends*!

> (JOMAMA *introduces the band and* THE VIBRATIONS.)

We have been called here to be with you.
At the Crossroads.
Perhaps you have been called here tonight as well?

Where together we will muse.

(Smiling mischievously at someone.)

Have you ever been a muse?
I can tell!
So have I.
I've been…sculpted…many times, by sensitive, artistic fingers.
Haven't we all been shaped by the encounters we have?
Perhaps we will have one such encounter tonight—here in [name the town], in [name the state], in these so-called United States of America.
We will consider the time we are in.
And what a time it is, indeed!

SHATTERED

JOMAMA & THE VIBRATIONS.
Language made to liberate
Now used to assassinate
The freeing impulse of the soul
And shame us into silence

Comfort sought at every turn
To suffering all blind eyes turn
And never once a sacrifice
Instead you say it's not your problem

Concepts of identity
Consume us like a cruel disease
Impede our vulnerability
Confuse our hearts for matter

Generations maimed and sidelined
'Til the flame is gone from their eyes
Once resilient spirits now are shattered
Now are shattered

All the bones swept under rugs
Are poking out from under edges
Blatant lies told to disguise
The truthful tale of nations

Rage and greed and fear and vengeance
Righteous dominating power
Are the contents we are told
Of every human's nature

Seconds turn to minutes
Turn to decades turn to centuries
Until the cord of time frays in our hands
And we are shattered

We who fail to greet life as it is
Not as we wish that it would be
Who fail to see all living beings
Umbilically connected

We who fail to recognize
The pulse of Earth
The pulse within
Who chose destruction not surrender
Here's our weeping hour

Take one last look in the mirror
See the mask reflected there
Was it worth it?
Ask yourself
As your illusions shatter

All illusions
All illusions
All illusions
All illusions
All illusions
All illusions
All illusions shatter

(JOMAMA *offers the "Casting Crossroads" gestures to* THE VIBRATIONS: *with the index and middle finger of the right hand extended, thumb folded over the ring and pinky fingers, two quick strikes toward the ground with sharp exhalations followed by quick raising of hand and arm up and out above the head and shoulder to the right with an inhalation. They repeat. A slow float of the hand down and toward the left hip, like a leaf falling through the air, with an almost-whispered exhalation. They repeat. Sharp strike out at an angle to the left corner then swift strike out at an angle behind to the rear right, drawing one "road," with a sharp exhalation each time on a "hah" sound. Then the opposite road, from the front right corner to the rear left, with a sharp exhalation each time on a "hah" sound. They repeat. She is pleased.*)

JOMAMA. Ahh! Very nice. Now, as you two are *my vibrations*, carry on with the call!

(JOMAMA *exits.*)

CASTING THE CROSSROADS

(THE VIBRATIONS' *open vowels and gestures
rise, weave with piano and drums, filling
the air and shimmering. They open the
Crossroads energy, consecrating the space.*)

THE VIBRATIONS.
Oh-oh-oh-oh-oh-oh ahhh-ahhh
Ahhh-ahhh
Ahhh-ahhh
Oh-oh-oh-oh-oh-oh ahhh-ahhh
Ahhh-ahhh
Ahhh-ahhh

(JOMAMA *returns in a dazzling gold suit
made of reversible sequins, one side shiny,
the other matte.*)

JOMAMA. Surprise!

(*To a nearby person*) May I look at you? Yes? Thank you.

(*To us all*) Yes, you see I've gotten consent. Consent is very
important in today's world. You must ask consent before you
go a-lookin'.

(*Back to them*) I give you permission to look at me. As a matter
of fact you may touch here...I offer my consent, yes! Go ahead.
If you rub this way it's bright and shiny, and if you rub that
way it's matte and spiky! I love this outfit, for it teaches us that
one must learn to rub the right way.

(*A wink. Then out to us all*) I give you *all* permission to take
me in.

Now quickly, close your eyes! Do you still see me in your mind's eye? Yes? Mmmm, I've left an impression. Much as the light from the stars above leaves an impression upon us. Even though that light travels to us from years and years and years and years and years ago when the star was young.

Can you imagine me as a young thing? A teenager? Yes? A high school student? I'll give you a hint: I didn't look that much different than I do now. I did have my fro, tho—(*gestures*) it was out to here.

I was quite a handful in high school. I was our regional track star; double-dutch champion; I was the certificate holder in arts and crafts—I won for making a popsicle stick replica of the Three Mile Island nuclear meltdown, it even had a cloud of nuclear fallout that wafted out, and everyone had to hide under their desks; I maintained a 4.0 GPA; and I was the all around go-to person for all sorts of dances and routines. But the thing of which I was most proud was being the star of my science class with my 11th grade science teacher, Miss Stutts. Miss Stutts was a bona fide Black scientist who taught at our school and we all wanted to be in her good graces. I'll never forget the day Miss Stutts introduced our unit on astrophysics. She told us we were going to be studying Black Holes. (*To an audience member*) Do you know what they are? Yes? They sort of suck everything up into nothingness. And their Event Horizons? (*To another audience member*) The Event Horizon is the edge of the Black Hole. It is the point beyond which nothing can escape. If you and I were to pay a visit to a Black Hole to say a fair hello, we wouldn't want to go past the Event Horizon because if you do, you're not coming out!

When I learned of these project presentations, ever the *artiste*, I knew in my bones what I had to do. I leapt to my feet. Miss

Stutts, I'm going to make a poem! Extemporaneously—I love extempore to this day—I recited the following poem:

> Black Hole.
> Yearning
> like the hearts of my people
> for freedom!
> Black Hole.
> Consuming
> like the cold, ruthless heart
> of the Man!
>
> *(Quick Black Power stance and fist with downcast eyes at the conclusion. Then...)*

Well, I thought it was something. But not Miss Stutts. She said we needed objectivity, data, facts, figures, scientific research! She set us all into working groups. I was assigned to a working group with my dear sweet friend...and rival, Tamika. I guess you could call her my best friend. She was always right there at my side, if ever so slightly behind. You see, I took being twice as good, twice as smart, twice as fast quite seriously. Much to the chagrin of my dear, sweet Tamika. Also in that working group were Tamika's cousins, the triplets: Faith, Hope, and Charity—the quiet one. Miss Stutts rolled out these big pieces of graph paper and gave us all china markers. We were to diagram the Black Holes and their Event Horizons. Now on this particular day, as she was wont to do, Tamika decided she wanted to stir up a bit of trouble.

At this point I should let you know the year in question was 19 and 79. Is there anyone here brave enough to admit they remember that year? A good number of things of historical significance happened in 1979. In addition to the aforementioned Three Mile Island Nuclear Meltdown, there was the Iranian

Hostage Crisis; Margaret Thatcher was elected Prime Minister of the UK; Assata Shakur busted out of prison and made her way to exile in Cuba. Indeed. None of these things have any bearing on my story. What does, however, is that in 1979 the gravitational center of our universe was Prince Rogers Nelson. That year, he released his second album, entitled *Prince*. It had the blue cover. His doe eyes were looking off in the distance and his hair was whipped back on the sides. And his little chest hairs were showing. There were 47 hairs. I counted them.

So, on this particular day, Tamika reached down into her book-bag and she withdrew a poster of Prince. This poster was the centerfold from *Right On!* magazine. Y'all remember *Right On!*? For those of you not in the know, it was the Black version of *Tiger Beat*. But it was much better, because we had better artists. What the album cover left to the imagination, this poster revealed. I mean *revealed*. Tamika put it right on the desk, leaned over to me and said...

(*A little scene.* JOMAMA *plays all the parts.*)

TAMIKA. Prince is my husband.

JO. That's alright, cuz he's my man.

TAMIKA. But...he slept with me last night.

JO. Girl, I know. I sent him to you to give him a break from the other six nights of the week with me.

That got under her skin. She took her china marker—with which she was supposed to be diagramming the Black Hole—and drew a circle around his eyes.

TAMIKA. His eyes are mine!

I snatched that marker and drew a circle around his heart.

JO. His heart is mine.

433

She then wrote her name all down his arms. T-a-m-i-k-a.

TAMIKA. His arms are mine.

I'll have you know, I drew a very secure rectangular box around Prince's, shall we say, miniscule leopard print bikini briefs and I said:

JO. All mine!

Back and forth it went, all sorts of body parts: belly button, fingertips, chesteseses, until, at the end of the line of the triplets, Charity, the quietest one, began to twitch. She leaned forward and whispered:

CHARITY. I want his leg.

We cut our eyes at Charity.

JO. Pssssh. What you gonna do with his leg?

And y'all, as though the Holy Ghost itself came down through the body of that little child she rose to her full height, which wasn't much, and in the middle of Miss Stutts's science class yelled out:

CHARITY. I don't care! I want his LEEEEGGGG!

The jig was up. Miss Stutts's hands swept down and confiscated that poster, with all of our names and circles and lines of demarcation. We knew we were in *trouble*. You see, this was a neighborhood school and Miss Stutts knew all of our parents, and she was gonna tell! Our heads hung low. We considered our research. The Black Hole. And its Event Horizon. The point beyond which nothing and nobody can escape.

Have you ever had a need like that? A need that led you to do things? This song is dedicated to the need in you, and it's most certainly dedicated to the need in me.

NEED IN ME

JOMAMA & THE VIBRATIONS.

Come see
The need in me
The yearning burning deep in me
Unfulfilled and smoldering
Raging where there once was love

It roars like an ocean
But don't be scared
I've kept it safe behind this wall
If one or two bricks start to fall
Don't you be alarmed at all

I'd never let you drown
Searched its depths in the sleepless night
Tried to keep it tight but I gave up the fight
Nothing I could do but stay true to the blue
I wonder where it came from—just like you

The longing to unite got deflected
The promises you made got infected
Left us with an empty tale to tell
High hopes gone straight to hell

The pain of the past rages in my bones
Staring at the future all alone
Like a flower calling to the sun
I'm crying won't you help me
I never let you down

I respect the need in me
Its ferocious vulnerability

Its luminous fragility
Its proof of my humanity

Betrayal wounds the heart you see
I don't take it lightly
Freedom has a heavy price
You don't have to tell me twice

Now is the time, I've got to take care
Time for me to hit the door
Go on and do what you've got to do
To deal with the need in you!

Deal with the need in you!

> (At this point in the song, drummer SEAN
> DIXON guides us through a piercing, shak-
> ing and cleansing drum solo, starting with
> sharp, almost arrhythmic strikes, and
> slowly piecing together statements of vary-
> ing length and tempo to reveal a trajectory
> with velocity increasing until the crescendo.
> A modulation in key accompanies the next
> vocal phrases. The final three repetitions of
> "Can I get a witness" are sung a cappella.)

Can I get a witness for the need in me?
Can I get a witness for the need in me?
Can I get a witness for the need in me?
Can I get a witness for the need in me?
Can I get a witness?
Can I get a witness?
Can I get a witness?
Can I get a witness?

Can I get a witness?
Can I?

> *(Transitional polyrhythmic, polyvocal music guides us Down South with a modified ring-shout dance.)*

JOMAMA. What do you know about that word? Witness. I'm not talking about being a passive observer. As in ... "I was standing there by the Astor Place cube and I witnessed a purse-snatching." Or "I was a witness to, say, a protofascist coup in my country." No. Not that kind of witness. I'm talking about witness in the Black American tradition. Meaning you take responsibility for what you see. You're willing to shoulder that load, and put your back into it! I learned that definition of witness from my Aunt Cleotha Down South. I wish that I could tell you she was my dear sweet Aunt Cleotha. She was anything but. At her warmest she might be best described as "taciturn."

You know there are some people you meet and you have that sort of instant spark of electricity between you? I feel it with you! (*To an audience member with whom* JO *feels it*) And if we had time we could sit down together and unpack it all! But it's there! With Aunt Cleotha and me? Polar opposites. An instant dislike. See, there were things about Aunt Cleotha that just irritated us as children, me and my little sister Clementine, when we would travel Down South with my grandmother to visit her sister, Cleotha. We would visit over the summer and sometimes over the holidays—Christmas and New Year.

Now the first thing—and, now, I'm going to build my relationship with you this evening based on honesty and trust, so, what I'm about to tell you is *true*, but not politically correct. Aunt Cleotha only had one good arm. Yeah, the other one, it just hung there. And we, as children, we said things about it.

JO. Mmmmm. She got that arm.

CLEMENTINE. It just hang there.

(*Scrutinizing gestures for a beat.*)

CLEMENTINE. How do she get dressed?

JO. I don't know but she do.

CLEMENTINE. Mmmmph.

JO. Then it just go right on back and hang there again!

CLEMENTINE. Why it's like that?

JO. I don't know.

CLEMENTINE. I don't like that. I don't *like...that...arm*!

It's true.

And the other thing, which confounded us as children, was that Aunt Cleotha slept until noon! Can you imagine a grown person sleeping until noon? Even today, you can't steal my joy in the morning. I'm up with the dawn, I have things to do, places to go, and people to see! As a child I had a play-agenda. Chock-full of activities. We were constantly chastised, be quiet! Stay indoors, simmer down, don't you wake your Aunt Cleotha. Can you imagine? This was particularly challenging for me because Down South there was something that we did not have in the North. Something that fascinated and delighted me.

Chickens!

No, it's true! I loved to play with the chickens! They had so much personality. *Joie de vivre*! They would run around the yard! My favorite was a fat copper-colored hen I nicknamed Penny. She was so smart, I could teach her all sorts of games and routines. Oh, I loved Penny. And of course, every time I set out to play with her I'd hear, "Simmer down! Quiet down! You're gonna wake Aunt Cleotha!"

Well, on the Fourth of July, Independence Day, I told Clementine, my little sister, to go down the road and fetch the little friend she'd made near Aunt Cleotha's house—a dusty little white girl named McClean. She brought McClean back and the three of us gathered around Penny and we taught her one of our favorite games from Up North:

Uno dos Sierra
Uno dos Sierra
I love coffee
I love tea
I love a Black boy and he loves me
So step back white boy you don't shine
I'll get a Black boy to beat your behind
Last night, night befo'
Met my boyfriend at the candy store
He brought me ice cream
He brought me cake
He brought me home with a bellyache
Mama mama I feel sick
Call the doctor
Quick quick quick
Doctor doctor shall I die
Count to five and you'll stay alive
(Go on Penny, count to five!)
One-two-three-four-five
Staying alive till the Fourth of July!

Y'all, Aunt Cleotha had come up out the house. She walked down the steps and came into the well of the yard where we were dancing. She reached down and with her good arm she snatched Penny by the neck and...

(*Quick violent whipping gesture.*)

my friend was gone.

Later that day the preacher came for Fourth of July dinner waving his little paper American flag. I can still hear his voice:

> PREACHER MAN. Sister Cleotha, I sure would enjoy another one of those drumsticks.
>
> JO. What? You mean Penny's leg?!

I was excused from the table for having poor home training. But I returned to clear the dishes. I scrupulously collected each and every one of Penny's bones.

(*By way of explanation to any of us who find this funny*) She was my friend. The next morning I rose before sunrise. I went outside Aunt Cleotha's bedroom window. I bent down in the dirt and scratched a shallow grave. I placed Penny's bones, covered them with dirt and tamped it down. Then I pressed my lips to Aunt Cleotha's window screen and serenaded her as the first rays of dawn filled the sky!

Oh, Death!
Death in the morning...
Death!
Death in the morning...
Death!
Death in the morning...
Spare me over another year!

Aunt Cleotha glared at me from behind that screen and I stared back at her and that set the tone for the remainder of our summer together.

(Somebody in the band plays a janky version of "Jingle Bells," garnering a raised eyebrow from JOMAMA.)

When I learned, much to my dismay, we were to return for the Christmas holiday into the New Year, I turned to my grandmother and said:

> JO. Ma'am, I cannot. Why does Aunt Cleotha sleep till noon?

> GRANDMOTHER. Because your Aunt Cleotha is a witness for the Lord.

> JO. But, every night?

> GRANDMOTHER. You'll have to take that up with your Aunt Cleotha.

Henceforth, I scrutinized Aunt Cleotha's every move. On New Year's Eve, at 10:30 at night, I noticed Aunt Cleotha's bedroom door suspiciously ajar. Gingerly, I spied through the crack. There she was, with her one good arm, buttoning up the last buttons of … *(Surprised, as little* JO *has never seen this side of* CLEOTHA) … a beautiful grey silk suit. She picked up a hat with all sorts of feathers and flowers on it then placed it on her head, acey-deucey. Then she reached into her bureau and withdrew—now, some of you may be old enough to remember this term—an electric torch. For you young folks in the room, that's what we used to call a flashlight. And before they were on your phones, they existed in real dimensional form. This electric torch weighed 900 pounds. You could kill a man with an electric torch. You stuffed them full of D batteries until they could take no more. I confronted her.

> JO. Aunt Cleotha, where are you going at this hour on New Year's Eve?

I knew she didn't have any friends.

> CLEOTHA. Young lady, I am a witness, and tonight is Watchnight.

> JO. Watchnight?

> CLEOTHA. When the slaves were freed, they learned their freedom was to take effect on the first day of the New Year. But given the track record of the United States of America, they did not believe for one moment that freedom would come easily if at all. And so they gathered together, to pray, to sing, to prepare, and to shout! Determined to ensure that when that New Year came their freedom came along with it. I go to commemorate that night. But I also go to do something else!

And she turned on that flashlight and she shone it in my face, as much as this light is shining in your faces now.

> CLEOTHA. I will stand in one of the corners of the church. The other ushers and the deacons will stand in the other corners and along the walls, and as midnight approaches, we will shine our lights. And we will watch, and we will watch, and we will watch! To make sure that as one year ends and the new year begins, the Devil himself doesn't slip through the cracks between years to wreak havoc upon the earth. I am a living witness!

And, *boom*! She was gone. Of late, I've been thinking a great deal about that. Wondering. Am I a living witness? Or have I become a passive observer? If there is no ritual without sacrifice, what am I willing to sacrifice? My comfort, my righteousness, my shame, or my name? Huh? The hour is nigh. Hit it!

GABRIEL'S HORN

JOMAMA & THE VIBRATIONS.
So many died just to get you free
But ignorant is all you seem to want to be
Glorifying everything material
'Til you end up looking like a carnival

Always pointing fingers at the other man
Shouting that nobody else can understand
Gonna get mine that's what you say
Step on anybody just to have your way

We should hang our heads in shame
This ain't why they overcame
You know that you ain't right

We need to do better
We need to do better
We need to do better
We need to do better
We need to do better
We need to do better
We need to do better
We need to do better
We need to do better
We need to do better
We need to do better
We need to do better

May we find the courage
To confront our contradictions
Reconcile our hatreds
Cross the boundaries of our longing

Recognize the ties that bind us
Amplify the love among us
Free ourselves from slaving stories
All they do is tear us down

Always gotta be your voice that's heard
Always gotta have the final word
You'll just remix history
To make sure it's your face we see

Won't let go even though you're dying
You'd rather drag us all to hell
Could be laughing could be crying
Such a damned liar you can't even tell

We'll all hang our heads in shame
If we don't reject this game
You know that you ain't right

Cowardice or bravery?
Greed or generosity?
Will our better choices
Be drowned by fearful voices?

We're bigger on the inside than we are outside
Turn it inside out eradicate the lie
That we're doomed to limitation
Unleash your imagination

Think of all who came before you
Sacrificed their blood and bone
Think of all who've yet to come
We're making theirs a broken home

Maintaining this abomination
Depends on all our supplication

To a system that consumes us
Each and every one

Activate the courage
Confront all our contradictions
Reconcile our hatreds
Cross the boundaries of our longing
Recognize the ties that bind us
Amplify the love among us
Free ourselves from slaving stories
Turn the world around!
If you live in truthful action, everything will change
You know that you ain't right

We need to do better, we need to do better
We need to do better, we need to do better
We need to do better, we need to do better
We need to do better, we need to do better
We need to do better, we need to do better
We need to do better, we need to do better
We need to do better, we need to do better
We need to do better, we need to do better

THE VIBRATIONS. North and South
And East and West
Above, Below, Within...
A song...
Crossroads

CROSSROADS

JOMAMA.

> Feet on the Earth
> Head in the clouds
> Hearts on fire
> At the Crossroads
>
> Venus says "yes"
> But Saturn says "no"
> Oh, my heart, my head
> Someone tell me where to go
>
> We can't confront it
> If we walk away
> And we'll feel the pain
> Either way
>
> But sometimes something shows itself
> In a sudden wonder
> And when I'm in its presence
> I have to call its name
>
> Sometimes there is magic
> Sometimes there is magic
> I think you are magic
>
> Are we ever ready?
> Will we ever know?
> When the fall will happen
> What the future holds
>
> Courage born from the soul within
> Help me as I choose
> Either way we could lose

But sometimes something shows itself
In a sudden wonder
And when I'm in its presence
I have to call its name

Sometimes there is magic
Sometimes there is magic
I think you are magic

JOMAMA. When last we left our heroines, a certain poster had been confiscated. Being that I was the most popular I was elected to go and speak with Miss Stutts. I waited until all the other students had left the classroom, and then I approached her door. Now, her door had glass in it, so you could see through to the outside window. There was a band of scarlet cutting across two shades of blue, it was twilight. And I could see her there, Miss Stutts in silhouette, scratching away at all of our papers, grading them. She cared so much for us that she would stay late every day to grade. That only doubled my shame. I approached her desk.

> JO. Miss Stutts, I think we all know what happened here.

> MISS STUTTS. Yes, we do.

> JO. Is there any way we could get the poster back?

> MISS STUTTS. You mean *this* poster?

And y'all, she unfolded that poster of Prince, full of our circles and lines of demarcation and names...

> MISS STUTTS. Look at what you did to this innocent young man. You carved him up like the Europeans did with Africa, motivated entirely by greed.

(Ouch.)

> JO. Yes, Ma'am.

MISS STUTTS. What were you thinking?

JO. Oh, we weren't thinking.

MISS STUTTS. Jo...

JO. Yes, Ma'am?

MISS STUTTS. What were you feeling?!

JO. Oh...Well, I felt excited. As though I could look into his eyes and and if I wished hard enough, *maybe, maybe, maybe* someday I might meet him and I'd say, "Hi, I'm Jo," and he'd say...

PRINCE. Hi, I'm Prince...

JO. How are you?

PRINCE. I'm good.

JO. Do you wanna get some ice cream?

PRINCE. Sure, as long as it's purple.

JO. I mean...ANYTHING COULD HAPPEN! And, Miss Stutts, I felt, I felt HOT. And a little bit sad like I might lose something, I don't know what, and, and a little bit afraid. I felt, I felt, I felt somanythingsalla-tonetime. I just...I just...

JOY {4 PRINCE}

JOMAMA & THE VIBRATIONS.
I brought you purple flowers
Gathered from the garden

448

Please take off your shirt
So I can hold them to your heart

I brought you purple fire
It shimmers on my skin
Would you like to touch it?
I want you to touch it

I brought you purple longing
I tucked it in my mouth
You gon' have to open wide
If you want to taste it

Tomorrow isn't promised
This day is almost done
We will touch eternity
Together we will hum

Now come into my bed and I will

Fill you up with joy
Joy
Joy
Fill you up with joy
Joy
Joy
Fill you up—

MISS STUTTS. Young lady, get down from on top my desk!

(*Awkward stumble down. Contrite teen pose.*)

MISS STUTTS. Jo...

JO. Yes Ma'am?

MISS STUTTS. I want you ...

JO. (*Braced*) Yes, Miss Stutts?

MISS STUTTS. I want you to feel all of those things.

JO. What?

MISS STUTTS. I want you to feel all of your feelings. That is your birthright. And don't you ever let anyone tell you otherwise, do you understand me, young lady?

JO. Yes, Ma'am.

MISS STUTTS. Just one thing.

JO. Yes, Miss Stutts?

MISS STUTTS. Don't feel them in my class.

Miss Stutts looked me in my eye, pulled out a china marker and wrote her name on Prince's leg! We got the poster back. Imagine having permission to feel all of your feelings. Now, I don't know if I want to feel all my feelings, with all the things we've got going on in this world. But imagine, if we gave ourselves permission, and perhaps more importantly, if we gave one another permission, and held space to feel all of those things we walk around with, tucked inside of ourselves like seeds.

SEEDS

JOMAMA.
Loose me from my name
Loose me from this place
Loose me from the stories
That always stay the same

Crack the skin I'm in
The habits of my bones
Liberate me from my
Paths and patterns

All this time I tried to be
The very best person I could be
All this time I looked to you
Looked through the walls you set up between us

We are seeds
Hearts called by the Sun
Yearning to come undone
Knowing our time has come

We are seeds
Trembling in the Earth
Wrestling with the birth
Of a way
We can't yet see

Violence
Surrounds me
The ravages of fear
Threaten to devour
The hope that seemed so near
Icy cold reactions
From others who want to hide
When I reach beyond the limit
I don't know what I'll find

But I can hide no longer
Silence brings no safety
I'm breaking open from within
I'm pushing past the boundary

I'm dying to the self I knew
I'm living just to break through
Won't you take the leap with me?
Can you feel me reaching
Green?

We are seeds
Hearts called by the Sun
Yearning to come undone
Knowing our time has come
We are seeds
Trembling in the Earth
Wrestling with the birth
Of a way
We can't yet see

We are seeds
Hearts called by the Sun
Yearning to come undone
Knowing our time has come
We are seeds
Trembling in the Earth
Wrestling with the birth
Of a way
We can't yet see

> (*Claps and dances. Everyone sings a chant*
> *for Elegba.*[1])

JOMAMA. On the very last night of my very last trip Down South as a little girl, something extraordinary happened. I couldn't sleep. Have you ever had those nights, no matter what you do, you toss and you turn and you just can't go down? I was at my own

---

[1]   Traditional.

sort of crossroads. The very next morning we were going to be heading back Up North, and I was going to be starting high school. I knew I was heading into terrain that was new, and it scared me a bit. And so, I did something that was forbidden in Aunt Cleotha's house. I snuck downstairs, pushed open the screen door, and, at three in the morning, went outside unaccompanied in the South!

Don't worry, I didn't go far. I stayed on the porch. But it was a big porch. Aunt Cleotha had one of those wraparound porches. The air was the same temperature as my skin. I could hear the cicadas overhead like waves of electricity. I came around back. Her yard opened onto a field and I could make out a line of trees in the distance. It was then, out of the corner of my eye, I saw a figure. In a rocking chair on the back porch, at three in the morning!

It was Aunt Cleotha. And beside her was the unmistakable silhouette of a shotgun. I made sure to announce myself before I came any closer ... "Aunt Cleotha!"

CLEOTHA. Girl! What are you doing up at this hour?

JO. I couldn't sleep.

(*Standoff.*)

Even though I couldn't see her I could feel her eyes boring into me. It was then the extraordinary thing began to happen. She did something she had never ever done.

CLEOTHA. Come here. Sit next to your Aunt Cleotha.

(JO *pauses, then chooses, yes.*)

I don't know if you remember that feeling, when you're little, and you sit next to someone grown, and you can feel their heart beating and their breath against you, yes? You feel secure, no?

Especially if they have a shotgun. I was very precocious, you see, things just tumbled out of my mouth:

> JO. Aunt Cleotha! What are you doing up at three in the morning?
>
> CLEOTHA. If I told you once, I told you a thousand times, I am a witness.
>
> JO. But, this isn't church.
>
> CLEOTHA. Ha! This is my church.

And she drew my attention outward. I could begin to make out the line of trees in the distance. On one of those trees, I could spy an owl looking back at us. I spied the crescent moon. And the sky was impossibly thick with stars.

Still, I couldn't keep things to myself:

> JO. But, Aunt Cleotha, why you got that shotgun?
>
> And she looked at me. I mean really looked at me.
>
> CLEOTHA. Hmmm. It's time, it's time, it's time, it's time, it's time I told you. About my arm.

She reached down and unbuttoned the sleeve of her nightgown. Some of y'all know that the old people Down South will wear that nightie with the long sleeves even in the middle of the summer!

> CLEOTHA. When I was your age, I used to love candy. Lemon stick candy. And my older brother Reggie would take me down to the town square and we would go to Mr. Harrison's store. Mr. Harrison was a white man, but he knew our family, and would let me and Reggie come around back, pay a penny, and get a bag of lemon stick candy and I'd start eating it right then and there. I loved that candy. But even more, I loved my brother

Reggie. He was called for a soldier for WWI. They called that the Great War. Like there wasn't ever gonna be no more war. The proudest day of my life was when he returned home from the army in his uniform. Oooh, he looked sharp. I grabbed him by the hand and paraded him down the road and around the town square and walked him right into Mr. Harrison's store, where Reggie reached in his pocket, took out a bright copper-colored penny and set it on the counter and bought me my lemon stick candy. It never tasted sweeter than it did on that day. Only thing 'bout it, some folk did not take kindly to Reggie walking through that square with his uniform on. That night I was awakened by a strange sound. I made my way down the stairs in the dark, pushed open the screen door and walked down onto the porch and onto the path and I...There was a mob of white men approaching the house. And smack dab in the middle of them, with his German Shepherd on a chain, was Mister Harrison.

> MISTER HARRISON. Cleotha, where is that brother of yours?

My feet rooted down into the earth. I looked him straight in the eye:

> CLEOTHA. You will not come into this house.

And he sicced that dog on me. It grabbed my arm and it shook, and shook, and shook.

> JO. Yes, ma'am.

She rolled down her sleeve and fastened it. And we sat together in silence for some time.

But my curiosity got the best of me, I couldn't help myself:

JO. But Aunt Cleotha...wasn't that the nineteen-hundred teens or something? Why do you have that shotgun now?

CLEOTHA. They're still out there moving, baby. I stay vigilant. So y'all can sleep.

JO. Yes ma'am. (*They are silent, breathing, then...*) You know, Aunt Cleotha, it's not really dark at all.

CLEOTHA. No, no, no, baby. I call this Black Light. If you look into the dark long enough, all sorts of things will reveal themselves to you.

And so, on the very last night of my very last trip Down South, I sat next to my Aunt Cleotha.

Waiting for dawn. And learning how to see in the dark.

SUPERNOVA

JOMAMA. I'm coming to visit! Hello!
Who here loves science as much as I do?

> (JOMAMA *improvises this section depending on response.*)

So I'm going to throw out a question here, and anyone can answer. What is a supernova?

An exploding star! So it is near the end of its life cycle, yes? And it cannot take the weight of its own gravity and it explodes. Sort of an allegory, no? I've been thinking about the supernova a lot, lately. Frankly, I've been thinking a lot about death. And I've been wondering if it is necessary for something to die in order for some new thing to come into being. Like the supernova, some good things come out of it. Like Joni Mitchell sang, "We are stardust," you know that song? I'm sure there are at least one or two Canadians here, tucked away in plain sight, sitting there with your health insurance.

(JOMAMA *approaches someone to demonstrate the following.*)

This is not exactly a scientific description, it's more like my poem for Miss Stutts...but the star explodes and the stardust traveled across vast distances of time and space, came to the galaxy over millions of years and then sort of rained down, and swirled and became our planet and rained on us and then we sprung up! Carbon-based life forms, here we are, eating our french fries. So something good came out of the bargain. But I wonder if something must die in order for some new thing to be born. Something like, say, an idea—an idea about ourselves, an idea about each other, the way that we relate to one another, maybe an idea that moves beyond all the categories, the boxes we love to put one another inside of, maybe even an idea as unwieldy, and contradictory, as the idea of a nation? Hmmm... will you do something for Jomama?

Will you, I can't hear you? Consent! Remember we practiced? Turn toward someone in this audience whom you are near but whom you do not know very well. Oh dear, don't be frightened. I would like for you to hold their hand. As you are holding this hand, consider that the universe I describe is not only out here, but that there may be a universe within this hand you're holding, with its own galaxies and Black Holes. Triumphs and losses. And stars, about to explode.

Hit it!

Now, keep holding hands!

JOMAMA & THE VIBRATIONS.
What words will you read
By the fading light?
Who will you hold
Through the coming night?

You searched for reasons
To say goodbye
Now our time has drawn nigh

A supernova means a star is dying
A supernova means a star is dying
A supernova means a star is dying

All of the colors
Revealed in time
All of the reason
And all the rhyme

Elegant questions
Up in the sky
Will pass just like
Memories fade

A supernova means a star is dying
A supernova means a star is dying
A supernova means a star is dying

Burning circles
Spreading spirals
Cresting longings
Gold and green

Pulsing rivers
Blinking eyes

Cosmic breezes
Passing by

Try to remember
Your very first touch
The sweetness of fingers
And arms intertwining

We hold beginnings
In rosy glow
But the way of all stars
They must go

A supernova means a star is dying
A supernova means a star is dying
A supernova means a star is dying

> (*Hard light snaps on in the room. Work lights. End-of-the-night lights. They are not at all theatrical. It should shock.*)

JOMAMA. Oh, oh dear. I call this my harsh light. A harsh light for harsh times. I believe we may agree, no matter what part of the so-called political spectrum we find ourselves on, these are harsh times in America, no? It's all well and good to talk about holding someone's hand and seeing their soul when everything is warm and fuzzy and magenta. But can we do it in the harsh light? When all of our faults, and our fears, and our failings are visible? I wonder. Does anyone have a smartphone? We carry them around with us everywhere. They go to bed with us, and they tell us when to wake up, and they tell us when to go to sleep, and they tell us how many steps to take, and they tell us what to eat, and I have a friend, she's a liberal, I don't know if there are liberals here? I make no assumptions, you see, and she has developed an app for the phone. It's called SOGÜTA, which stands for the Stages of Grief Under This Administration. It scans her, and it tells her which particular stage of grief she is moving through on a given day. Is she in denial? Or anger? Or depression? Or bargaining? Or is she moving ever so slowly toward the final stage of acceptance and transformation? You know, I told her I didn't want her app. I want an app for the Stages of Black Rage. Some of the steps may be the same, I don't know. I know one of them must be Lord, I'm Weary. Another, perhaps, How Did We Get Here Again? A third might be Unwilling but Necessary Steely Resolve. But that final stage, Acceptance and Transformation…I don't know what we would compare it to—we've never even been close in this country.

You know my smartphone did come in handy. Tamika texted me. When Prince died. She wrote: Girl…

I wrote back: I know…And I put the umbrella emoji, the Purple Umbrella with the rain falling on it…

She wrote back: The music lives on…

I said, Yes, yes…

But I've been thinking about Prince. A star who has died. And another loss we endured in our family. Aunt Cleotha.

She passed right before the last election. No one there to shine a light that night, I'll tell you. Who was watching that night? But she was one of the old people who, she knew her time was coming so she went around and put pieces of tape and wrote names on things so they would go to the right people so that there wouldn't be fussing and fighting at the funeral. Some of us have been to that funeral. It's like, "I'm gonna miss her so much—wait, get your hands off my china!"

I learned that a box was on its way to me when she passed away.

So I opened it. The most extraordinary smell. She had packed it herself full of pine needles, and it took me instantly back to childhood, that smell. And I rummaged around in the box and pulled out Aunt Cleotha's electric torch. She gave it to me. It still works. Things built in the 1960s still work! Sometimes you have to jiggle them a bit, but they turn on eventually! I thought this was an awfully big box just for an electric torch so I continued to rummage around until my fingers touched something at the bottom. Aunt Cleotha's shotgun.

And I stood in my room with the light in one hand and the shotgun in the other. Building my relationship based on honesty, I will tell you: I am still standing right there. I have not made up my mind. I don't know about you. I want to think about death only in the abstract. Magenta. Supernova. I don't want it to mean me! What would happen to all the fashion? No, I don't want it to mean me. And I don't want it to mean you. But we just don't know. At this particular juncture where we find ourselves, this crossroads.

HE VIBRATIONS. What if I told you it's going to be alright?
What if I told you not yet?
What if I told you there are trials ahead beyond your deepest fears?
What if I told you you will fall down, down, down?
What if I told you you will surprise yourself?
What if I told you you will be brave enough?
What if I told you you're not alone?
What if I told you that we won't all make it through?
What if I told you this is as it must be?
What if I told you that I've already seen it come to pass?
What if I told you that I've seen the future?
What if I told you we're from the future?
What if I told you it has already begun?

Tonight. Here, at the Crossroads.

JOMAMA. The future is a funny place to be from. All of its secrets are held under lock and key and only our choices will reveal them. Choices at the crossroads. What if I told you it has something to do with your imagination? Imagination, that tricky word, no? Allow me to reframe it for you. I come from a long line of people with radical imagination. Stretching back through my grandmother and Aunt Cleotha, across generations, through slavery time, when people imagined a freedom they knew they themselves might never experience firsthand. Still they held it in their mind's eye, and they prayed, and they sang, and they shouted. Faced with an impossible crossroads, they dared to imagine possibility.

Sometimes, all you need to get the imagination going is a little sign, a little nudge, from the other side. So I brought my Tarot deck! My personal Tarot deck from home, to put a little skin in the game, as they say.

> (JOMAMA *turns to* THE VIBRATIONS *and gets them to shuffle the deck. One of them pulls the card.*)

We pull one card and I'll read it for you, a different card every night. There, now tap this deck three times, one two three, and withdraw any card. Exciting, no?

THE VIBRATIONS. The High Priestess of the Crossroads.

JOMAMA. Oh, look at this, why she's very pretty. So we read the symbols of this you see, to give us a sense of where things are. There's a crescent moon, there's a glowing world, there's a flashlight, there's a shotgun, there's a chicken ... *ghost*. And there's a poster of Prince. All these stories, all these signs and

signifiers, woven, finding their way into your subconscious to
help you as you choose what you must choose.

THE VIBRATIONS.
Future light within me
Future light within you
Future light within me
Future light within you

JOMAMA. What if I told you we are equal to this time, but not if we
don't imagine ourselves to be so.

SEE (THINGS AS THEY ARE)

JOMAMA & THE VIBRATIONS.
Went to the rock to hide your face
Rock cried out no hiding place
Can't cover your mouth, your ears, your eyes
This time

Fear that the pain will undo you
But your brave heart will renew you
Turn around, lift your head

See things as they are
By the light of day
Don't you turn your gaze away
See things as they are
Act on what is true
You will find your own way through

Chaos in these streets around
Everything lost and nothing found

Took so long to climb
But no time at all to fall

Odds are too steep
So much fear in the air
But you are stronger
I can tell you still care

See things as they are
By the light of day
Send despair on its way
See things as they are
Truth will amplify
The courage that is deep inside you

See things as they are
See
See
See

JOMAMA. We thank you.

> (*She names the band members again. Everyone sets down their instruments, save the guitarist, and everyone moves into proximity with the audience to sing the following song a cappella and unmic'd. Just the voices and the breath in the room at the end of the night.*)

SKINS

JOMAMA & THE VIBRATIONS.
When I'm inside you
And you're inside me
We embody
A mystery

We shared the secrets we held within
Now what to do with these skins?
Now what to do with these skins?

Oh, oh, oh, oh

Walk into the day
And this will fade away
Walk into the day
And this will fade away
Walk into the day
And this will fade away

Oh, look at the Sun

> (*The light sets and once again darkness*
> *envelops the room as* BAND MEMBERS *and*
> THE VIBRATIONS *exit the space, bells chim-*
> *ing. The only light comes from the candle*
> *that* JOMAMA *holds as she exits slowly. Just*
> *before leaving the space she pauses to ask*
> *a final question.*)

JOMAMA. What if I told you—choose?!

SONG CREDITS

"BLACK LIGHT"—Lyrics by Jomama Jones; music by Jomama Jones and Josh Quat

"NEED IN ME"—Lyrics by Jomama Jones; music by Bobby Halvorson and Samora Pinderhughes

"SHATTERED"—Music and lyrics by Jomama Jones

"CASTING THE CROSSROADS"—Music by Samora Pinderhughes

"GABRIEL'S HORN"—Lyrics by Jomama Jones; music by Bobby Halvorson

"CROSSROADS"—Lyrics by Jomama Jones; music by Dylan Meek; arrangement by Samora Pinderhughes

"JOY"—Lyrics by Jomama Jones; music by Bobby Halvorson

"SEEDS"—Lyrics by Jomama Jones; music by Bobby Halvorson

"SUPERNOVA"—Music and lyrics by Jomama Jones; arrangement by Bobby Halvorson

"FUTURE LIGHT"—Lyrics by Jomama Jones. music by Jomama Jones and Bobby Halvorson

"SEE (THINGS AS THEY ARE)"—Lyrics by Jomama Jones; music by Jomama Jones and Josh Quat

"SKINS"—Lyrics by Jomama Jones; music by Josh Quat; arrangement by Samora Pinderhughes and Tariq al-Sabir

GRATITUDES

Any list of gratitudes is incomplete. I am certain I will have left some folk off unintentionally, and for that I ask that you, as the people say, "charge it to my head, not my heart."

Elissa Adams
Chris Agosto
Tariq al-Sabir
Tea Alagic
Jesse Alick
Herb Alpert
The Alpert Foundation
Erika Amato
Nehprii Amenii
Laura Jean Anderson
Adelina Anthony
Corinna Applegate
ArtMatters
Deborah Asiimwe
Truth Bachman
Sharon Rula Backos
Lawrence Bagwell
e. g. bailey
Samiya Bashir
Karen Baxter
Marisa Becerra
Lou Bellamy
Sarah Bellamy
Sarah Benson
Dr. Constance E. Berkley
Ron Berry
Rajasvini Bhansali
Dr. Joyce Bickerstaff
Carl Bishop

Robert Blacker
MaYaa Boateng
Eyenga Bokamba
Gigi Bolt
Vicky Boone
Irene Borger
Kate Bornstein
Danielle Boutet
Kay Bourne
Oana Botez
Djola Branner
George Brant
Erik Braund
Ed Brennan
Maria Brennan
Mary "O.B." Brennan
Moira Brennan
Barbara Rose Brown
Carlyle Brown
Jyana Browne
Peggy Brunache & Family
Florinda Bryant
Vinie Burrows
Duana Butler
Emilya Cachapero
Sha Cage
Ben Cameron
Sandra Camp
Dr. P. Carl

Diane Carpenter
Mike Carpenter
Marissa Chibas Preston
Tanisha Christie
Anne Clark
Jeremy Cohen
Catherine Cole
Grisha Coleman
Jacques Colimon
Marlene Cooper
Whealon Costello
Dr. Aimee Meredith Cox
Creative Capital
Angie Cruz
Jackie Cuevas
Fran Kumin
Lisa D'Amour
Ishani Das
Darby Davis
Eisa Davis
Helga Davis
Will Davis
Thomas DeFrantz
Suzy Delvalle
Baraka de Soleil
Diana DiMenna
Stephen DiMenna
Sean Dixon
Martina Downey

George Drance
Barbara Duchow
Elizabeth Duffel
Alec Duffy
Doris Duke Foundation
Noma Dumezweni
Dr. Elliot Dyer
Linda Earle
Matt Edlund
Kristy Edmunds
Mary Edwards
Erik Ehn
Janine Ekulona
Saidah Arrika Ekulona
Daniel Dodd Ellis
Normandi Ellis
John Emigh
Ullie Emigh
Oskar Eustis
Diane Exavier
Robert Faires
Pattie Farley
The Fire & Ink Conference
Dan Fishback
Kimberly Forastiere-Schulz
The Forastiere Family
Jason Finkleman
Leon Finley
The Fire & Ink Conference
Cynthia Flowers
Dr. Stacey Floyd-Thomas
Gracie Fojtik
Olase Freeman
Kimberlee Koym-Murtiera
Greg Gagnon
Angelique Gagnon

Philippe Gagnon
Katie Gamelli
Denise Kumani Gantt
Lucinda Garthwaite
Jeremy Garza
Leigh Gaymon-Jones
Noel "Paco" Gerald
Matthew Glassman
Ebony Noelle Golden
Kirsten Greenidge
Virginia Grise
Guggenheim Foundation
Dr. Alexis Pauline Gumbs
Cat Gund
Tenzin Gund-Morrow
Dr. Frank Guridy
Barbara Maier Gustern
Jessica Hagedorn
Priscilla Hale
Bobby Halvorson & Family
Rachel M. Harper
Chris Harrison
Henry Harrison
Rita Harrison
Deborah Hay
Aleta Hayes
Krystal Hawes-Dressler
Philip Himberg
Zach Hodges
Jen Hofer
The Howard Foundation
Sylvia Humphrey-Spann
Keenan Hurley
Naomi Iizuka
Jake Inman
Maricella Infante

Ako Jacintho
Joia Jacintho
Carla Jackson
Gale Jackson
Tonia Jackson
Barbara Dalia Jasmin
Morgan Jenness
The Jerome Foundation
Dr. E. Patrick Johnson
Vanessa Johnson
The Jones Family
Jake-ann Jones
Dr. Omi Osun Joni L. Jones
Ursula Jones
Melanie Joseph
Swen Kaehlert
Colleen Keegan
Kimberly Kelly
Dennis Kim
Garrett Kim
Caroline King
Donald King
Andrew Kircher
Walter Kitundu
Maurine Knighton
Alex Knowlton
Wendy Knox
Kristen Kosmas
Lady Krishna
Aaron Landsman
Oni Faida Lampley
Jenny Larson
Randy Sue Latimer
Alyce Jones Lee
Patrick Lee
Ruby Lerner

Stephen J. Lewis
Clarissa Marie Ligon
Maira Liriano
B. Loewe
Todd London
Taylor Mac
Wayne "Juice" Mackins
Matthew Maguire
Sydné Mahone
MAP Fund
Elizabeth Margid
Ruth Margraff
Jen Margulies
Renita Martin
Adrienne Martini
Chad McCarver
Jonathan McCrory
Emilie McDonald
Shaka McGlotten
Meg McHutchison
Giuseppe Mele
The Mellon Foundation
David Mendizábal
Jasson Minadakis
Megan Monaghan-Rivas
Jessie Montgomery
Kym Moore
Lisa C. Moore
Carmen Morgan
Rev. J.P. Morgan, Jr.
Elmo Terry-Morgan
Emily Morse
A.J. Muhammad
Carlos Murillo
Christopher Myers
Erica Nagel

New Dramatists
NEFA
Valerie Curtis-Newton
Kate Nicoll
Oak Kalawakan
Michael O'Brien
Jeanie O'Hare
Cynthia Oliver
Michelle Marie Osbourne
Sterling Overshown
Lenora Pace
Nicky Paraiso
Deborah Paredez
Alexander Paris
Sonja Parks
Helen Patmon
Eva Patton
Katie Pearl
Tom Pecinka
PEN America
Ana Luisa Perea
Sonja Perryman
Naimah Zulmadelle Petigny
Jason Phelps
Pillsbury House Theatre
Samora Pinderhughes &
Family
The Playwrights' Center
Penumbra Theatre Co.
Sayra Pinto
Alyson Pou
Suzanne Pred Bass
Lisa Preston
Travis Preston
Faye Price
Pablo Prince

Josh Quat
Aishah Rahman
Marlene Ramirez-Cancio
Clint Ramos
Phylicia Rashad
Noel Raymond
Toshi Reagon
Lady Red
Marcie Rendon
Yoruba Richen
Dr. Ramon Rivera-Servera
Stacey Robinson
Rhonda Ross
Joel Ruark
Sarah Ruhl
Carl Hancock Rux
Abe Rybeck
Dawn Akemi Saito
Esther Saks
Jane M. Saks
Benny Sato Ambush
Eleanor Savage
Tony Senecal
Kaneza Schaal
Bonnie Schock
Bret Schneider
Stephanie Schneider
Charles Schuminski
Patrick Scully
Kyla Searle
Buffy Sedlachek
Margery Segal
Joanna Settle
Ntozake Shange
Porn Siphanoum
Carlos Sirah

Ana Sisnett

Nick Slie

Namir Smallwood

Anna Deavere Smith

Roger Guenveur Smith

Vuyo Sotashe

Anuson Souvannasane

Justin Speranza

John Steber

Leilah Stewart

NaTanya' Davina' Stewart

Tawanna Sullivan

Annie Suite

Quita Sullivan & Family

Colin Denby Swanson

Cynthia Taylor-Alexander

Eric Taylor

TED Fellows Program

Mei Ann Teo

Elmo Terry Morgan

Lisa Thompson

Shanta Thake

Shanti Tom Thake

The Theater Offensive

Dr. Stacey Floyd-Thomas

Lucy Thurber

Shelby Jiggetts-Tivony

Liesl Tommy

John Townsend

korde arrington tuttle

Rose Twofeathers

Roberta Uno

Arlene Uribe

USA Artists

Malaika Uwamaharo

Joel Valentin-Martinez

Laura Verallo de Bertotto

Shelley Vermilyea

Regina Victor

Paula Vogel

Shirin Vossoughi

Rebecca Walker

Naomi Wallace

Sangodare Wallace

Mike Wangen

Bettye Webb

Chris Wells

Deborah White

Courtney Williams

Eder J. Williams

Jacqueline T. Wigfall

Michelle Witt

Tanya Wright

Mia Yoo

Shay Youngblood

Dr. Fawzia Zawahir

Suzan Zeder

Appreciation to all my current and former colleagues and students over the years at Goddard College, MIT, The University of Texas at Austin, Fordham University, and CalArts, as well as in those schools, community centers, and private homes who welcomed me as a teacher.

Thanks to all those folks who called my name, lifted my work in conversation, in rooms, on panels, etc. and who advocated with quiet generosity and kindness. I continue to pay it forward. Deb, Aaron, Jacques, korde/khat, Vicky, Eisa, and Dr. Omi—it is appropriate that we are all up in this book together; I respect each of you artists so much. And Sister Shay, you opened the way for me, demonstrating a life filled with incalculable magic, and I will never forget.

Thank you to all who have supported my work in process and production—you invested your time, lifeforce, wisdom, and heart. From the waitstaff at Joe's Pub who ensured that the spell of *Black Light* happened right every night, to the front desk workers at Pillsbury United Communities who ensured that anyone entering that building was met with kindness and care, to the celebrated dramaturgs and performers who were collaborators of record, I recall you all with gratitude and take none of what you gave me for granted.

As the old-folks would say, "everybody is not for you and you are not for everybody." I understand the roles of discord and dissonance within our life journeys. There are those folks who I struggled with or who struggled with me, sometimes resulting in burned bridges and bad tastes. As I've gained perspective on once painful passages, I honor the impetus for change and growth coded within. May love and forgiveness someday resurface in the seemingly barren field.

To an emerging generation of artists, some of whom I've been honored to work with, who are actively embodying freedom of expression and unlimited imagination in the service of healing and quantum dreaming, I celebrate you. May this book give you evidence, fuel, and an oasis for reflection.

To my late mentors Dr. Constance E. Berkley, Laurie Carlos, Dr. Blanche Foreman, Kathryn Gagnon, Robbie McCauley, Aishah Rahman, and Rebecca Rice: you suffuse all of this work with sunset glow. I pray you are proud. I will always call your names.

To my "Jedi Council" of loved ones, who have walked with me through the peaks and valleys and crossroads, offered counsel, who grabbed me by the ear when necessary, who challenged and affirmed my evolving understandings, and who continue to believe in my mission, I thank you, I thank you, I thank you. I bow deeply to my Dad, Art Jones, whose life is a testimony to community service; my brother, Todd Jones, the human being I most admire; Bridget Carpenter, my forever writing buddy and thought partner; and Sharon Bridgforth, my forever first reader and responder. None of this work would exist were it not for you.

IMAGE CREDITS

BLOOD:SHOCK:BOOGIE

Open: Daniel Alexander Jones as Josephine Baker, Frontera@Hyde Park Theatre. Photo by Bret Brookshire

Gallery (photos by Bret Berkshire): **1:** Jomama Jones is greeted during a 1996 photo shoot in Austin, TX by a stranger who suggests that Jo "angle her leg and lift her heel for a sexier legline." **2:** (l-r) Daniel Dodd Ellis, Daniel Alexander Jones, and (tucked in the corner) Jason Phelps backstage at Frontera@Hyde Park Theatre. **3:** Jason Phelps and Daniel Dodd Ellis at Boston Center for the Arts, Theater Offensive. **4-6:** Daniel Alexander Jones at Boston Center for the Arts, Theater Offensive. **5-8:** Daniel Dodd Ellis, Jomama Jones, and Jason Phelps. **9:** Jomama Jones.

PHOENIX FABRIK

Open: Robbie McCauley as Mother Dixon, Todd Mountain Theatre Project. Photo by Daniel Urie.

Gallery: 1: Robbie McCauley as Mother Dixon, Namir Smallwood as the Boy, Todd Mountain Theatre Project. Photo by Daniel Urie. (Remaining gallery photos by Usry Alleyne from Pillsbury House Theatre Project production): **2.** Vinie Burrows as Mother Dixon, Namir Smallwood as The Boy. **3:** Namir Smallwood as The Boy (Barbara Duchow as Inga in back). **4:** Rhonda Ross as Eleanor, Barbara Duchow as Inga. **5:** Vinie Burrows as Mother Dixon, Rhonda Ross as Eleanor. **6:** Rhonda Ross as Eleanor, Namir Smallwood as The Boy. **7:** Namir Smallwood as The Boy, Barbara Duchow as Inga. **8:** The river of doll dresses created by Leilah Stewart.

BEL CANTO

Open: Merle Perkins as Marian Anderson and Burl Mosely as Benjamin Turner, Theater Offensive and Wheelock Family Theatre. Photo by Mirta Tocci.

Gallery: 1: Merle Perkins as Marian Anderson, Theater Offensive and Wheelock Family Theatre. Photo by Mirta Tocci. **2:** Faye Price as Barbara Scarlatti. Photo by Michal Daniel. **3:** (l-r) Josie Burgin-Lawson as Marian Anderson, Theroun Patterson as Benjamin, and Vinie Burrows as Barbara Scarlatti, Actor's Express, Atlanta (courtesy of Actor's Express Archive). **4:** Will Sturdivant as Benjamin Turner, Pillsbury House Theatre. Photo by Michal Daniel. **5:** Will Sturdivant as Benjamin and William Grier as Terence, Pillsbury House Theatre. Photo by Michal Daniel.

DUAT

Open: (l-r) Kaneza Schaal as Thoth, Tenzin Gund-Morrow as the Ba, Toussaint Jeanlouis as Anubis, and Stacey Karen Robinson as Ma'at, Soho Rep. Photo by Sam Horvath.

Gallery (photos by Julieta Cervantes from Soho Rep production): 1: Tenzin Gund-Morrow. 2: Daniel Alexander Jones and Jacques Colimon. 3. Jomama Jones as Miss Jones and Tenzin Gund-Morrow as Sweet T. 4: Kaneza Schaal as Lalibela, Stacey Karen Robinson as Miss Robinson, Jacques Colimon as Alex, Toussaint Jeanlouis as Saint. 5: Jacques Colimon (reclined on table) as Alex, Toussaint Jeanlouis as Saint, Tenzin Gund-Morrow as Sweet T, Jomama Jones as Miss Jones, and Kaneza Schaal as Lalibela.

CLAYANGELS

Open: Todd Jones and Daniel Alexander Jones. Photo by Bret Brookshire.

Gallery (photos by Bret Brookshire): 1: Todd Jones and Daniel Alexander Jones. 2: Todd Jones and Daniel Alexander Jones. 3: Daniel Alexander Jones and Todd Jones.

BOOK OF DANIEL

Open: Thompson Street, Springfield, MA, early 1980s: Daniel Alexander Jones, Joia Jacintho, Keiyan Crump, Ako Jacintho, Todd Jones.

Gallery (photos by Bret Brookshire from *The Book of Daniel, Chapter Five* at allgo in Austin, TX): Daniel Alexander Jones and Walter Kitundu.

BLACK LIGHT

Open: Jomama Jones, the Public Theater. Photo by Joan Marcus.

Gallery (photos by Joan Marcus from the Public Theater production): 1: Josh Quat, Jomama Jones. 2: Josh Quat, Truth Bachman, Vuyo Sotashe, Jomama Jones, Tariq al-Sabir, Michelle Marie Osbourne, and (barely visible on drums) Sean Dixon. 3: Jomama Jones.

DANIEL ALEXANDER JONES

Daniel Alexander Jones exemplifies the artist-as-energy worker. His wildflower body of original work includes plays, performance pieces, recorded music, concerts, music theatre events, essays, and long-form improvisations. He explores the esoteric and the everyday through his own distinctive dramaturgy.

Jones's critically-acclaimed pieces include *Radiate* (Soho Rep and National Tour); *Black Light* (Public Theater, Greenwich House Theatre, American Repertory Theatre, Penumbra Theatre); *Duat* (Soho Rep); *An Integrator's Manual* (La MaMa, etc. and Fusebox Festival). Jones has recorded six albums of original songs as his alter-ego, Jomama Jones. Daniel's current project, www.aten.life, significantly expands his digital media work. He has been a part of arts communities in New York City, Minneapolis/St. Paul, Austin, Boston, and Los Angeles, where he bases his practice.

Jones directed world-premieres of new plays and performance pieces by E. Patrick Johnson, Erik Ehn, Renita Martin, and Shay Youngblood, among others. He is a company member of Penumbra Theatre Company in St. Paul; an associate company member of Pillsbury House Theatre in Minneapolis; an alumnus of New Dramatists, and was a company member of Frontera@Hyde Park Theatre in Austin.

Jones was honored with the PEN America Laura Pels Foundation Theatre Award in 2021. Daniel was a 2020 TED Fellow, a Guggenheim Fellow, and the recipient of the Helen Merrill Playwriting Award, a Doris Duke Artist Award, an Alpert Award in the Arts, a USA Artist Fellowship, an Arts Matters grant, an inaugural Creative Capital Grant, a McKnight National Residency and Commission, a Howard Foundation Fellowship, a NEA/TCG Playwriting Residency, a Jerome Fellowship, and a Many Voices Playwriting Fellowship. Jones was the lead artist on five projects awarded support by the MAP Fund and is a NEFA National Theatre Project grantee. Daniel has been a Mellon Creative Research Fellow at the University of Washington, a Hume Fellow at Occidental College, a Fellow at the Hemispheric Institute at NYU, and has been in residence at a number of colleges and universities across the country, including CalArts and UCLA's Center for New Performance. Jones received a Bistro Award for Outstanding Performance Artistry for Jomama Jones, and a Franky Award from the Prelude Festival in recognition of long-term, extraordinary impact on contemporary theatre and performance.

Daniel Alexander Jones completed his undergraduate study at Vassar College in Africana Studies with a focus on literature and the arts under the guidance of Dr. Constance E. Berkley, and his graduate study at Brown University in Theatre where he worked with Rites and Reason Theatre and was mentored by Aishah Rahman. He is a widely respected, innovative educator who has taught across the United States and held faculty positions at Goddard College, The University of Texas at Austin, and most recently at Fordham University, where he is a Full Professor in the Department of Theatre and Visual Arts. He is a frequent essayist, with contributions published by *Theater* magazine and *HowlRound*. The Herb Alpert Foundation noted that Daniel Alexander Jones "creates multi-dimensional experiences where bodies, minds, emotions, voices, and spirits conjoin, shimmer, and heal."

COMPLETE WORKS OF DAJ

PLAYS & PERFORMANCE PIECES:
Aten
Black Light
Duat
An Integrator's Manual
Bright Now Beyond
Radiate
Phantasmatron
Hera Bright
Qualities of Light
Phoenix Fabrik
The Book of Daniel (Chapters 1-10)
Bel Canto
Cab and Lena
Clayangels
Ambient Love Rites
Blood:Shock:Boogie
Earthbirths, Jazz and Raven's Wings

ALBUMS (as Jomama Jones):
Aten
Anew
Flowering
Six Ways Home
Radiate
Lone Star

CONTRIBUTORS

Vicky Boone is a casting director and film producer based in Austin, Texas. She is currently developing a feature film adapted from Carrie Fountain's young adult novel *I'm Not Missing*. Other film works include the festival projects *Adventure Story*, *Attack of the Bride Monster*, and *Fall to Grace*. She also directed the music video *Bones* in collaboration with Jomama Jones. As a casting director, Boone works closely with many auteur directors including Terrence Malick, Richard Linklater, David Lowery and Julie Andem. Her casting director credits include *Where'd You Go, Bernadette*, *The Tree of Life*, *Ain't Them Bodies Saints* and the English-language remake of the hit Norwegian series *SKAM*. Before working in film, Boone directed and produced new plays. For ten years, she was the Artistic Director of Austin's ground-breaking Frontera @ Hyde Park Theatre. She has an MFA in Directing from Boston University School for the Arts.

Jacques Colimon is a rising actor, producer, and singer/songwriter. Upcoming, Colimon will star as the male lead of Josephine Decker's A24/Apple film *The Sky Is Everywhere*, slated for release later this year. Additionally, Colimon will star as 'Gaia' in *Endless Light*, a drama sci-fi about a bipolar woman who conjures the mysticism of Alaska's wilderness to communicate with her deceased brother. Most recently, Colimon was seen in the Blumhouse thriller mystery *Nocturne*, which follows a gifted pianist who makes a Faustian bargain to overtake her older sister at a institution for classical musicians. The film is part of a 4-episode anthology series now streaming on Amazon. Prior, he starred in the Halloween episode of the Hulu anthology series *Into the Dark: Uncanny Annie*, and as 'Will LeClair' in the hit Netflix drama series *The Society*. A modern take on *The Lord of the Flies*, the series follows the teen residents of West Ham, Connecticut as they forge their own society in an effort to survive after realizing that all the adults have mysteriously vanished. Colimon's additional film credits include *Collection*, *Ugly Dolls*, and *Sweet Old World*. Off-screen, Colimon's theater credits include the critically acclaimed production of Daniel Alexander Jones's *Duat* at Soho Rep in New York and Gabriel Jason Dean's *Terminus*, for which he received the B. Iden Payne Lead Actor award. In addition to his work on and off-screen, Colimon is also a dedicated human rights activist and musician.

Eisa Davis is a Brooklyn-based, Berkeley-born multidisciplinary artist working onstage, screen, and hybrid performance spaces. A 2020 Creative Capital Awardee, Herb Alpert Award recipient, Cave Canem fellow, and Obie winner for Sustained Excellence in Performance, Eisa was a finalist for the Pulitzer Prize in Drama for her play *Bulrusher*, and wrote and starred in the stage memoir *Angela's Mixtape*. Alongside her thirteen full length plays, she has written episodes for both seasons of the Spike Lee Netflix series *She's Gotta Have It*, penned the narration for Cirque du Soleil's first ice show *Crystal*, and released two albums of music. She lives in Brooklyn. www.eisadavis.com

Omi Osun Joni L. Jones brings Black Feminist praxis and theatrical jazz principles to her artmaking, pedagogy, and facilitation. Her dramaturgical work includes August Wilson's *Gem of the Ocean* and Shay Youngblood's *Shakin' the Mess Outta Misery*—both under the direction of Daniel Alexander Jones, as well as Sharon Bridgforth's *con flama* under the direction of Laurie Carlos. Her most recent book is *Theatrical Jazz: Performance, Àse, and the Power for the Present Moment* (The Ohio State University Press). She is Professor Emerita from the African and African Diaspora Studies Department at the University of Texas at Austin.

korde arrington tuttle is a multidisciplinary maker, poet, and playwright from charlotte, nc. as a curator of emotional space, the expansion of human consciousness, healing, and play live at the center of their work. love is the reason. korde is the author *falling is the one thing i*, a book of haiku and photography published by candor arts. they are the author of award-winning plays such as *graveyard shift* and *clarity*. they received their mfa at the new school. korde is grateful to have been asked to contribute to the temple of light daniel alexander jones is constructing.

Aaron Landsman is a theater artist, writer, and teacher, an Abrons Arts Center Social Practice Artist in Residence, a recent Guggenheim Fellow, ASU Gammage Residency Artist and Princeton Arts Fellow, an eternal Capricorn bean counter and childlike aging crank. His performance works, including *Empathy School/Love Story*, *City Council Meeting*, *Appointment*, and *Open House*, have been presented by The Foundry Theatre, Abrons, The Chocolate Factory Theater and other venues in New York, regionally and in the UK, Serbia, Norway and The Netherlands. His book, *No One Is Qualified*, about democracy, participation and performance, co-authored with Mallory Catlett, comes out with the University of Iowa Press in 2022. He has appeared in the work of Elevator Repair Service and many other artists.

Deborah Paredez is a poet, essayist, and performance scholar. She is the author of two poetry collections, *This Side of Skin* and *Year of the Dog*, and the critical study, *Selenidad: Selena, Latinos, and the Performance of Memory*. Her work has appeared in the New York Times, Los Angeles Review of Books, Boston Review, Poetry, and elsewhere. She is the co-founder on CantoMundo, a national organization for Latinx poets, and is a professor of creative writing and ethnic studies at Columbia University. She lives in New York City where she's currently at work on a book about the impact of divas on her life that includes, of course, a chapter on Jomama Jones.

Shay Youngblood is an Atlanta-based writer, visual artist, and educator. Author of several novels including *Soul Kiss* and *Black Girl in Paris*, collections of short stories and numerous essays, her published plays, including *Shaking the Mess Out of Misery* and *Talking Bones*, have been widely produced and her short stories have been performed at Symphony Space and recorded for NPR's Selected Shorts. She teaches advanced fiction at City College New York and the Harvard Extension School. In 2021 she was appointed Commissioner to the Japan U.S. Friendship Commission and serves as a board member of Yaddo artists' community. Her current projects include *Mama's Home*, an illustrated children's book, *LUNA*, a super hero graphic novel collaboration and Tent Cities, a multi-media performance work about architecture, memory and the environment inspired by research in Japan, China and the U.S. www.shayyoungblood.com

ABOUT THE PRESS

53rd State Press publishes lucid, challenging, and lively new writing for performance. Our catalog includes new plays as well as scores and notations for interdisciplinary performance, graphic adaptations, and essays on theater and dance.

53rd State Press was founded in 2007 by Karinne Keithley in response to the bounty of new writing in the downtown New York community that was not available except in the occasional reading or short-lived performance. In 2010, Antje Oegel joined her as a co-editor. In 2017, Kate Kremer took on the leadership of the volunteer editorial collective. For more information or to order books, please visit 53rdstatepress.org.

53rd State Press books are represented to the trade by TCG (Theatre Communications Group). TCG books are exclusively distributed to the book trade by Consortium Book Sales and Distribution, an Ingram Brand.

LAND & LABOR ACKNOWLEDGMENTS

53rd State Press recognizes that much of the work we publish was first developed and performed on the unceded lands of the Lenape and Canarsie communities. Our books are stored on and shipped from the unceded lands of the Chickasaw, Cherokee, Shawnee, and Yuchi communities. The work that we do draws on natural resources that members of the Indigenous Diaspora have led the way in protecting and care-taking. We are grateful to these Indigenous communities, and commit to supporting Indigenous-led movements working to undo the harms of colonization.

As a press devoted to preserving the ephemeral experiments of the contemporary avant-garde, we recognize with great reverence the work of radical BIPOC artists whose (often uncompensated) experiments have been subject to erasure, appropriation, marginalization, and theft. We commit to amplifying the revolutionary experiments of earlier generations of BIPOC theatermakers, and to publishing, promoting, celebrating, and compensating the BIPOC playwrights and performers revolutionizing the field today.

53rd STATE PRESS

The Book of the Dog // Karinne Keithley
Joyce Cho Plays // Joyce Cho
No Dice // Nature Theater of Oklahoma
When You Rise Up // Miguel Gutierrez
Montgomery Park, or Opulence // Karinne Keithley
Crime or Emergency // Sibyl Kempson
Off the Hozzle // Rob Erickson
A Map of Virtue + Black Cat Lost // Erin Courtney
Pig Iron: Three Plays // Pig Iron Theatre Company
The Mayor of Baltimore + Anthem // Kristen Kosmas
Ich, Kürbisgeist + The Secret Death of Puppets // Sibyl Kempson
Soulographie: Our Genocides // Erik Ehn
Life and Times: Episode 1 // Nature Theater of Oklahoma
Life and Times: Episode 2 // Nature Theater of Oklahoma
Life and Times: Episode 3 + 4 // Nature Theater of Oklahoma
The 53rd State Occasional No. 1 // Ed. Paul Lazar
There There // Kristen Kosmas
Seagull (Thinking of You) // Tina Satter
Self Made Man Man Made Land // Ursula Eagly
Another Telepathic Thing // Big Dance Theater
Another Tree Dance // Karinne Keithley Syers
Let Us Now Praise Susan Sontag // Sibyl Kempson
Dance by Letter // Annie-B Parson
Pop Star Series // Neal Medlyn
The Javier Plays // Carlos Murillo
Minor Theater: Three Plays // Julia Jarcho
Ghost Rings (12-inch vinyl) // Half Straddle
A New Practical Guide to Rhetorical Gesture and Action // NTUSA
A Field Guide to iLANDing // iLAND
The 53rd State Occasional No. 2 // Ed. Will Arbery
Suicide Forest // Haruna Lee
Rude Mechs' Lipstick Traces // Lana Lesley + the Rude Mechs
MILTON // PearlDamour
The People's Republic of Valerie, Living Room Edition // Kristen Kosmas
Uncollected Trash Collection // Kate Kremer
A Discourse on Method // David Levine + Shonni Enelow
Severed // Ignacio Lopez
Ann, Fran, and Mary Ann // Erin Courtney

Particle and Wave: A Conversation // Daniel Alexander Jones & Alexis Pauline Gumbs
Love Like Light // Daniel Alexander Jones

FORTHCOMING

SKiNFoLK: An American Show // Jillian Walker
WATER SPORTS; or insignificant white boys // Jeremy O. Harris
I Understand Everything Better // David Neumann + Sibyl Kempson
ASTRS // Karinne Keithley Syers
Wood Calls Out to Wood // Corinne Donly
Karen Davis: Bitter Pill, Mistook Acerbic for Advil // Jess Barbagallo
12 Shouts to the Ten Forgotten Heavens: Springs // Sibyl Kempson
Broken Clothing // Suzanne Bocanegra

Love Like Light is made possible by the New York State Council on the Arts with the support of Governor Andrew M. Cuomo and the New York State Legislature.

For me, a memorable person made these plays. Sometimes we forget a writer is first a person. It is a person who created these words. And Daniel Alexander Jones is a person. I remembered him for decades. I first met him when he was a young scholar standing in the lobby of Churchill House at Brown University. So passionate, so gracious—he was like the hero from a play. He came to me and told me he was working on my play *The Owl Answers* with Rhonda Ross. The play would start in minutes. But he said I was waiting for you. I do want to tell you I read *Funnyhouse* and it was on my mind for a long time. The production he and Rhonda created was superb. But I always remembered this passionate young man with a heroic manner and grace. And he is the creator of the plays in these pages. As he did then he has a connection like electricity to the word. He totally understands the human issues at the core of theatre and what makes it important to our lives. When a person is unforgettable like that that young scholar was, you sense he is important. And Daniel, his vision, his narratives—he sees beyond the realities. He sees invisible realities. He sees beyond horizons.

– Adrienne Kennedy

53ʳᵈ State Press
new writing for performance